# LEARNED IN THE LAW;

OR,

## EXAMPLES AND ENCOURAGEMENTS

FROM THE

## Lives of Eminent Lawyers.

BY

## W. H. DAVENPORT ADAMS.

THE LAWBOOK EXCHANGE, LTD.
Clark, New Jersey

ISBN 978-1-58477-238-5

Lawbook Exchange edition 2002, 2019

*The quality of this reprint is equivalent to the quality of the original work.*

THE LAWBOOK EXCHANGE, LTD.
33 Terminal Avenue
Clark, New Jersey 07066-1321

*Please see our website for a selection of our other publications
and fine facsimile reprints of classic works of legal history:*
www.lawbookexchange.com

### Library of Congress Cataloging-in-Publication Data

Adams, W. H. Davenport (William Henry Davenport), 1828-1891.
    Learned in the law, or, Examples and encouragements from the lives of
        eminent lawyers.
        p. cm.
    Originally published: London: S.W. Partridge & Co., 1882.
    Includes index.
    ISBN 1-58477-238-7 (cloth: acid-free paper)
    1. Lawyers—Great Britain—Biography. 2. Practice of law—Great Britain—
        History. I. Title: Learned in the law. II. Title: Examples and
        encouragements from the lives of
    eminent lawyers. III. Title.

    KD536 .A32 2002
    340'.092'24 1 —dc2 1

                                                                [B] 2002025948

*Printed in the United States of America on acid-free paper*

# LEARNED IN THE LAW;

OR,

EXAMPLES AND ENCOURAGEMENTS

FROM THE

## Lives of Eminent Lawyers.

BY

## W. H. DAVENPORT ADAMS.

London:

S. W. PARTRIDGE & CO., 9 PATERNOSTER ROW, E.C.

# PREFACE.

THE biographies included in the present volume have been compiled from the best authorities. They contain no new facts, and put forward no startling theories; but they have been written from an independent and an impartial standpoint, and the expression of opinions which they contain is at least honest and sincere. As the title indicates, they are devoted to eminent lawyers; but in making the selection, it has been the aim of the writer to deal with men who have been eminent lawyers—and something else. He has sought to show, more or less directly, that conspicuous success in some particular department of human effort does not necessitate failure in all other departments, but that, on the contrary, the broader and deeper a man's general attainments, the more thorough will be his knowledge of the calling to which he has specially devoted himself. It may be true that a versatile man is generally a smatterer; it is not less true that a specialist is usually narrow-minded. He so confines his vision to a particular object, that it becomes incapable of any extended scope or range. Other morals are necessarily taught in these

5

pages; those old, old morals, so valuable that they cannot be too often repeated, which enforce the value of patience and perseverance, of the resolute will, the fixed purpose, the steadfast adherence to principle. Every man's life is full of lessons for his fellows; much more so the lives of those who have risen out of the mass, and helped to make the history, or literature, or jurisprudence of a nation.

Some objection may be offered to the inclusion of Edmund Burke among eminent lawyers; but he was certainly "learned in the law," and his knowledge of the higher principles of the law helped him largely in his public career.

Primarily this work is intended for the young, and every page, it is believed, bristles with examples and encouragements or warnings, which, if duly heeded, will assist them not a little in the battle of life. But the author hopes that older people will derive some interest from its very unpretending but faithful sketches of men who ever played an important part in our national life, and whose names are for ever associated with much valuable and enduring work.

W. H. D. A.

# CONTENTS.

# INTRODUCTION.

IT is a curious and interesting fact that most of our great lawyers have owed nothing of their success in life to adventitious aids—such as high birth, rank, or wealth. They have sprung, with few exceptions, from the middle classes, and even from the lower section of the middle classes, and made their way to eminence by their resolution, perseverance, and patience. I have often wondered that writers for the young, when seeking examples by which to stimulate their ardour and sustain their hopes, have not sought them more frequently and freely in the honourable profession of the law; for in no other are they so numerous or so brilliant. The lives of men like Tenterden and Eldon show us in the most striking manner what may be achieved by a brave heart and a clear brain; and convey a lesson which it is impossible to misunderstand—a lesson of high encouragement well calculated to awaken the energies and nourish the wholesome ambition of youth.

But they convey another and even more valuable lesson by illustrating the advantages of culture; the pleasure and profit derivable from the pursuit of knowledge. They teach us, moreover, the value of self-reliance; that quality which distinguishes the wise man

B

from the fool. A Roman politician when captured by traitors was tauntingly asked : " Where is thy stronghold now ? " Placing his hand upon his heart, he answered, " Here ! " And this must be the stronghold of every seeker after knowledge. No good work will be done by young men who accustom themselves to lean upon others, who are always finding new leaders, and professing themselves disciples of new Gamaliels. They must learn to think their own thoughts, to form their own opinions ; valuing authority justly, but not submitting to it slavishly. " Every one," writes Thierry, the historian, " can make his own destiny, every one employ his life nobly, or at least usefully."

A century ago there lived at Canterbury a respectable barber and hairdresser named Abbott, who endeavoured to do his humble work in life to the best of his ability. He had a son named Charles, a decent, grave, and primitive-looking youth, who in his childhood, when not learning to read at a dame's school, was employed in carrying home the wigs on which his father had exercised his skill. The boy was next admitted on the foundation of the King's School, where his master's quick eye detected his latent capacity, and he was cordially encouraged in the prosecution of his studies. He soon came to be distinguished for his industry and intelligence, and his skill in Latin verse and prose composition—an acquirement more valued then as a test of scholarship than it is now. It is said that to every man once in his life comes his opportunity; assuredly to every man comes once in his life the risk of failure by diverting his energies into the wrong channel. Charles Abbott was fourteen when this risk befell him. A chorister's place was vacant at the cathedral, and his father put him forward as a candidate, satisfied that his long connection with the cathedral authorities as their *perruquier* would secure the prize for his son; but, happily, the Dean and Chapter decided that his voice was too husky; and he was left to succeed as a great lawyer instead of failing as a mediocre singer. Long years afterwards, the Lord Chief-Justice of England, while "going circuit" with another judge, visited St. Augustine's ancient minster, and pointing to a singing-man in the choir, "Behold, brother Richardson," he exclaimed, "the only human being I ever envied. When at school in this town, we were candidates together for a chorister's place; he obtained it, and if I had gained my wish, he might have been accompanying you as Chief-Justice, and pointing me out as his old school-fellow, the singing-man." This is more than doubtful. There is no reason for supposing that the singing-man had a tithe of Tenterden's ability, or resolution, or force of character.

For three years more Charles Abbott continued at school, and fought his way energetically to the captain-ship. Then it seemed good to his father that since he could not be a singing-man he should become a barber, and shave the chins and clip the hair of Canterbury citizens after the paternal example. The head-master of the King's School interfered. His promising pupil was worthy of something better; and with the aid of some leading townsmen, and a grant from the school's trustees, he raised a small sum to enable him to go to college. Entering Corpus Christi College at Oxford, he won a classical scholarship, which contributed materially to the expense of his maintenance. Writing to a young friend he says : " But a little while past, to be a scholar of Corpus was the height of my ambition; that summit is (thank Heaven) gained, when another and another appears still in view. In a word, I shall not rest easy till I have ascended the rostrum in the theatre." That is, until he had gained the Chancellor's medal, and recited a prize composition from the rostrum of the Sheldonian. He competed for the prize Latin poem, " Calpe Obsessa," on the recent successful defence of Gibraltar by General Elliot and his gallant followers. The prize fell to William Lisle Bowles, afterwards the genial and accomplished sonneteer; but the examiners commended Abbott's effort as " quam proxime accessit." In the following year (1784) on the subject of balloon voyages, " Globus Aerostaticus," Abbott's muse was more propitious. He won the prize,* and fulfilled his ambition by reciting his poem from the rostrum of the Sheldonian theatre. Afterwards he gained the Chancellor's medal for a tersely written essay on " The Use and Abuse of Satire." So far Abbott had lost nothing by starting " without a shilling."

In 1785, he took his degree of B.A., obtained a fellowship, and was appointed junior tutor. Though in improved circumstances, he lived with the most rigid economy, in order to contribute freely to the support of his mother, who had been left a widow. He was

---

* The Latin is certainly elegant and the expression is sometimes ingenious, as in the following lines :—

> " Quid dicum, et quales novit tibi chymicus artes ?
> Quod mode effusum resoluto e sulphure acetum,
> Et chalybis ramenta, levisque a flumino rores
> Ille docet miscere, utrumque exsolvere in ignem ?
> Nempe ea cum proprio jam collabefacta calore
> In sua se expediunt iterum primordia, et arctos
> Dissolvunt rexus, et vincla tenacia laxant."

meditating the important step of taking holy orders, when fortune again interfered to direct him into his proper career. He was invited to become tutor to a son of Mr. Justice Buller, one of the most eminent of the many eminent men who have illustrated the English bench; and the judge's quick eye, detecting the logical power of Abbott's intellect, strongly advised him to adopt the legal profession, as better suited to him than the clerical. "You may not possess," he said, "the garrulity called *eloquence*, which sometimes rapidly forces up an impudent pretender, but you are sure to get early into respectable business at the bar, and you may count on becoming in due time a puisne judge." Acting on this encouraging advice, Abbott articled himself for a year to a special pleader of the name of Wood, who, at the end of the year, told him he had learned all he had to teach.*

"With characteristic prudence," says his biographer, "he then resolved to practise as a special pleader below the bar, until he had laid the basis firm and wide of an enduring reputation; and, hiring chambers in Brick Court, with a small boy as clerk at ten shillings a week, he sat down to wait for clients. These came to him more numerously and more quickly than his most sanguine dreams could have anticipated; for it was soon known that his advice was sound and promptly given, and that he possessed an almost unrivalled faculty for despatching business. After seven years of this laborious apprenticeship, he was called to the bar (1796), and started on the Oxford circuit. He had previously taken to himself a wife. The father of the lady he loved, a country squire, called upon him at his chambers, and

* "He seemed intuitively to catch an accurate knowledge of all the most abstruse mysteries of the *Doctrina Placitandi*, and he was supposed more rapidly to have qualified himself to practise them than any man before or since."—CAMPBELL, "Lord Chief Justices," iii. 270.

inquired how, when married, he proposed to keep up his house-hold. 'By these books in this room,' he answered, 'and two pupils in the next.' A year or two afterwards the Canterbury barber's son was making £8000 a-year."

In 1816, he accepted a puisne judgeship, and fulfilled Judge Buller's prophecy. But two years later he went beyond it, being appointed Lord Chief-Justice of England on the retirement of Lord Ellenborough. In this high office his peculiar intellectual qualifications, his quickness of perception, his closeness of reasoning, his solidity, and his patience, found a fitting arena for their exercise; and all lawyers agree that his administration of the business of his court was beyond praise. His tenure of office was, indeed, a golden age for lawyers and suitors.

" Every point made by counsel was then understood in a moment ; the application of every authority was understood at a glance ; the counsel saw when he might sit down, his case being safe, and when he might sit down, all chance of success for his client being at an end. During that golden age law and reason prevailed. The result was confidently anticipated by the know-ing before the argument began, and the judgment was approved of by all who heard it pronounced, including the vanquished party. Before such a tribunal the advocate becomes dearer to himself by preserving his own esteem. I do not believe that so much important business was ever done so rapidly and so well before any other court that ever sat in any age or country."

The climax of the barber's son's successful career was reached when, in 1827, he was raised to the peerage by the title of Baron Tenterden, a promotion acknowledged by all to be but the due reward of his merits as a scholar, a gentleman, a lawyer, and a judge.

When Wilberforce asked Lord Eldon how two young

friends of his could best make their way at the bar, the great ex-Chancellor replied, " I have no rule to give them, but that they must make up their minds to live like a hermit, and work like a horse." He spoke from his own experience. Born the son of a Newcastle coal-filler, he started on his career with no special advantages. His education was indifferent; and at school he gave no promise of future distinction. His father was actually hesitating whether he should bring him up to his own trade, or apprentice him to a grocer, when his elder brother William (afterwards Lord Stowell), having just gained a scholarship at Oxford, wrote to him, " Send Jack up at once, I can do better for him." At all events, Jack did better for himself. He went to Oxford, applied himself to his studies with assiduity, and carried off a fellowship. When at home in the vacation, he met and fell in love with a beautiful girl, who was rich in every-thing but that which the world values as wealth—eloped with her, married her, and entered upon life without home or fortune. By this marriage he had forfeited his fellowship, and hence was compelled to abandon all in-tention of joining the Church. He turned his attention to the study of law, repaired to London, took a small house in Cursitor Street, and devoted all his energies to his new pursuit.

No worker ever exhibited greater self-command or more determined perseverance. Rising at four in the morning, he studied until far into the following night, though frequently compelled to bind a wet towel round his head to keep himself awake. As he was too poor to pay the fee of a " special pleader," he copied out no fewer than three folio volumes of " precedents " from a manuscript collection ; and when the day's labours were at an end, he and his wife would sit down to a supper of sprats. At length he was called to the bar; but even then few clients came to his door, and his first year's earnings did not exceed nine shillings. However, that opportunity eventually came which patience and energy sooner or later never fail to command, and he had the skill and courage to make the most of it. Succeeding in a very difficult case, he rose at once into favour with solicitors and clients; and so rapid was his progress that, at the age of thirty-two, he was appointed King's Counsel. In due time he became Solicitor-General, Attorney-General, and finally Lord Chancellor, holding the last distinguished position for a quarter of a century.

When a person thought to compliment the great Chancellor Thurlow by asking him whether he was not sprung from the family of Thurlow, the secretary of Cromwell, the "law-lion" replied: "There were two Thurlows in my country. Thurlow the secretary, and Thurlow the carrier. I am descended from the latter." His father was a clergyman, occupying a small poor benefice at Ashfield, in Suffolk. Poor as he was, he contrived to give his son a decent education, and to send him to college, selecting Peter House, Cambridge, which is one of the least expensive. Most of our great lawyers have been remarkable for their studious youth; and, indeed, it would seem that in no profession is early application more indispensable than in that of the law. But Thurlow was an exception. He devoted much of his time to pleasure, acquiring by his irregular habits an unfavourable reputation in the university. His natural powers, however, were so great that he contrived in his occasional intervals of study to gain a considerable knowledge of the classics; a knowledge much more highly valued in those days than it seems to be in ours.

Having chosen the law as his road to fortune, Thurlow became a member of the Inner Temple, where he studied with more persistency and punctuality than he had at the university.

"It was generally supposed," says one of his contemporaries, "that Thurlow-in early life was idle; but I always found him close at study in a morning, when I have called at the Temple; and he frequently went no farther in an evening than to Nando's (a noted oyster-shop), and then only in his *déshabillé*. At the age of twenty-two he was called to the bar (1758). Like most aspirants in the legal profession, he remained for some time without practice; and as his father was unable to afford him much pecuniary assistance, he suffered much of the wretchedness and humiliation of debt. He sometimes began his circuit without the means of paying the necessary travelling expenses; and on one occasion could reach the town where the assizes were held only by the ingenious but not altogether honourable expedient of taking a horse on trial. At length he was employed in a case of some importance, and which afforded him an opportunity of exhibiting his intellectual acumen and legal knowledge. He rose at once into celebrity, and being afterwards retained in the celebrated Douglas case, his success was fully established. In 1770 he was appointed solicitor-general; in the following year attorney-general; and in 1778 reached the summit of a lawyer's ambition by being promoted to the woolsack. He was immediately raised to the peerage by the title of Baron Thurlow, of Ashfield."

Upon this occasion Cowper, the poet, who had been his fellow-student in the Temple, addressed him in some verses, from which a deduction must be made on the score of friendly enthusiasm and poetical license. We have seen that it is hardly accurate to say that

> " Round Thurlow's head in early youth,
>      And in his sportive days,
>   Fair Science poured the light of truth,
>      And Genius shed his rays."

And it must be owned that his career failed to justify so
strong a panegyric as the following :—

> "' See !' with united wonder cried
>      Th' experienced and the sage,
>   ' Ambition in a boy supplied
>      With all the skill of age !

> "' Discernment, eloquence, and grace *
>      Proclaim him born to sway
>   The balance in the highest place,
>      And bear the palm away !'

> " The praise bestowed was just and wise ;
>      He sprung impetuous forth,
>   Secure of conquest, where the prize
>      Attends superior worth.

> " So the best courser on the plain,
>      Ere yet he starts, is known,
>   And does but at the goal obtain
>      What all had deemed his own."

Of the early life of the great orator and lawyer, John
Dunning (born at Ashburton, 10th October, 1730), few
reminiscences have been preserved.   He came of a
respectable family, and received a good education, but, his
father being unable to give him much assistance, he was
compelled as a student to go through that experience of
rigid economy which seems so often to strengthen the
character and develop all that is best in a young man's
nature.   His two most intimate friends were Kenyon
(afterwards Lord Kenyon), and Horne Tooke, and all

---

\* " Grace " is about the last epithet that could fairly be applied to
the elephantine Thurlow !

three lived with a frugality that was hardly distinguishable from poverty.

"I have been frequently assured,"says Horne Tooke's biographer, "that they were accustomed to dine together, during the vacation, at a little eating-house in the neighbourhood of Chancery Lane, for the sum of sevenpence halfpenny each." . . . "As to Dunning and myself," added he, "we were generous, for we gave the girl who waited upon us a penny a piece ; but Kenyon, who always knew the value of money, sometimes rewarded her with a halfpenny, and sometimes with a promise."

Lord Campbell, speaking of the famous Lord Chief-Justice Ellenborough, says :—" He was a man of gigantic intellect ; he had the advantage of the very best education which England could bestow ; he was not only a consummate master of his own profession, but well initiated in mathematical science, and one of the best classical scholars of his day. He had great faults, but they were consistent with the qualities essentially required to make him to fill his high office with applause."

This illustrious judge was an exception to the rule which has so generally prevailed with respect to great lawyers. He did not come of low birth, nor in his early career was he impeded by the restraints of circumstance. His ancestors had long been " statesmen " in Westmoreland, that is, substantial farmers cultivating their own property. His father was Dr. Edmund Law, Bishop of Carlisle. He himself was born in 1750, at the parsonage of Salkeld, before his father's elevation to the episcopal bench. Until eight years old he was kept at home, acquiring that strong Cumbrian pronunciation and accent which marked his speech down to the day of his death. After spending a few months in a school at

Bury St. Edmunds, he was admitted a scholar of the Charterhouse in London, in 1761, and there laid the solid foundation of his vast classical and mathematical knowledge. He remained there six years, and rose to be captain of the school. He was wont to say that, while holding this dignified position, he felt himself of much more importance than when he rose to be Chief-Justice of England and a Cabinet Minister. This was no doubt the case, for at eighteen we have not learned how little we know !

From the Charterhouse he went to Cambridge, where he took his degree of M.A. His father was anxious for him to enter the Church, but he himself felt that it was not his vocation, and at last obtained leave to enter himself of Lincoln's Inn, on the understanding that he was not to begin the study of the law till he obtained a fellowship, so that he might have the certainty of at least a moderate subsistence, — that if he failed, he should take holy orders. "It was," as Lord Campbell says, "a fortunate circumstance for him that he embraced the profession of the law against the earnest wishes of a father whom he sincerely respected and loved. He thus took a tremendous responsibility upon himself, and had the most powerful motives for exertion, that he might justify his own opinion and soothe the feelings of him whose latter days he hoped to see tranquil and happy. He spurned the idea of retreating upon the Church after a repulse of the law, and he started with the dogged resolution to overcome every difficulty which he might encounter in his progress." Here an important subject of discussion opens upon us : How far is a young man fitted to decide upon his own career ? Our parents and guardians will not allow that it is one on which a second

opinion is possible, and are always solicitous to shape the
future lives of the young according to their own perception of what is best and most desirable. But in choosing
a pursuit it is surely necessary that the natural instinct
should be carefully studied, that we should satisfy ourselves of the eligibility of the plant for the soil in which
we intend to set it. And when we know that the
parents of Claude Lorraine would have made him a pastry-
cook, that Hogarth's father placed him under a silver-
smith, that the father of Sir Joshua Reynolds was intent
that he should be a physician, that Jackson the artist
was started in life as a tailor, that Chantry the sculptor
lingered for awhile in a small grocer's shop in Sheffield,
and that the mother of William Etty apprenticed him to
a printer—we cannot but feel some doubt whether the
choice of a young man's vocation is always safe in the
hands of his " natural guardians; " and in Law's case, it
is tolerably certain that he who became so great a lawyer
would have made but an indifferent divine.

Obtaining a small set of chambers in Lincoln's Inn,
Law addressed himself to his work with all the determination of his nature. In his time a student intended
for the common-law courts was expected to toil for at
least a couple of years in a special pleader's office, copying
musty precedents, drawing up pleas and declarations, and
studying practice and precedents rather than principles.
After duly submitting to this drudgery for the conven-
tional period, he began his independent career as " special
pleader under the bar," and in this vocation met with
very considerable success. He was called to the bar in
1780, joined the circuit at York, and, by his eloquence
and knowledge, almost immediately leapt into reputation.
In 1787 he obtained the silk gown of a K.C., and in

the same year made a start for the highest prize in the profession by being appointed to conduct the defence of Warren Hastings. In Macaulay's famous description of the famous trial, he alludes to " the bold and strong-minded Law," who, with unfailing energy and audacious skill, confronted the eloquence of the managers of the impeachment, Fox and Sheridan, Burke and Windham, and proved himself not unworthy of crossing swords with those notable adversaries.

The following sketches of the lives of great lawyers all point the same old moral—that moral which, in the ears of the young, the elders of each generation are always so assiduously repeating—that everything in this world falls to the patient. To labour and to wait, that is the true secret of success. The biography of every man who has risen to eminence is nothing more than a commentary on the commonplace truth which has been expressed by poets and teachers in so many different ways, but always with the same application; as, for instance, " In life, nothing bears fruit except by toil of mind and body;" or, as the poet puts it—

> " Rich are the diligent, who can command
>     Time, nature's stock! and could his hour-glass fall,
>   Would, as for seed of stars, stoop for the sand,
>     And by incessant labour gather all."

Labour ! that is the keynote not only of a successful but of an honourable life. A shrewd observer, Sir Thomas Fowell Buxton, writes :—" The longer I live, the more I am certain that the great difference between men, between the feeble and the powerful, the great and the insignificant, is energy, invincible determination, a purpose well fixed, and then death or victory. That quality will do anything that can be done in this world, and no talents, no circumstances, no opportunities will make a two-legged creature a man without it."

And yet another lesson do they teach—the importance of keeping open the mind for the reception of all kinds of knowledge. A man of no pursuit is necessarily a narrow-minded man. The great lawyers portrayed in the following pages were great lawyers because they were something more than lawyers—were scholars, philanthropists, reformers, or statesmen.

# Francis Bacon (Lord Verulam).

1561-1626.

———•◦•———

"For my name and memory, I leave it to men's charitable speeches, and to foreign nations, and to the next age."—*From Lord Bacon's Will.*

Afar, upon a sea all unexplored,
  A gallant vessel rides with venturous prow;
And soon, with precious spoils of Ophir stored,
  Returns to port exultant. Vainly now
Each envious eye has marked its ragged poles,
  Its torn and shattered sides has rudely scanned!
Alas, the jealousy of little souls
  When dwarfed before the great they shivering stand!
Such was thy fortune, Verulam, whose mind,
  Informed with living wisdom, roamed the vast
  And glorious realms of Science, and the Past
Despoiled of all the treasures it enshrined!
  But these our times have done thee justice; late
  Thy laurels have been wrung from partial Fate.

## I.

FRANCIS BACON, Lord Verulam, the father of Inductive Philosophy, best known in English history and English literature as Lord Bacon, was the son of Sir Nicholas Bacon, Queen Elizabeth's Lord-Keeper, by his wife, Anne Cooke, one of the accomplished daughters of Sir Anthony Cooke, tutor to Edward VI.

He was born on the 22nd of January, 1561, at York House, in the Strand,—not then, as now, a busy highway of trade and commerce, shut out from the river by lines of stuccoed houses and shops, but a broad tract of green fields and blooming hedgerows, besprinkled with noble mansions, the gardens of which descended to the very margin of the "royal towered Thames." York House, held as a fief from the Crown, was situated not far from the queen's palace. It had at one time been occupied by the Bishops of Norwich as their "inn" or town-residence; but, reverting to the Crown in the reign of Henry VIII., was bestowed upon Charles Brandon, Duke of Suffolk, the husband of Mary Tudor, the widowed Queen of France. Queen Mary gave it to Lord Chancellor Heath, the Catholic Archbishop of York, upon whose downfall it passed, by lease, to his successor in office, Sir Nicholas Bacon. It was a spacious and pleasant mansion, commanding a fine view of the river, then gay with water-pageants and processions, from the gray towers of Lambeth to the picturesque span of London Bridge.

Like most great men, Bacon was much indebted to the admirable parts and acquirements of his mother, who was a firm adherent of the Reformed faith, and a versatile scholar. She and her sister had been carefully imbued with the spirit of the ancient learning. She conducted a controversial correspondence in Greek with Bishop Jewel, whose "Apologia" she translated into English with rare fidelity. She also rendered from the Italian some abstruse sermons on "Fate and Free Will," by Bernardo Ochino. At the same time, she bore a high repute as a notable housewife, who was versed in all the mysteries of

domestic economy. Her husband, Sir Nicholas,—fifty-
one years old, when Francis, his youngest son, was born,
—if not endowed with genius, was a man of sound clear
judgment, excellent discretion, and lively humour. It
was said of this urbane and portly "courtier of the
queen's," that "some men look wiser than they are; the
lord-keeper is wiser than he looks." Some happy sayings
of his have been preserved. "Let us take time," he
would exclaim, "that we may be sooner done." When
a thief, named Hogg, put in a plea for a mild sentence
on the ground that a kinship existed between *Hogg* and
*Bacon*, he drily remarked: "Nay, nay, you and I cannot be of kin until you have been hanged." Queen
Elizabeth, visiting him at his country seat of Redgrave,
observed: "My lord, what a little house you have
gotten!" "Madame," replied the lord-keeper, "my house
is well, but you have made me too great for my house."

While he derived his sense of humour, his shrewd-
ness, and what I would call his "practical turn of mind"
from his father, it was to his mother that Bacon owed his
finer qualities, his rare intellectual powers, and his thirst
after knowledge. She superintended his education until
he was thirteen, and grounded him thoroughly in the
classics. A picturesque sketch of this remarkable woman
has been drawn by Mr. Hepworth Dixon, and as it is free
from exaggeration I shall transfer it to these pages:—

"More loving and more taking," he describes her, "slower
in her opinions, gentler in her deeds, than the majority of her
sex; a little high and masterful; apt, as many good women are,
to give strong advice. In her motherly eyes, her two sons
remained always the same little fellows who had played in the
galleries of York House, or rolled on the sward at Gorhambury;
boys needing a mother's eye and a mother's voice; and, in

truth, when they were grown up into men, full of the experience of travel, the knowledge of books, she continued to feed them from her own barn and cellars ; to look sharp after their pills and confections ; to send them game from her own larder, and beer from her own vats ; to lecture them soundly on what they should eat and drink, when purge or let blood, how far they might ride or walk, when safely to take supper, and at what hour of the morning to rise up from bed."

Believing that " the child is father of the man," the world is always eager to collect anecdotes of the early intelligence of its great men. We possess but few of Francis Bacon; those we have, however, may be taken as confirmatory of the popular belief. Queen Elizabeth, who, in allusion to the precocious gravity of his demeanour, was wont to call him her " young lord-keeper," once asked him, "How old are you?" A veteran minister might have envied the adroit reply : " Just two years younger than your Majesty's happy reign." His bias for inquiry comes out in the circumstance that on one occasion he abandoned the society of his playmates in order to investigate the source of a curious echo which he had discovered in a vault in St. James's Fields ; and he was but twelve when his attention was drawn to the recondite secrets of the art of legerdemain.

In his thirteenth year, he went to Trinity College, Cambridge, then under the rule of the learned and devout Whitgift, afterwards Archbishop of Canterbury. He remained there for three years, with the exception of those considerable intervals when outbreaks of the plague compelled his removal. All that was taught he did not fail to learn ; but the curriculum in those days was pitifully narrow, and wholly unsuited to a strong, keen intellect like Bacon's. He detected at once the weakness of the

Aristotelian philosophy, and "disliked" it heartily. "Not for the worthlessness of its author," says his earliest biographer, "to whom he would even ascribe all high attributes, but for the unfruitfulness of the way—being a philosophy (as his lordship used to say) only strong for disputations, but barren of the production of works for the life of man. In which mind he continued to his dying day."

The next three years he spent in France; at first residing in Paris under the charge of Sir Amias Paulet, Queen Elizabeth's able ambassador to the French court. For a youth of Bacon's parts no better education could have been devised. It opened up to him all the pomp and splendour of French royalty, all the arts and subtle intrigues of courtiers and diplomatists. It brought him into contact with the bright, quick ladies who sunned their charms in the train of the queen—herself a woman of great loveliness and rare mental gifts; with the glittering nobles of chivalrous France; with the astute leaders of the rival factions of Huguenot and Catholic. Thus his powers of observation and reflection were early developed, and he gained that wide and varied knowledge of the world which is an important part of a statesman's education. When Sir Amias was recalled to England, Bacon went on a tour through the western and southern provinces, the results of which seem to be gathered up in his "Notes on the State of Europe."

On the death of his father, in 1579, he returned to England. The lord-keeper's end was sudden and unexpected. The winter had been sharp and severe; but a genial thaw succeeding to the frost, the portly Sir Nicolas, at all times afflicted with a difficulty of breathing, seated himself by an open window while his barber trimmed his hair and beard. During the process he fell asleep. Waking with a chill and a fit of shivering, he inquired of his servant, " Why did you let me sleep ? " " Why, my lord," was the answer, " I durst not wake your lordship." " Then you have killed me with kindness," retorted the asthmatic judge ; and, taking to his bed, he died on the 20th of February.

At his father's death, Francis Bacon found himself inadequately provided for, and could no longer hope to enter public life as the equal and companion of men of good estate. " He had to think how to live, instead of living but to think." At first he solicited some public office ; and, as the son of the late lord-keeper and a nephew of Lord Burleigh, might reasonably have hoped for success. But his application to Lord Burleigh was made in vain. The Cecils had a strong dread of able men, and Bacon had already earned a reputation for ability. So that he was left to derive what consolation he could from his studies, and to starve on his mother's slender means, or on the small advances he obtained from the Jewish usurers. The sole source of a livelihood which seemed available was the profession of the law; and, in 1580, in his twentieth year, he began to keep his terms in Gray's Inn, where he had entered himself as a member as early as November, 1576. At this time he lived at No. 1 Gray's Inn Square, one of the " historic places " of Old London, which to this day retains much of its ancient character, and by Bacon's admirers must always be regarded as a shrine full worthy of a pilgrimage. In depth of interest it is second only to the old timbered house at Stratford-on-Avon, just as Bacon in largeness and grasp of intellect is second only to Shakespeare.

That he applied himself with all his powers of mind,

all his subtle acumen and rare patience, to the literature
of his profession is not to be doubted, for he certainly
became not only a great philosopher, but "learned in the
law." On that point we may take the evidence of a
lawyer, who, if incompetent to measure at its full extent
the genius of Francis Bacon, was unquestionably capable
of pronouncing a fair estimate of his legal acquirements.

"There can be no doubt," says Lord Campbell,* "that he
now diligently and doggedly sat down to the study of his profession, and that he made very great progress in it, although he
laboured under the effect of the envious disposition of mankind,
who are inclined to believe that a man of general accomplishments cannot possibly be a lawyer, and e converso, if a man has
shown himself beyond all controversy to be deeply embued with
law, that he is a mere lawyer without any other accomplishment.
A competent judge who peruses Francis Bacon's legal treatises,
and studies his forensic speeches, must be convinced that these
were not the mere result of laboriously getting up a title of law
pro re natâ, but that his mind was thoroughly familiar with the
principles of jurisprudence, and that he had made himself complete master of the common law of England, while there might
be serjeants and apprentices who had never strayed from
Chancery Lane to 'the Solar Walk or Milky Way,' better versed
in the technicalities of pleading and the practice of the courts.
He must have sedulously attended the 'readings' and 'mootings'
of his time, and abstracted many days and nights from his
literary and philosophical pursuits to the perusal of Littleton and
Plowden."

Bacon was always a "sociable" man, and one who
affected the amenities of life ; and in the intervals of his
studies he found leisure to join in the revels and pastimes
of the period. He laid out walks in his garden, having,
as one of his pleasantest essays proves, a strong love of

---

* Lord Campbell, "Lives of the Lord Chancellors," ii. 274.

gardening, and planted numerous trees, some of which, on a slight eminence named "Lord Bacon's Mount," were standing as late as the reign of William IV.

On the 27th of June, 1582, he was called to the bar; and immediately, according to use and wont, walked in Fleet Street in his serge and bands, to intimate his willingness to practise for fees.   In 1584, he had made so much progress as to obtain a seat in the House of Commons, having been elected member for the Dorsetshire port of Melcombe Regis.   The House at that time was graced by many illustrious statesmen and brilliant speakers, men whose names are now enrolled on the list of "the immortals," whose deeds are part and parcel of English history; but, after a brief interval of preparation, Bacon stood forward among them as equal to the brightest and best in the keenness of his wit, the felicity of his humour, the force of his reasoning, and the scope of his sagacity.   A critic so complete as Ben Jonson bears the fullest testimony to his exalted oratorical powers.

"There happened in my time," he says, "one noble speaker who was full of gravity in his speaking.  His language, when he could spare or pass by a jest, was nobly censorious.  No man ever spoke more neatly, more pressly, more weightily, or suffered less emptiness, less idleness, in what he uttered.  No number of his speech but consisted of his own graces.  His hearers could not cough or look aside from him without loss.  He commanded where he spoke, and had his judges angry and pleased at his devotion (that is, at his will).  No man had their affections more in his power.  The fear of every man that heard him was lest he should make an end."

Bacon was early admitted to the inner bar, and immediately afterwards was elected a Bencher of the Society.  Within two years he was made Lent Reader;

and so wide and great was his reputation for learning and eloquence that Elizabeth, in order to secure the benefit of his advice, created for him the office of Counsel Extraordinary. But it was fame and social consideration, rather than any substantial position or solid advantage, the brilliant lawyer had as yet acquired. Sir Robert Cecil's powerful influence worked against him; and he was represented as no real lawyer, but as a speculative and painful theorist, who indulged himself in philosophical reveries, and was far more likely to perplex than promote public business.*

It is not improbable that his slow advancement may in part have been due to the courage with which he had presented himself in the House of Commons as a reformer. He did not speak with bated breath or whispering humbleness, but strongly protested, in language as clear as it was forcible, against the abuses which clogged the wheels of administration. This was not a line of action calculated to recommend him to the Cecils or to their sovereign.

We gather from his correspondence, that Bacon, like Shakespeare, felt cribbed, cabined, and confined, by the profession he had chosen. His large mind was above "the ordinary practice of the law," and he longed for the means and the leisure to pursue the lofty speculations in which he loved to indulge. Writing to Lord Burleigh, he says :—

"I wax now somewhat ancient; one-and-thirty years is a great deal of sand in the hour-glass. My health, I thank God, I find confirmed, and I do not fear that action shall impair it; because I account my ordinary course of study and meditation to be more painful than most parts of action are. I confess that

* Basil Montagu, "Bacon's Works, with a New Life" (edit. 1825-34).

I have as vast contemplative ends as I have moderate civil ends, for *I have taken all knowledge to be my province ;* and if I could purge it of two sorts of errors—whereof the one with frivolous disputations, confutations, and verbosities; the other with blind experiments and auricular traditions and impostures, hath committed so many spoils—I hope I should bring in industrious observations, grounded conclusions, and profitable inventions and discoveries."

But he was sore beset by his straitened circumstances :

"If your Lordship," he continues, "if your Lordship will not carry me on, I will not do as Anaxagoras did, who reduced himself with contemplation into voluntary poverty; but this I will do—I will sell the inheritance that I have, and purchase some lease of quick revenue, or some office of gain, that shall be executed by deputy, and so give over all care of service, and become some sorry bookmaker, or a true pioneer in that mine of truth which lies so deep."

With the lofty assurance of genius—that self-knowledge and self-reliance which breathe in Horace's " Exegi opus perennius," and Milton's " Which the world will not willingly let die "—he felt that high achievements were within his reach, and that from the mine of truth he had the strength and will to bring up inestimable treasures to the light of day.    Nor did this belief ever desert him. In his last will he wrote : " My name and memory I leave to foreign nations, and to mine own countrymen after some time be over."   Time, as the elder Disraeli remarks, seemed always personified in the imagination of our philosopher; and with Time he wrestled in the full consciousness of triumph.

In the parliament that assembled on the 19th of February, 1593, Bacon took his seat as knight of the shire for Middlesex.   He at once plunged into the debates in his capacity of reformer, attacking the excessive expenditure, and protesting against the subsidy demanded by the queen's ministers. He asked, in reference to it, that three questions might be answered :—

" The first, impossibility or difficulty; the second, danger and discontentment; and thirdly, a better manner of supply. For impossibility, the poor man's rent is such as they are not able to yield it. The gentlemen must sell their plate, and farmers their brass pots, ere this will be paid: and as for us, we are here to search the wounds of the realm, and not to skin them over. We shall breed discontentment in paying these subsidies, and endanger Her Majesty's safety, which must consist more in the love of her people than in their wealth. This being granted, other princes hereafter will look for the like, so that we shall put an evil precedent on ourselves and our posterity."

This language now-a-days would not disturb the most jealous courtier; but Elizabeth had been unaccustomed to opposition, and her ministers and adulators broke out into indignant reproof of this audacious, plain-speaking lawyer. Elizabeth keenly resisted his presumption, and caused the offender to understand that he must expect from her neither favour nor promotion. Yet Bacon's fault had surely been venial; he had not refused to vote supplies for the public service, but had simply condemned the unconstitutional manner in which the queen's ministers proposed to levy them. Bacon sued humbly for pardon, and promised to abandon all further resistance to the policy of the Court. The incident furnishes a clue to the complexities of his character, to its strange combination of strength and weakness, of intellectual strength and moral weakness. At the same time, we must not condemn the inconsistency of his conduct as we should condemn a similar inconsistency in the statesmen of a later age. The men of Elizabeth's generation entertained for her a reverence which was so excessive that we are scarcely able to understand it, and therefore feel disposed to stigmatise it as adulation. But, then, they knew what she was and what she represented; how in her had centred all England's hopes of religious freedom, and national independence, and manly growth. It was natural they should shrink from wounding or offending her. With Bacon, moreover, another motive was powerful. His strong and active mind teemed with great social and political ideas—" the reform and codification of the law, the civilisation of Ireland, the purification of the Church," the diffusion of knowledge, the improvement of the social condition of the people; and these, in the Elizabethan period, could be realised only by the initiative of the Crown. Hence he supported without hesitation the privileges and prerogatives claimed by the Throne; and while eloquently enlarging on the necessity of redressing many grievances, he remained the servant of the Crown and the defender of the Queen.

It was about this time that the restless jealousy of the Cecils brought Bacon into a close connection with their brilliant opponent, the Earl of Essex, then rising like a star of the first magnitude on the political horizon. Young, daring, and gay, the bright young nobleman won hearts without thought or trouble. He was in high favour with the queen, who, as he was her cousin's grandson, claimed the privileges of kinship. Between him and Bacon a warm and cordial intimacy arose. The young Earl was drawn towards Bacon by his genius, learning, and acquirements; Bacon towards him by his splendour and refinement, and, probably, by a secret hope of rising through the influence of his young and powerful patron.

Early in 1594, Egerton, the attorney-general, was made master of the rolls. To the vacant attorneyship Essex endeavoured to secure the promotion of Bacon, and it is recorded that on this subject the following conversation took place between himself and Sir Robert Cecil :—

"*Cecil.* 'My Lord, the queen has determined to appoint an attorney-general without more delay. I pray, my lord, let me know whom you will favour.'

"*Essex.* 'I wonder at your question. You cannot but know that resolutely against all the world I stand for your cousin, Francis Bacon.'

"*Cecil.* 'I wonder your lordship should spend your strength on so unlikely a matter. Can you name one precedent of so raw a youth promoted to so great a place?'

"*Essex.* 'I have made no search for precedents of young men who have filled the office of attorney-general; but I could name to you, Sir Robert, a man younger than Francis, less learned, and equally inexperienced, who is suing and striving with all his might for an office of far greater weight.'

"*Cecil.* 'I hope my abilities, such as they are, may be equal to the place of secretary, and my father's long services may deserve such a mark of gratitude from the queen. That although Her Majesty can hardly stomach one so inexperienced being made her attorney, if he would be contented with the solicitor's place, it might be of easier digestion to her.'

"*Essex.* 'Digest me no digestions. The attorneyship for Francis is that I must have, and in that I will spend all my power, might, authority, and amity, and with tooth and nail procure the same for him against whomsoever.'" *

Sir Edward Coke, the solicitor-general, succeeded

---

* Dr. Nares, "Life of Lord Burleigh," iii. 436. There is an apocryphal air about this conversation.

Egerton.   Bacon can hardly have expected to have leaped over his head into the higher office; and it was upon the vacant solicitor-generalship that he concentrated his hopes and energies.   He addressed himself to Burleigh, to the lord-keeper, to the master of the rolls.   At first the Cecils were not indisposed to favour him, but Essex interposing with his usual impetuosity, they turned against his nominee in order to inflict a fresh defeat on the powerful young noble.   In this strait Bacon appealed directly to Elizabeth, in a letter which is not wholly wanting in manliness of tone :—

"Madam," he wrote, "remembering that your Majesty has been gracious to me, both in countenancing me and conferring upon me the reversion of a good place,* and perceiving that your Majesty had taken some displeasure towards me, both these were arguments to move me to offer unto your Majesty my service, to the end to have means to deserve your favour and to repair my error.   Upon this ground I affected myself to no great matter, but only a place of my profession, such as I do see divers younger in proceeding to myself, and even of no great note, do without blame aspire unto.   But if any of my friends do press this matter, I do assure your Majesty my spirit is not with them. It sufficeth me that I have let your Majesty know that I am ready to do that for the service which I never would do for mine own gain.   And if your Majesty like others better, I shall, with the Lacedemonian, be glad that there is such choice of abler men than myself.   Your Majesty's fervour, indeed, and access to your royal person, I did ever, encouraged by your own speeches, seek and desire, and I would be very glad to be reintegrate in that.   But I will not wrong mine own good mind so much as to stand upon that now, when your Majesty may conceive I do it but to make my profit of it.   But my mind turneth

---

* The Registrarship of the Star Chamber, worth about £1600 a-year ; but this did not fall into his hands for some years.

upon other wheels than those of profit. The conclusion shall be, that I wish your Majesty served answerable to yourself. *Principio est virtus maxima nosse suos.* Thus I must humbly crave pardon of my boldness and plainness. God preserve your Majesty ! "

It would be wronging Bacon to suppose that he hungered after office for the sake of its emoluments. He was conscious of the ability to do good service to the State, and when he compared himself with his competitors, could not but recognise his intellectual superiority. That he thirsted after an opportunity of proving this to the world in a way honourable to himself and advantageous to his country is not to his discredit. His entreaties, however, and the recommendations of Essex, were alike ineffectual. Mr. Sergeant Fleming was appointed to the vacant office; a man whose chief distinction is that on this occasion he defeated Bacon.

That Bacon keenly felt the disappointment we gather from a letter which his mother addressed to his elder brother :—

"*3rd June,* 1595.

"I am sorry your brother with inward secret grief hindereth his health. Everybody saith he looketh thin and pale. Let him look to God, and confer with Him in godly exercise of hearing and reading, and continue to be noted to take care. I had rather ye both, with God's blessed favour, had very good health, and were well out of debt, than any office. Yet, though the Earl showed great affection, he marred all with violent courses.

"I pray God increase His fear in his heart, and a hatred of sin ; indeed, halting before the Lord, and backsliding, are very pernicious. I am heartily sorry to hear how he [the Earl of Essex] sweareth and gameth unreasonably. God cannot like it.

"I pray show your brother this letter, but to no creature else. Remember me and yourself.—Your mother,

"ANNE BACON."

To soften Bacon's disappointment, the queen bestowed upon him the estate of Zelwood in Somersetshire, and appointed him her counsel learned in the law. What he valued more, perhaps, was her generous gift of a reversion of the lease of Twickenham Park, a beautiful sylvan solitude to which he was exceedingly partial. Thither he retired to enjoy "the blessings of contemplation in that sweet solitariness which collecteth the mind, as shutting the eyes does the sight." He received from Essex a grant of land in the same neighbourhood, worth about £1500, as an acknowledgment of the services he had rendered.

He took an admirable method of proving his fitness for the office he had coveted and lost, by publishing, or rather circulating in MS., a "recondite and accurate" treatise "Upon the Elements and Use of the Common Law," which contains one of the earliest examples of his system of inductive reasoning. Early in 1597, he published a book more congenial to his own tastes, and certainly of greater utility to the world at large—his famous "Essays," a small but precious volume of noble thoughts and apt and pregnant images, embodied in stately language. These he counted simply as "the recreation of his other studies," flinging them out on the world right royally, as an Oriental prince lavishes the rarest gems with indifferent hand. They are remarkable for their wide range of subject, their worldly wisdom, their compactness of thought, their felicity of expression ; but yet more remarkable for the power and success with which their author applies to human life and human motives that "experimental analysis," which, at a later date, he was to apply with such great results to Science.

It was at this time that Bacon, whose fame had steadily ripened, without any corresponding development of his worldly fortunes, offered his hand to the well-born and opulent widow, Lady Hatton, a grand-daughter of Lord Burleigh. She was rich, handsome, clever, witty, and—a shrew. In his suit he was strongly supported by his steadfast patron, Essex, who wrote in his favour both to the lady and her father ; but happily for Bacon, she chose for her husband his elderly and powerful rival, Attorney-General Coke, whom, as Macaulay says, she did her best to make as miserable as he deserved to be. This mercenary courtship of Bacon's does not raise our opinion of his character, which, indeed, was pitifully deficient in moral fibre and the elements of true greatness. Its sole excuse is to be found in his pecuniary difficulties, which would seem to have been very grave, as he was arrested by a money-lender, named Simpson, on a bond for £300, apparently as soon as the failure of his matrimonial venture became known. "A dispute had arisen about the bond, and the matter having been argued during Trinity Term, 1598, the settlement was postponed, with Simpson's consent, until Michaelmas Term. On the 24th of September, two or three weeks before the time of settlement arrived, Bacon, going down to the Tower on Her Majesty's affairs, had been arrested at the suit of Simpson, and lodged by his captors in a sponging-house in Coleman Street, whence he sent to Lombard Street for Simpson, who, perhaps aware that he had no power to arrest a queen's officer actually engaged in Her Majesty's service, even if the days of grace were fully expired, refused to come. Bacon appealed to the Lord Keeper and to the Secretary of State against this illegal arrest. The bond was discharged before it was due, and Bacon returned to his lodgings in Coney Court.

The principal importance of this incident arises from the use made of it by Attorney-General Coke, with the view and for the purpose of injuring his great rival. It chanced that Bacon, having to move in the Court of Exchequer for the confiscation of certain lands belonging to a recusant papist, George More, had occasion to refer to Coke, and though his language was mild and moderate, he did not fail to excite Coke's fervent indignation. The attorney-general broke out—

"'Mr. Bacon, if you have any tooth against me, pluck it out, for it will do you more hurt than all the teeth in your head will do you good.'

"*Bacon.* 'Mr. Attorney, I respect you; I fear you not; and the less you speak of your own greatness, the more I will think of it.'

"*Coke.* 'I think scorn to stand upon terms of greatness towards you, who are less than little; less than the least.'

"*Bacon.* 'Mr. Attorney, do not depress me so far; for I have been your better, and may be again, when it pleases the queen.'

"With this," says Bacon, who is himself the chronicler of the occurrence, "with this he spake neither I nor himself could tell what, as if he had been born attorney-general; and in the end bade me not meddle with the queen's business, but with mine own; and that I was unsworn, &c. [That is, had not taken the oath of allegiance as attorney or solicitor-general.] I told him, sworn or unsworn was all one to an honest man; and that I ever set my service first, and myself second, and wished to God he would do the like. Then he said it were good to clap a *capias ut legatum* [a reference to the arrest for debt] upon my back! To which I only said he could not; and that he was at fault, for he hunted upon an old scent. He gave me a number of disgraceful words besides, which I answered with silence, and showing that I was not moved with them."

D

In the same year, Bacon gave further illustration of
the solidity and extent of his legal learning by the production of his "History of the Alienation Office," which,
according to Lord Campbell, shows "a most copious and
accurate acquaintance with existing law and with our
legal antiquities." Another learned tractate "On the
Statutes of Uses" is characterised as possessing "the
legal acuteness of a Fearne or a Sugden."

This, as Lord Campbell says, was the most auspicious
period of Bacon's career, and the one to which, in later
life, he probably looked back with the greatest satisfaction. As yet he had not forfeited his self-respect, nor
the esteem of men whose esteem was an honour. His
pecuniary difficulties were being rapidly relieved by the
increase of his practice at the bar. He was in high
favour with the queen, who had conquered her prejudice
against him, and consulted him more frequently than
she did her attorney-general. Not only did she receive
him in audience at the Palace, but often visited him in
his retirement among the green shades of Twickenham.
It was on one of these occasions that he dexterously
turned aside the royal wrath from a young, hot-headed
doctor of civil law, who had published a wild and almost
treasonable book about the deposition of Richard II., and
had hinted at the Earl of Essex as a future Bolingbroke.

"There was treason in it," exclaimed the suspicious sovereign;
and, appealing to Bacon, she inquired, Could he find no places
in it that might be drawn within case of treason?

"For *treason*, Madame," replied Bacon, "I surely find none;
but for *felony*, very many." Felony was hanging matter as
well as treason; so the queen, well-pleased, replied—

"Wherein? Felony? Where?"

"Madame," said Bacon, with a grave smile, "the author hath

committed very apparent theft, for he hath taken most of the sentences of Cornelius Tacitus, translated them into English, and put them into his text."

"But Hayward," continued Elizabeth, "is a fool; some one else hath writ the book. Make him confess it; put it to the rack."

"Nay, Madame," answered Bacon, with evident enjoyment of his own humour, "rack not his body, rack his style. Give him paper and pens and ink, with what help he needs of books; bid him carry on his tale. By comparing the two parts, I will tell you if he be the true man."*

## II.

The poet Pope, in a well-known couplet, has made use of Bacon to point a moral and adorn a tale, and has contrived to embody the praises of his admirers, as well as the censures of his detractors, in the famous line—

"The wisest, brightest, *meanest* of mankind."

But Pope was not a profound student, and probably based his epigrammatic estimate of the philosopher's character upon the gossip of the old diarist, Sir Symond d'Ewes, who, in evil alliance with the notorious Anthony Weldon and Sir Edward Coke, Bacon's life-long adversary, may be regarded as the source of most of the foul and black aspersions cast upon his fame. In our own time, Lord Macaulay has lent the force of his brilliant rhetoric, and Lord Campbell the weight of his legal acumen, to the unfavourable view of Bacon's character. The kindlier and more generous judgment, originally put forward by

---

* Bacon's "Apology," in his Works (Basil Montagu's edit.), vi. 220-222.

Ben Jonson, Aubrey, and the philosopher Hobbes, has
been supported by Basil Montagu, and of late, with
greater exactness and more complete research, by Mr.
Hepworth Dixon and Mr. James Spedding, who, while
not concealing his moral weakness, has vindicated his
memory against the graver charges, and established his
claims to the love and gratitude of his countrymen.   To
the impartial critic I think he will be, what he was to
Ben Jonson, " one of the greatest men and most worthy
of admiration that had been in many ages."

Respecting no part of Bacon's career have his assail-
ants and defenders more hotly contested than that which
involves his intimate relations with the Earl of Essex.
The unfriendly biographer represents his conduct as marked
by the blackest treachery and meanest ingratitude ; the
panegyrist sees in it the action of a wise and honest man,
who loved the vain and gay young noble much, but his
queen and country more.   I believe that the true course
is to accept a mean between these extreme opinions, and
to believe that Bacon laboured honestly in the cause of
Essex, and would gladly have saved him if his own levity
and ill-regulated ambition had not rendered it impossible ;
but that he refrained, like a prudent man and a loyal
subject, from hopelessly entangling himself in his patron's
ruin.   He stood manfully by the earl until it was evident
that he could no longer serve him, but might bring about
his own destruction ; and to me it is not clear why,
because he was the author of the "*Novum Organum*," he
should yet have acted without the least worldly discretion.
Nor do I see that the guilt of Essex can reasonably
be doubted.   His execution was a political necessity;
his crime was a crime which Elizabeth could not have
pardoned if she would ; and Bacon, as a lawyer and a

faithful subject, was bound to declare his abhorrence of the treason, whatever feelings of compassion and old friendship he might secretly cherish towards the traitor. Lord Campbell admits—what is indeed a truism—that "friendship cannot justify treason or any violation of the law;" "but," he asks, "are the sacred ties of friendship to be snapped asunder by the caprice of any crowned head?" This is the merest sophistry. Friendship does not require a man to defend a traitor, and we should be loath to recognise its "sacred ties" if our former friend proved ready to betray both his queen and fatherland.

From the earliest date of Bacon's connection with Essex, he showed himself a frank and a sincere friend. Even Lord Macaulay admits that the advice which he gave was generally most judicious. He did all that he could to dissuade the earl from accepting the perilous charge of the Irish Government—then, as now, a burden bringing with it more pain than honour. "For," says Bacon, "I did as plainly see his overthrow, chained as it were by destiny to that journey, as it is possible for a man to ground a judgment upon future contingents." His foresight was vindicated; Essex returned in disgrace. Bacon then attempted to mediate between his friend and the queen, and, we believe, honestly employed all his address for that purpose. But the task which he had undertaken was too difficult, delicate, and perilous even for so wary and dexterous an agent. He had to manage two spirits equally proud, resentful, and ungovernable. At Essex House he had to calm the rage of a young hero incensed by multiplied wrongs and humiliations, and then to pass to Whitehall for the purpose of soothing the peevishness of a sovereign whose temper, never very gentle, had been rendered morbidly irritable by age, by

declining health, and by the long habit of listening to
flattery and exacting implicit obedience.   In a word, he
had to choose between Essex and his queen.   It is the
fashion to speak of the earl as Bacon's " noble benefactor,"
but I cannot find that he overpaid Bacon's services.   It is
not less the fashion to speak lightly of the earl's crime;
to refer to it as the mere indiscretion of a passionate and
wounded nature; and yet he could scarcely have sinned
more deeply than he did sin against his generous queen
and patron.

It was due to the influence which Bacon now enjoyed
with the queen that Essex was forgiven for his strange
and wayward conduct in Ireland; but no sooner did he
feel himself personally safe than he renewed his desperate
intrigues.   Abandoned by his old Protestant friends, he
filled their places with subtle, designing Papists, the
meanest of conspirators and most reckless of adventurers.
Then the plot went bravely on.   Lord Mountjoy was to
bring over an army from Ireland; the queen's person
was to be seized, and her deposition effected; Raleigh,
Cobham, and Cecil, her chief advisers, were to be slain;
and then Essex might play at dictator, or call in James
of Scotland, if he were not previously overthrown by the
dark intriguers into whose hands his passion had thrown
him.   Bacon made one more attempt to dissipate Elizabeth's anger, but by this time she was aware of the full
compass of the earl's guilt.   Every hour increased the
weight and added to the fulness of the evidence against
him.   When Bacon pleaded for him, her wrath blazed
up, and for three months the unlucky advocate was shut
out from her favour.   From Michaelmas to Christmas
this burst of royal anger lasted.   At the New-Year
Bacon contrived to gain admittance to her presence.

"Madame," he said,* "I see you withdraw your favour from me; and now I have lost many friends for your sake, I lose you too. You have put me like one of those that the Frenchmen call *enfans perdus*, that serve on foot before horsemen; so have you put me into matters of envy without place or without strength; and I know at chess a pawn before the king is usual played upon. A great many love me not, because they think I have been against my Lord of Essex; and you love me not, because you know I have been for him. Yet will I never repent me that I have dealt in simplicity of heart towards you both, without respect of caution to myself; and, therefore, *vivus vidensque pereo.* If I do break my neck, I shall do it in a manner as Master Dorrington did it, who walked on the battlements of the church many days, and took a view and survey where he should fall. And so, Madame, I am not so simple but that I take a prospect of mine overthrow; only I thought I would tell you so much that you may know that it was faith and not folly that brought me into it. And so I will pray for you."

The simplicity and candour of this appeal much moved the queen, who took him again into favour, while giving him clearly to understand that he must refrain from further advocacy of Essex.

A great man would doubtlessly have remained true to his friend though the heavens had fallen, but Bacon was a man of great genius, not a great man. He had nothing of the heroic in him; nothing of the stuff that makes martyrs; and he acted as, I suppose, all prudent men in his place would have acted. His intellectual and moral natures differed vastly; nothing was too bold for his mind to grasp at, but his nervous and timid temperament shrunk from self-denial or self-sacrifice. It was easier for him to yield than to stand firm; and no

---

* Bacon's "Apology," Works, vi. 231.

doubt he was always able to satisfy his conscience by considerations of expediency.

The dark drama of the fate of Essex hastened rapidly to its *dénouement*. It was in the hush and calm of a Sabbath morning that, suddenly and all unexpectedly, the highest officials in the realm—Lord-Keeper Egerton, Lord Chief-Justice Popham, and the Lord Comptroller Knollys—appeared at the gate of Essex House. The plotters arose to discover that their intrigues were known. All was immediately confusion and dismay. The earl's house of cards tumbled to pieces in a moment. But, relying on his popularity with the Londoners, they determined on an effort of resistance. They sallied forth into the streets to rouse the citizens against the queen's government. With drawn sword Essex advanced at their head, shouting, "For the Queen! for the Queen! a plot is laid for my life!" But there was no response. No citizen joined the ranks of that despairing company. Sorely dismayed, Essex took boat at Queenhithe, and returned to his mansion, surrendering quietly on the arrival of the Lord Admiral Nottingham with the trainbands. In a few hours he was a prisoner in the Tower; and thus disastrously ended the "Ride of the Mad Earl."

On the 19th of February, 1601, he was brought up for trial. His guilt was clear; the evidence of it indisputable. The simplest of tasks lay before the prosecutors, and we could wish, therefore, that Bacon had refrained from undertaking it. He might have left it to Attorney-General Coke and Solicitor-General Henning. Though it is true that he acted in discharge of his official duty; if for once he had put that duty by, none would have blamed him. But he yearned to make his favour with the queen; and in his anxiety to please the sovereign, forgot the delicacy he owed to the friend and patron. Nay, he plunged into such severities of language as to justify the earl's warning to his judges to be on their guard against "those orators who, out of a form and custom of speaking, would throw so much criminal odium upon him, while answering at the peril of his life a particular charge brought against him." Let the reader, however, take for what it is worth Bacon's own justificatory plea, that what he did at the bar in his public service, " by the rules of duty," he was bound to do " honestly and without prevarication."

After the earl's execution, it was judged advisable to put before the public a narrative of his crimes, and Bacon was chosen to be the penman. Sending for him to the Palace, the queen commanded him to draw up, from materials furnished by herself and her Privy Council, such a State Paper as should satisfy the world that Essex had justly been condemned and had justly suffered. It was a labour of pain, however accomplished; for if there were much that Elizabeth wished to conceal, out of regard for the memory of the young kinsman she had once loved, there was much that it was necessary to publish in vindication of the course she had adopted. Bacon's first essay was so gently worded that the queen and her counsellors took it in hand, strengthened its expressions, and elaborated its points. Then she bade him write it out afresh. Even when " the Declaration of the Practices and Treasons of the late Earl of Essex and his Complices" had been thus embittered, she sent again for its author, complaining of the leniency of the sentiment and the tenderness of the language. " It is my Lord of Essex, my Lord of Essex," she said, " on every page ! You can't forget your old respect for the traitor. Strike it out; make it Essex, or the late Earl of Essex." But as thus amended, it still remains "the most gentle and moderate State Paper ever published in any kingdom."

There was a sumptuousness—or, shall we say, a sensuousness—in Bacon's intellectual nature which was keenly responsive to the beauty of form and colour. He delighted in the bloom and fragrance of flowers, in the harmonies of sweet music, the richness of rare tapestries, and gems, and marbles, and the glory of a well-ordered garden, with its murmur of fountains and shade of cedar alleys. When he sought a wife, he looked, therefore, for comeliness of person as well as the graces of an accomplished mind. For, as he himself says, with his usual rhythm of language : " Beauty is as summer fruits, which are easy to corrupt, and cannot last; and, for the most part, it makes a dissolute youth, and an age a little out of countenance; but yet certainly again, if it light well, it maketh virtues shine and vices blush."

Writing to Sir Robert Cecil, he says : " I have found an alderman's daughter, a handsome maiden, to my liking." This was Alice Barnham, the daughter of Alderman Benedict Barnham and Dorothy his wife. Mistress Dorothy, about 1603, had become a widow, but being beautiful, accomplished, and ambitious, she aimed at making a second marriage which should give her rank and social position. She obtained her desire, wedding Sir John Pakington, of Hampton Court. Her ambition expanded farther, and she looked out for a splendid match for her lovely daughter. When Bacon presented himself, she by no means encouraged his suit; and it was not until he had won a knight's spurs from James I. (21st July, 1603), had distinguished himself as a debater in the House of Commons, and burst upon the world with his great work on "The Advancement of Learning," that Dame Pakington could be induced to yield her assent.

And then the marriage-day was named—10th May, 1606. Of the festivities which graced it, a vivid picture has been sketched by Mr. Hepworth Dixon :—

"Feathers and lace lighted up the rooms in the Strand [where Sir John Pakington, the bride's step-father resided]. Cecil [Sir Robert] was invited to come over from Salisbury House and taste the feast; but the hunchback earl would not cross the street. Three of his gentlemen—Sir Walter Cope, Sir Baptist Hicks, and Sir Hugh Baston—hard drinkers, and men about town, struted over in his stead, flaunting in their swords and plumes; yet the prodigal bridegroom, sumptuous in his tastes as in his genius, clad in a suit of Genoese velvet, purple from cap to shoe, outbraved them all. The bride was richly dight; her whole dowry, as her guests observed, seeming to be piled on her in cloth of silver and ornaments of gold. The wedding rite was performed at St. Marylebone Chapel, two miles from the Strand, among the lanes and suburbs winding towards the foot of Hampstead Hill. Who that is blessed with sympathy or poetry cannot see how that glad and shining party rode to the rural church on the sunny 10th of May? How the girls would laugh, and Sir John would joke, as they wound through lanes then white with thorn and the bloom of pears? How the bridesmaids scattered rosemary, and the groomsmen struggled for the kiss? Who cannot imagine that dinner in the Strand, though Salisbury would not come over to Sir John's lodging to kiss the bride? We know that the wit must have been good, for Bacon was there; we may trust Sir John for the quality of his wine. Alice brought to her husband two hundred and twenty pounds a-year, with a further claim, on her mother's death, of one hundred and forty pounds a-year. As Lady Pakington long outlived Bacon, that increase never came into his hands. Two hundred and twenty pounds a-year was his wife's whole fortune. What was not spent in lace and satin for her bridal dress he allowed her to invest for her separate use. From his own estate he settled on her five hundred pounds a-year."

I am unable to see that such a match deserves the epithet of "mercenary" which Bacon's calumniators have applied to it. With more justice, I fear, it may be styled "unhappy." There was no scandal, no open rupture ; but the alderman's daughter cannot have been a "helpmeet" for a man like Bacon. At all events, it is impossible to ignore the significance of the fact that Bacon, in a codicil to his will, revoked "for just and great causes" all previous bequests to his wife, and left her nothing but her marriage settlement.

When James I. ascended the English throne in 1603, Sir Francis Bacon did not fail to address himself to the new sovereign and the new sovereign's favourites, in the hope of obtaining a share of the royal patronage. This is the manner of his appeal to the pedantic taste of Buchanan's pupil :—

"It is observed," he began, "by some upon a place in the Canticles, *Ego sum flos campi et lilium convallium,** but, *a dispari,* it is not said, *Ego sum flos horti et lilium montium,** because the majesty of that person is not enclosed for a few, nor appropriated to the great. And, therefore, most high and mighty king, my most dear and dread sovereign lord, I think there is no subject of your Majesty's which loveth this island, and is not hollow and unworthy, whose heart is not set on fire not only to bring you peace-offerings to make you propitious, but to sacrifice himself a burnt-offering or holocaust to your Majesty's service."

---

\* I am the flower of the field, and the lily of the valley.
† I am the flower of the garden, and the lily of the mountain.

Bacon's keen estimate of his royal master's character we gather from a confidential letter which he wrote to the Earl of Northumberland :—

"His speech is swift and cursory, and in the full dialect of his country; in speech of business, short; in speech of discourse, large. He affecteth popularity by gracing such as he hath heard to be popular, and not by any fashions of his own. He is thought somewhat general in his favours, and his virtue of access is rather because he is much abroad and in fears than that he giveth easy audience. He hasteneth to a mixture of both kingdoms faster than policy will well bear. I told your lordship once before that methought His Majesty rather asked counsel of the time past than of the time to come ; but it is yet early to ground any settled opinion."

Cecil and Bacon were now allies if not friends, and at the instigation of the former, Bacon received, as we have already stated, the honour (if such it were) of knighthood. He desired it simply to gratify the alderman's daughter, who wished to be known as "Dame Alice Bacon." Soon afterwards, in order to silence effectually the slanderous tongues of his many enemies, he published his remarkable "Apology of Sir Francis Bacon in certain imputations concerning the late Earl of Essex ;" a noble piece of self-vindication (as it appears to us), absolutely candid and straightforward, which, as it was certainly accepted by his contemporaries, should hardly be denied by posterity.

In the House of Commons, where he now sat for the borough of Ipswich, his influence rapidly increased. He was the most powerful debater within its walls; while the largeness of his views gave a peculiar dignity and value to his eloquent speeches. He lent a hearty support to the king's favourite project of the Union of England and Scotland, while he did not scruple to maintain his

independence of action by exposing the numerous defects which existed in every department of the administration. Such a man could no longer be neglected, and
in 1607 he became solicitor-general. This office he held
for six years. Though its duties were arduous, and
his practice at the bar had largely increased, he found
time to enrich the literature of his country with the logic
of his " *Cogitata et Visa*," and the wit and fancy of his
" *De Sapientia Velerum.*" He was active also in his
support of the companies of adventurers at whose risk
English colonies were settled in Newfoundland and
Virginia. Nor did he neglect any opportunity of self-
advancement. In order to secure his promotion to the
attorney-generalship when a vacancy occurred, he wrote to
King James the following characteristic letter :—

"It MAY PLEASE YOUR MAJESTY,—Your great and princely
favours towards me in advancing me to place, and, that which
is to me of no less comfort, your Majesty's benign and gracious
acceptation from time to time of my poor services, much above
the merit and value of them, both almost brought me to an
opinion that I may sooner, perchance, be wanting to myself in
not asking, than find your Majesty wanting to me in any very
reasonable and modest desires. And, therefore, perceiving how
at this time preferments of law fly about mine ears, to some
above me and to some below me, I did conceive your Majesty
may think it rather a kind of dulness or want of faith, than
modesty, if I should not come with my pitcher to Jacob's well
as other do. Wherein I shall propound to your Majesty that
which tendeth not so much to the raising of my fortune as to the
settling of my mind ; being sometimes assailed with this cogi-
tation, that by reason of my slowness to see and apprehend
sudden occasions, keeping in one plain course of painful service,
I may, *in fine dicrum*, be in danger to be neglected and forgotten, and if that should be, then were it much better for me

now, while I stand in your Majesty's good opinion, though unworthy, and have some little reputation in the world, to give over the course I am in, and to make proof to do you some honour by my pen, either by writing some faithful narrative of your happy though not untraduced times; or, by recompiling your laws, which I perceive your Majesty laboured with, and hath in your head, as Jupiter had Pallas, or some other the like work, for without some endeavour to do you honour I would not live, than to spend my wits and time in this laborious place wherein I now serve, if it shall be deprived of those outward ornaments which it was wont to have, in respect an assured succession to some place of more dignity and rest, which seemeth now to be an hope altogether casual, if not wholly intercepted. Wherefore, not to hold your Majesty long, my humble suit to your Majesty is that, than the which I cannot well go lower, which is, that I may obtain your royal promise to succeed, if I live, into the attorney's place whensoever it shall be void; its being but the natural and immediate step and rise which the place I now hold hath ever in sort made claim to, and almost never failed of.    In this suit I make no friends but to your Majesty, rely upon no other motive but your grace, nor any other assurance but your word ; whereof I had good experience when I came to the solicitor's place, that it was like the two great lights which, in their motions, are never retrograde.    So, with my best prayers for your Majesty's happiness, I rest." *

In 1613, Bacon's desire was fulfilled.  He was appointed attorney-general, on the elevation of Hobart to the bench as Lord Chief-Justice of the Common Pleas.    He received a further honour in his election by the members of Cambridge University as their representative.    His attorneyship was distinguished by the prosecution of Edmond Peachem, " one of the most despicable wretches who ever brought shame and trouble on the Church," yet

---

* Bacon's Works (edit. Basil Montagu), v. 322.

one whom Bacon's hostile biographers have thought fit to
represent as a martyr and a victim, tortured and racked
almost to the death by the vindictive attorney-general.
In truth, the man was a dishonest scribbler of libels and
treasonable pamphlets, who had malignantly plotted to
involve in ruin some of his staunchest and kindest
patrons, the friends of Bacon, and richly deserved exemplary
punishment.   It is not the less a matter of regret, however, that he was subjected to the torture by order of
the commissioners appointed to inquire into his guilt, and
that among these commissioners should have been the
greatest intellect of the age.   We are not concerned to
represent Bacon as a perfect man.   We admit the flaws
which weakened his character.   Our sole object is to
judge him fairly and tolerantly; to do him that justice
which the world willingly renders to meaner men; and
not to exaggerate errors into crimes, or to take a base
delight—as some of his biographers have notably done—
in enlarging upon the deficiencies of his moral nature.

It was about this time that "a star" of surpassing
brilliancy rose above the horizon of the Court in the
person of George Villiers, afterwards Duke of Buckingham,
the handsomest, cleverest, most brilliant, and most generous of all the favourites of the weak James.   Between
him and Bacon a cordial alliance was gradually cemented;
and to this radiant, volatile youth the grave lawyer-
philosopher inscribed a composition of noble eloquence, entitled, "Advice to Sir George Villiers," indicating the whole
course of duty of an English statesman, and laying down
the true principles of government.   He considers his
subject under eight heads:—(1) Religion and the Church;
(2) Justice and the Laws; (3) The Council and the Great
Officers of the Kingdom; (4) Foreign Negotiations and

embassies ; (5) War, the Navy, and Ports ; (6) Trade at Home ; (7) Colonies ; and (8) The King's Court. It may have been the sumptuousness, the brilliancy, and the many graces of Villiers which touched the fancy and commanded the sympathies of Bacon ; it must have been the vast intellectual power of Bacon which drew the admiration of Villiers. Partly through the latter's influence with the king, and partly through the force of his own great services, Bacon at last obtained the prize of his ambitious hopes, the Great Seal, and on the 7th of March, 1617, was appointed Lord-Keeper of England, in succession to Lord Ellesmere. His accession to this high dignity was the subject of very general congratulation ; and when, on the first day of Easter term, he took his seat on the Chancery Bench, he was attended by a splendid retinue of English notables. The rules he laid down for his guidance in his inaugural speech were excellent :—

"Concerning speedy justice," he said, "I am resolved that my decree shall come speedily upon the hearing. Fresh justice is the sweetest. Justice ought not to be delayed. There ought to be no labouring in causes but that of the counsel at the bar. And because justice is a sacred thing, and the end for which I am called to this place, and therefore is my way to heaven (and if it be shorter it is none the worse), I shall, by the grace of God, as far as God will give me strength, add the afternoon to the forenoon, and some fortnight of the vacation to the terms, for clearing the causes of the Court. Only, the depth of the three long vacations I would reserve for studies of arts and sciences, to which in my nature I am most inclined." *

Bacon nobly fulfilled these voluntary promises. He worked with so much assiduity and energy that in Easter

---

* "Domestic Papers, tempore James I.," xiii. 18. Basil Montagu, "Life and Works of Lord Bacon."

and Trinity terms he settled no fewer than 3658 suits. To his admirable administration of his high office, even Lord Campbell, the most captious and carping of his biographers, who is always ready to hint a suspicion or suggest some depreciatory circumstance, bears testimony :—

"He sat forenoon and afternoon, coming punctually into Court, and staying a little beyond his time to finish a matter, which if postponed might have taken another day; most patiently listening to everything that could assist him in arriving at a right conclusion, but giving a broad hint to counsel by a question, a shrug, or a look, when they were wandering from the subject; not baulking the hopes of the suitors by breaking up to attend a cabinet or the House of Lords; not encouraging lengthiness at the bar to save the trouble of thought; not postponing judgment till the argument was forgotten; not seeking to allay the discontent of the bar by "nods, becks, and wreathed smiles !"

On the 4th of January, 1618, he had the higher distinction of Lord Chancellor bestowed upon him; and, a few months later, he was raised to the peerage by the title of Lord Verulam. By a later creation he became Viscount St. Albans, but posterity has persisted in ignoring both these titles, and in recognising the "father of experimental philosophy" only as Lord Bacon.

These honours he wore with dignity; and, despite the feebleness of his physical frame, induced by incessant application, Bacon might reasonably count on a long and prosperous career. But it is generally in the hour of our greatest success that evil-handed Fortune prepares a poisoned chalice for our lip. The bolt breaks from the unclouded blue. At this moment of triumph the Lord Chancellor was suddenly brought to the very verge of ruin. Sir Edward Coke, his old and persistent rival and enemy, had married his daughter and heiress to Sir John Villiers, the brother of the all-powerful favourite. Bacon did what he could to avoid an alliance which boded him no good; and, in so doing, aroused the indignation of Buckingham, and through him, of the king. His down-fall was imminent, and he averted it only by the most profuse apologies, which Buckingham, after awhile, conde-scended to accept.

It is pleasant to turn from these petty intrigues to record the publication, in October, 1620, of the "*Novum Organum*," the great work which had employed his meditations for thirty years, and was destined to lay the foundation of a new and comprehensive system of inductive philosophy. Its author was more fortunate than poets and philosophers usually find themselves. His genius was permitted at once to enjoy the fruition of its labours. His reputation grew by no small degrees, was watered by no bitter tears of sorrow and disappoint-ment; for the world spontaneously hailed, and with ungrudging applause, the rich and lofty gift—the "noblest birth of time"—laid before it by Bacon's luminous intellect.

Bacon's fortunes had now reached their zenith; he was in the full enjoyment of almost everything which the heart or mind can covet—fame, affluence, high posi-tion, the means of doing good service to his country and humanity, ripe intellectual vigour, the admiration of friends, the applause of the learned. All classes of the community paid him their homage. In the splendour of his renown as philosopher, orator, lawyer, judge, the faults of his character were scarcely perceptible. The energy with which he did his judicial work, and the justice of his decisions, provoked general approval. The king smiled upon his distinguished subject, who was also fortunate enough to be upon good terms with the king's favourite, and it was supposed that he would retain the Great Seal for the full term of his prosperous career.

At Kew he had a pleasant villa, to which, during his busy seasons, he would repair for a day's leisure : and at Gorhambury, where he spent his vacations, he had erected, at a cost of £10,000, a commodious mansion, in which and in its grounds he had indulged his luxurious taste.    In London he kept an ample state at York House, gathering around his hospitable board all that was most distinguished in the society of the day.    It was here that, on his sixtieth birthday, he gave the grand banquet which Ben Jonson has commemorated :—

> " Hail, happy Genius of this ancient pile !
> How comes it all things so about thee smile ?
> The fire, the wine, the men !  And in the midst
> Thou stand'st, as if some mystery thou didst !
> Pardon, I read it in thy face, the day
> For whose return, and many, all these pray ;
> And so do I.   This is the sixtieth year
> Since Bacon, and thy lord, was born, and here ;
> Son to the grave wise Keeper of the Seal—
> Fame and foundation of the English weal.
> What then his father was, that since is he,
> Now with a little more to the degree ;
> England's high Chancellor, the destined heir,
> In his soft cradle, to his father's chair :
> Whose even threads the Fates spin round and full
> Out of their choicest and their whitest wool."

On the 30th of January, 1621, a parliament, which had been summoned by Lord Bacon's advice, assembled at Westminster.    Both at home and abroad the aspect of affairs was so lowering, that the king found it absolutely necessary to seek the support of his " faithful

Commons;" and his Lord Chancellor urged him to win their confidence by redressing the grievances under which the country impatiently groaned. His scheme included a reform in the administration of the law; an abolition of the nefarious monopolies, which impoverished the people; to assail the myrmidons and hangers-on of the Court; an immediate increase of the naval force of the kingdom; and a vigorous foreign policy in the interests of Protestantism.

But each of these proposals was an offence to one or other of James's profligate courtiers, and simply intensified the hatred which they already bore towards the Lord Chancellor. By the able but unscrupulous Dean (afterwards Archbishop) Williams, who secretly coveted the Lord-Keepership; by Sir Lionel Cranfield, whose ambition rested on the Lord Treasurer's staff; and by Sir Edward Coke, whose increasing years brought no diminution of the ancient enmity, a conspiracy was formed against the chancellor, in order to secure his immediate destruction. The circumstances of the time greatly favoured their attempt. A strong feeling of anger and disgust had arisen in the country at the shameless venality which disgraced the administration of justice; and the House of Commons, reflecting the temper of the people, resolved on the punishment of the principal offenders. The judge of the Prerogative Court was impeached for venality, and the Bishop of Llandaff for being accessory to a matter of bribery. Bacon's enemies saw their opportunity, and having made sure that neither Buckingham nor the king would shield him, struck at once, availing themselves of the fee system which existed in the Court of Chancery. The Lord Chancellor and his principal officers received no, or very trivial, salaries, and maintained their dignities and their establishments by means of the presents, fees, " benevolences " —or to use a plainer word—bribes, which they received from the suitors of the court. Such a system was obviously open to abuse; but Bacon, a profuse man, with no apparent power of regulating his expenditure by economical principles, made no attempt to reform it. He took presents from suitors, as probably his predecessors had done, and never paused to inquire, or shrank from inquiring, whether the practice was defensible. But the country had grown weary of it, and was resolved that the administration of justice should be purged of all suspicion and discredit.

Soon after the meeting of parliament, Sir Edward Coke obtained a committee of the whole House to sit on Wednesdays, and hear complaints relative to the Courts of Justice. It soon became known that its object was to obtain evidence in support of a charge of bribery and corruption against the chancellor; and on the 19th of March, their charge was openly preferred at the bar of the House of Lords. It took cognisance of two-and-twenty items. Bacon, at the time, lay at York House, very sick and feeble; but he hastened to address to the Lords the following dignified and pathetic letter :—

" MY VERY GOOD LORDS,—I humbly pray your Lordships all to make a favourable and true construction of my absence. It is no feigning, nor fainting, but sickness, both of my heart and of my back, though joined with that comfort of mind that persuadest me that I am not far from heaven, whereof I feel the first fruits. And because, whether I live or die, I would be glad to preserve my honour and fame as far as I am worthy. Hearing that some complaints of base bribery are come before your Lordships, my requests unto your Lordships are :--

"First, that you will maintain me in your good opinion, without prejudice, until my cause be heard; secondly, that, in regard I have sequestered my mind at this time, in great part, from worldly matters, thinking of my account and answer in a higher court, your Lordships would give me some convenient time, according to the course of other events, to advise with my counsel and to make my answer, wherein, nevertheless, my counsel's part will be the least; for I shall not, by the grace of God, trick up innocency with cavillations, but plainly and ingenuously (as your lordships know my manner is) declare what I know and remember; thirdly, that, according to the course of justice, I may be allowed to except to the witnesses brought against me, and to move questions to your lordships for their cross-examination, and likewise to produce my own witnesses for discovery of the truth; and, lastly, if there were any more petitions of like nature, that your lordships would be pleased not to take any prejudice or apprehension of any number or muster of them, especially against a judge that makes two thousand decrees and orders in a year (not to speak of the courses that have been taken for hunting out complaints against me), but answer them according to the rules of justice, severally and respectfully.

"These requests, I hope, appear to your lordships no other than just.

" And so, thinking myself happy to have so noble peers, several prelates, to discern of my cause, and desiring no privilege for subterfuge of guiltiness, but meaning (as I said) to deal fairly and plainly with your lordships, and to put myself upon your honours' favours, I pray God to bless your counsels and your persons, and rest your lordships' humble servant,

"FR. ST. ALBAN, *Cane*."

It seems to me that this letter was not unworthy of Bacon. It is the language of a *mens conscia recti*, and it was language which, to the last, he continued to hold. "I know," he said, "I have clean hands and a

clean heart." He addressed himself privately both to
the king and the Duke of Buckingham; but the latter
had set his eye upon York House, and the former, though
at first inclined to support his chancellor, was soon persuaded that, by flinging so great a victim before the
Commons, he might check them from pursuing their
perilous investigations. Bacon saw that his ruin was
predetermined, and, like the old Roman, he drew his
cloak around him, and prepared to fall with dignity. It
may be that, by resigning the Seals, he hoped to propitiate his enemies, and avert a struggle for which his
ill-health unfitted him; and he was doubtlessly moved
by the urgent and repeated solicitations of the king, who,
with tears in his eyes, besought the Lord Chancellor to
abandon his defence, surrender his office, and trust his
honour and his fortunes to the Crown. The bitterness
of his enemies, however, was not to be so easily satisfied.
He had not acknowledged his guilt, because he had not
received particulars of the actions alleged against him.
They were now set forth, with the view of wringing from
him a plea of "guilty." Twenty-two were charges of
corruption, one was of carelessness. The majority of
them, however, were speedily abandoned by the accusers
themselves, who confined their indictment to four only.[*]

Bacon was about to be put upon his trial, when, on
the 24th of April, perceiving that he was helpless in the
hands of his enemies, he sent to the Lords, through the
Prince of Wales, his "humble submission and supplication." In this he says :—"I do ingenuously confess and
acknowledge that, having understood the particulars of

---

[*] These have been minutely examined by Mr. Hepworth Dixon in
his "Story of Lord Bacon's Life," and I think he shows very clearly
that an impartial jury would decide that they were "not proven."

the charge not formally from the House, but enough to inform my conscience and memory, I find matter sufficient and full both to move me to desert the defence, and to move your lordships to condemn and answer me."

This is not the confession of a criminal, but rather the submission of a man who feels that he has by his weakness given colour to the accusations of his enemies, and that, as he cannot offer a complete defence, he will attempt no partial explanation. He had done some things weakly, foolishly, thoughtlessly. He had allowed his servants, through want of supervision, to drag their master's high office through much foul mire. He had allowed the continuance of a practice which, as it led to bribery and corruption, he could not excuse; and having allowed it, he owned his responsibility, but "never had he bribe or reward in his eye or thought when pronouncing sentence or order." No fair judgment can be pronounced on the subject of Bacon's moral criminality until, as Mr. Spedding says, four questions have been considered. "1. What was the understanding, open or secret, upon which the present, or 'bribe,' was given or taken? 2. To what extent was the practice prevalent at the time? 3. How far was it tolerated? 4. How stood it with regard to other abuses prevailing at the same time?" No one will deny the reprehensibility of the practice, and Bacon himself, when his conscience was awakened, saw it clearly. It was in this sense that he spoke to Dr. Rawley: "I was the justest judge that was in England these fifty years, but it was the justest censure in Parliament that was there these two hundred years."

The sentence passed upon the ex-chancellor (3rd May) was to the following effect :—

"That the Lord Viscount St. Albans shall undergo fine
and ransom of £40,000; that he shall be imprisoned
in the Tower during the king's pleasure; that he shall
for ever be incapable of any office, place, or employment
in the State or Commonwealth; that he shall never sit
in Parliament, nor come within the verge of the Court."

Thus was compassed the ruin and disgrace of the
greatest Englishman of his time, and his enemies
triumphed in his downfall.  Cranfield became Lord-
Treasurer and Earl of Middlesex; Buckingham obtained
a lease of York House; Williams obtained the Seals.
While these men rejoiced in their spoils, Bacon, on the
31st of May, was carried to the Tower, bearing with him
in his hour of darkness the love and friendship of such
fine natures as Ben Jonson, the learned Selden, the
Church poet George Herbert, Hobbes of Malmesbury, Sir
Robert Cotton, and Sir Henry Savile.

He was moved from the Tower, however, on the following day, through the interposition of Prince Charles,
and allowed to retire to Gorhambury.  At first he yearned
to return to the movement and action of political life;
and his fine being remitted, and a pension of £1200
a-year granted to him, he was not without some hope of
being eventually reinstated in office.  In this he was
disappointed.  In 1624, he received a full pardon, an-
nulling his exclusion from the House of Lords; but by
that time advancing years and increasing weakness had
disabled him from participation in parliamentary contention.  Meanwhile he had renewed the studies and
learned pursuits in which he had always delighted, and
gradually he recovered his composure and intellectual
tranquillity.  His leisure hours were cheered by his birds
and his dogs, his blooming gardens, his thriving planta-

tions, his organ music, his "nicotian weed," and a game at bowls. To this period of calm the world owes a more complete edition of his "Essays," his weighty but too partial "History of Henry VII.," and a Latin translation of his "Advancement of Learning."

---

## NOTE—GORHAMBURY.

A picturesque writer supplies the following sketch of his retreat at Gorhambury :—

"The Gothic pile, enlarged by Sir Nicholas for Lady Anne, which had come into his possession on his brother's death, stood high and dry above the water; and as the stream would not flow up to his house he took his house down to the stream. Avenues of stately trees sloped from the hall-door to the little lakes which, four or five acres in extent, were kept bright as crystal, filled with brilliant fish, and paved with pebbles of various hues. On the banks of one of these lakelets he had built Verulam House, a tiny but enchanted palace, one front leaning on the water, the other glancing, under oak and elm, up the long leafy arcade to his mother's house. This place was furnished and complete. The larders and kitchens were underground; through the centre of the blocks ran a staircase delicately carved; on the rests and landings a series of figures—a bishop, a friar, a king, and the like—not one repeated either in idea or execution; on the door of the upper story statues of Jupiter, Apollo, and the round of gods. Beauty and luxury combined. Chimneypieces prettily wrought, rooms lofty and wainscotted, baths, oratories, divans. Shafts from the chimneys ran round the rooms, with cushions on these shafts so as to garner up the heat. The roof, which was flat and leaded, in the Eastern manner, commanded views of wood and water, plain

and upland, with the square plain Saxon tower of St. Alban's
Abbey high above all.   In the centre pond was a Roman temple
or banqueting-room, paved with black and white marble.   One
of the doors had a device of mirrors, so that a stranger fancied
he was looking into the gardens when the door was closed."—
*Hepworth Dixon.*

An excellent account of Bacon's Gorhambury is given by
Bishop Hind in a letter to Bishop Warburton, 14th June,
1679 :—

"This ancient seat . . . stands very pleasantly on high ground
in the midst of a fine park, well wooded.   There is a gentle
descent from it to a pleasant vale, which again rises gradually
into hills at a distance, and those well cultivated, or finely
planted.   The house itself is of the antique structure, with
turrets, but low, and covered with a white stucco, not unlike
the old part of your lordship's palace at Gloucester.   It is built
round a court, nearly square, the front to the south, with a little
turn, I think, to the east.   The rooms are numerous, but small,
except the hall, which is of moderate size, but too narrow for
the height : the chapel neat and well-proportioned, but damp
and fusty, being (*as is usual with chapels belonging to the lay
lords*) seldom or never used.   On the west side of the house
runs a gallery, about the length of that at Prior Park ; the
windows, especially the oriel window at the west, finely painted ;
the niches covered with pictures of the great men of the time of
the Stuarts ; and the ceiling, which is coved, ornamented with
the great men of antiquity, painted in compartments.   At the
end of the gallery is a return, which serves for a billiard-room.
Underneath the gallery and billiard-room is a portico for walking, and that too painted.   I should have observed that the
chamber floor of the front is a library, furnished, as it seemed to
me on a slight glance, with the books of the time, as the gallery
is with the persons.   The furniture altogether unique, and suitable to the rest.   It is impossible that any fine man or woman
of these times should endure to live at this place ; but the whole

has an air of silence, repose, and recollection very suitable to the idea one has of those

'Shades, that to Bacon could retreat afford ;'

and to me is one of the most delicious seats I ever saw."*

The present mansion, the seat of Earl Verulam, was built in 1778-1785, by Lord Grimston, from the designs of Sir Robert Taylor. It is a spacious semi-classical structure, consisting of a centre of stone, with a grand portico supported on Corinthian columns, and two wings of brick covered with stucco. The hall, library, and reception-rooms are spacious, well-proportioned, and contain a good collection of pictures. Among these are portraits of Sir Nicholas Bacon, the Lord-Keeper; of Francis Bacon, by Vansomar; and of his half-brother, Sir Nathaniel Bacon, painted by himself. There are also portraits of Queen Mary, of Queen Elizabeth (painted by Hilliard), James I., Earls of Pembroke and Cumberland, Archbishop Abbot of Canterbury, Queen Catherine of Braganza, and many other illustrious personages.

On Lord Bacon's death, Gorhambury descended to Sir Thomas Meantys, his cousin and heir, whose widow married Sir Harbottle Grimston. His son purchased the reversion of the estate, which has since continued in his descendants, created successively Viscount Grimston, and, in 1815, Earl of Verulam.

Gorhambury stands in the midst of a noble and well-wooded park of six hundred acres, about a mile and a-half to the north-east of St. Albans. Some remains of Bacon's house are still extant.

---

### III.

I have said that a full pardon being granted to Bacon, he was entitled once more to take his place among his peers. But no parliament was summoned during the

---

* "Letters from a late Eminent Prelate to one of his Friends," p. 429.

remainder of James I.'s reign, and, after the accession of Charles I., he was prevented by his age and
infirmities from taking his seat. Already the silver cord
was loosed, the golden bowl broken. A frame, naturally weak, was bent and bowed by severe study, physical
as well as mental suffering, disease as well as the consciousness of errors committed and wrongs endured. The
unwearied fingers still plied the eloquent pen; but Bacon
felt that the sun was sinking, and prepared to meet his
end with Christian heroism. He effected a reconciliation
with his enemies, even with the specious and crafty
Williams, and made his last testamentary arrangements.
Still, from all parts of Christendom came the great and
learned, anxious to pay their homage to the Apostle of
Experimental Philosophy. Visited by the Marquis d'Effiat
—who had accompanied Queen Henrietta Maria to England—and disliking to expose the ravages of a cruel
disease, Bacon received him in a darkened bed-chamber,
and with curtains drawn. "You resemble the angels,"
said the Frenchman courteously, "we hear them frequently spoken of, we know them to be superior to
mankind, and yet we have never the consolation to see
them." "My infirmities," rejoined Bacon gravely, "tell
me I am a man."

It was when thinking of this noble close to the great
philosopher's career, that Ben Johnson wrote:—

"My conceit towards his person was never increased by his
place or honours; but I love and do reverence him for the greatness that was only proper to himself, in that he seemed to me,
ever by his works, one of the greatest men, and most worthy of
admiration, that had been in many ages; in his adversity I ever
prayed that God would give him strength,—for greatness he
would not want; neither could I condole in a word or syllable

for him, as knowing no accident could do harm to virtue, but rather help to make it manifest."

At home his popularity was due, I think, more to his eloquence as a speaker, and his repute as a man of great parts and learning, than to any general appreciation of the grandeur of his philosophical work. Writing a few years after Bacon's death, Dr. Rawley, his chaplain and biographer, observes :—" His fame is greater and sounds louder in foreign parts abroad than at home in his own nation, thereby verifying that divine sentence, 'A prophet is not without honour, save in his own country and his own house.'" Even the scholar and the man of science did not comprehend the true value and significance of the new philosopher. "Bacon was no great philosopher," said Harvey, contemptuously; "he writes philosophy like a Lord Chancellor." Sir Edward Coke received a presentation copy of the "*Novum Organum*." A device on the title-page represented a ship sailing between the Pillars of Hercules, with the proud motto of "*Plus ultra*." The narrow-minded sciolist wrote above it, in allusion to the German satire of "The Ship of Fools," a miserable distich, which embalms for ever his pretentious ignorance :—

> "It deserveth not to be read in schools,
> But to be freighted in the Ship of Fools."

Thanks to the sweet air of Gorhambury, Bacon's health during the autumn of 1625 made some improvement, but the rigorous winter which followed compelled him to return to London for the benefit of medical advice. He lodged at Gray's Inn, and busied himself in the preparation of a new edition of his "Natural History." As he was investigating the nicest methods of preventing putrefaction of animal substances, it occurred to him

that snow might prove as good a preservative as salt.
To test the idea, he ordered an excursion into the
country, where, owing to the protracted severity of the
weather, snow might yet be found. Accompanied by
Dr. Witherborne, the king's physician, he drove out to
Highgate, where he stopped at a small cottage at the foot
of the hill, purchased a hen lately killed, and stuffed its
body with snow, which he thrust in with his own hands.
He was almost immediately seized with a chill, and finding himself too unwell to return to Gray's Inn, he was
conveyed to Lord Arundel's house at Highgate. There
he was warmly welcomed; but, being a peer and an ex-
chancellor, the attendants could do no less than put him
into the State bed, which was unhappily damp, and sorely
aggravated his disease. For a day or two, indeed,
nature seemed to rally, but the cold was followed by
fever, the fever induced congestion of the lungs, and, in
the calmness of an assured hope, his pure and noble spirit
passed away to that Heaven of which only it was worthy
—"*cœtum conciliumque divinum animorum immor-
talium*"—early in the morning of Easter Sunday, the
9th of April, 1626.

> " Full of repentance,
> Continual meditations, tears, and sorrows,
> He gave his honours to the world again,
> His blessed part to Heaven, and slept in peace."

" My name and memory," says Bacon, in words I have
already quoted, " I leave to men's charitable speeches, and
to foreign nations, and to the next ages." The legacy is
one in which England—though England is not named—
must have a share. She can neither surrender her claim
to his writings as a precious portion of her literature, nor

abandon the advantage which her sons may derive from his character and example.

No doubt, as we have already acknowledged, he was deficient in moral strength. He loved pomp, and beauty, and brightness, and in the indulgence of these tastes, yielded to a profuse living, which plunged him frequently into pecuniary difficulties. He was too easily drawn aside from absolute rectitude of purpose by his regard for power and place ; yet consciously dishonest he was not, and if he condescended to accept presents, he never allowed them to bias his judgment. He was not "the meanest of mankind," but he was not the strongest. His intentions were loftier than his practice ; his aspirations were purer than his ambition. Yet when this defective-ness has been admitted, how much remains to command our admiration and esteem. And first, he was an in-defatigable student, sacrificing even his life to a philo-sophical experiment. Neither the stir and excitement of a Court, nor the pressure of his high judicial dignity, could abstract him from his beloved studies. Knowledge was the constant object of his labours ; his thoughts, hopes, and desires were concentrated on the acquisition of knowledge. It was the mistress from whose endearing bosom he sorrowed to be torn ; the star, which shed its serenely consoling light on his darkest hour.

Then, again, Bacon, I take it, was a sincere Christian. The light of a tranquil, steadfast, religious spirit seems to radiate from every page of his writings. He recognised in it "the bond of charity, the rule of evil passions, the consolation of the wretched, the support of the timid, the hope of the dying." It was a stay and a support when the storms of adversity buffeted him so rudely; it cheered and sustained him as he entered the valley of the

F

shadow.  His most malignant enemies have not ventured
to accuse him of an irreligious life.  His worst slanderers
do not say that he was insolent in the day of triumph or
abject in the day of dejection ; for in both, his higher and
purer inspiration moderated and restrained him.  He
forgave with ready forgiveness those who had most
deeply injured him, and poured coals of fire on the heads
of his persecutors.  By adversity his character was
ennobled, purified, strengthened ; it developed fresh
graces as troubles pressed more heavily upon him.  He
had learned the sublime lesson — that out of sorrow
springs the highest wisdom.  As he himself says, in that
grand rythmical style of his :—

" Prosperity is the blessing of the Old Testament ; adversity
is the blessing of the New, which carrieth the greater benedic-
tion and the clearer wisdom of God's favour.  Yet, even in the
Old Testament, if you listen to David's lays, you shall hear as
many hearse-like airs as carols ; and the pencil of the Holy
Ghost hath laboured more in describing the afflictions of Job
than the felicities of Solomon.  Prosperity is not without many
fears and distastes ; and adversity is not without comforts and
hopes.  We see in needleworks and embroideries it is more
pleasing to have a lively work upon a sad and solemn ground
than to have a dark and melancholy work upon a lightsome
ground.  Judge, therefore, of the pleasure of the heart by the
pleasure of the eye.  Certainly, virtue is like precious odours,
more fragrant when they are incensed or crushed ; for prosperity doth but discover vice, but adversity doth but discover
virtue."

And so the adversity which overtook Francis Bacon,
brought out all the highest and loveliest qualities of his
nature.

To "the next ages" and "to men's charitable speeches,"

Bacon left the legacy of his philosophy—the grand work of a grand mind, of the most comprehensive genius the world has ever known. Its object was defined by himself to be " usui et commodis hominum," for the advantage and welfare of mankind. " Meditor," he says, " instaurationem philosophiæ ejusmodi quæ nihil inanis aut abstracti habeat, quæque vitæ humanæ conditiones in melius provebat "—I contemplate the inauguration of a system of philosophy, which shall have in it nothing of the vapid or abstruse, but provide for the greater happiness of human life. The Baconian philosophy is essentially practical : it deals with facts, not theories; with experiments, not speculations. Macaulay, in a rhetorical passage, sums up the benefits which it has conferred upon man :—

" It has lengthened life," he says ; " it has mitigated pain ; it has extinguished diseases ; it has increased the fertility of the soil ; it has given new securities to the mariner ; it has furnished new arms to the warrior ; it has spanned great rivers and estu-aries with bridges of form unknown to our fathers ; it has guided the thunderbolt innocuously from heaven to earth ; it has lighted up the night with the splendour of the day ; it has extended the range of the human vision ; it has multiplied the power of the human muscles ; it has accelerated motion ; it has annihilated distance ; it has facilitated intercourse, correspondence, all friendly offices, all despatch of business ; it has enabled men to descend to the depths of the sea, to soar into the air, to penetrate securely into the noxious recesses of the earth, to traverse the land in cars which whirl along without horses, and the ocean in ships which run ten knots an hour against the wind. These are but a part of its fruits, and of its first fruits. For it is a philo-sophy which never rests, which has never attained, which is never perfect. Its law is progress. A point which yesterday was in-visible is its goal to-day, and will be its starting-point to-morrow."

This is eloquent and impressive; but it is over-
coloured. The merit of Bacon did not lie in indicating
the method of modern science, which he did not, which
perhaps it would have been impossible for him to fore-
cast. Of the science of his own day he knew little, and
understood less. The magnetic researches of Gilbert he
despised; the astronomical theory of Copernicus he
refused to accept. He lived, moreover, before the great
sciences of physics and astronomy had taken shape.
But what Bacon did, and in doing conferred an inestimable benefit on later generations, was to demonstrate the
existence of a Philosophy of Science—" to insist on the
unity of knowledge and inquiry throughout the physical
world, to give dignity by the large and noble temper in
which he treated them to the petty details of experiment
in which science had to begin, to clear a way for it
by setting scornfully aside the traditions of the past,
to claim for it its true rank and value, and to point
to the numerous results which its culture would bring in
increasing the power and happiness of mankind."

To natural science he ascribed a place of pre-eminence
which it had never before, but has ever since, been permitted to occupy :—

"Through all those ages," he says, "wherein men of genius
or learning principally or even moderately flourished, the smallest
part of human industry has been spent on natural philosophy,
though this ought to be esteemed as the great mother of the
sciences; for all the rest, if torn from this root, may perhaps be
polished and formed for use, but can receive little increase." . . .
"Let none," he continues, "expect any great promotion of the
sciences, especially in their effective part, unless natural philosophy be drawn out to particular sciences; and, again, unless
these particular sciences be brought back again to natural philo-

sophy. From this defect it is that astronomy, optics, music, many mechanical arts, and (what seems stranger) even moral and civil philosophy and logic, rise but little above the foundations, and only skim over the varieties and surfaces of things."

It was because he found and enunciated to the world this grand conception of the value, importance, and lofty destiny of natural science, that Bacon may justly be honoured by the title so often given to him on erroneous grounds—the Father of Inductive or Experimental Philosophy.

The two books of Francis Bacon, of the " Proficiencie and Advancement of Learning, Divine and Human," were first published in 1616. In 1623, they were translated into Latin, and expounded, under the title of " De Augmentis Scientiarum," libri ix.; in this shape they form a portion of his *magnum opus*, the " Instauratio Magna, or Great Reconstruction of Science." Bacon wrote in Latin from the mistaken belief that it was more permanent than those "modern languages, which would one day play the bankrupt with books;" but his writings have frequently been translated. The " Advancement " should, of course, be read in Bacon's own English, which, if less stately than Hooker's, is rich, strenuous, and musical. In the first book he dilates on the excellence of knowledge, pointing out that its supposed defects originate in human errors, in the mistaken choice of subjects of study, or in imperfect methods of dealing with them. Knowledge was not to be sought, he said, as if it was a couch whereon a searching and restless spirit might repose; or a terrace for a wandering and variable mind to walk up and down with a fair prospect before it; or a tower of state for a proud mind to elevate itself upon; or a fort or commanding ground for strife and contention ; or a shop for profit or sale ; but as a rich storehouse for the Creator's glory and the relief of man's estate. Having vindicated the dignity of knowledge, Bacon, in his second book, proceeds to survey the whole field of human learning, and to inquire what parts thereof lie fresh and waste, and not improved and converted by human industry ; to the end that such a plot, made and recorded to memory, may both minister light to any public designation and also serve to stimulate voluntary effort. He divides knowledge into the three branches, of history, poetry, and philosophy, which he refers to the three parts of man's understanding—memory, imagination, and reason ; and having examined what has been done in each, he comments upon revealed religion, and proceeds to show the inquirer the course or path he should follow in his endeavour to compass a cultivated mind ; the right path being that by which we can most easily contribute to the stock of human learning something worth labouring for, something that will prove to the glory of the Creator and the relief of man's estate.

In the " Instauratio," as the title implies, Bacon's object is to effect a " renewal " or " repair " of human knowledge. We have seen the ground-plan he laid down in the " Advancement ; " that he proved the existence of deficiencies, and arranged and systematised the work to be done. In the " Novum Organum " (1620), of which the first part only was completed after the labour of thirty years, he develops the " new method " by which defects were to be remedied and the bounds of knowledge extended. This is done in a series of aphorisms, spread over two books, arranged in logical sequence, and leading naturally the one to the other, like a succession of terraces.

The first of these is the key-note, the clue or the foundation of the whole Baconian philosophy; and, though a truism now, was, when first enunciated, a revelation.

Man, the servant and interpreter of Nature, can do and understand no farther than he has, either in art or in contemplation, observed the order and method of Nature. Human power and human science are co-incident. The dominion of man over things depends upon the arts and sciences; because, to govern Nature, you must first obey her. The cause and root of all the evils in the sciences was this, that while men ignorantly wondered at and vaunted the powers of the human mind, they forbore to rule its true aids. How little assistance had the useful arts obtained from science! how little had science benefited by the labours of practical men! Whence arose the vagueness and sterility of the physical systems which had been put before the world? Not certainly in anything in Nature itself, for the steadfastness and regularity of its laws mark them out clearly as objects of certain and precise knowledge. Not in any want of ability in the inventors of these systems, many of whom were men of the highest genius of the ages in which they flourished. No, this vagueness, this sterility, originated solely in the perverseness and inadequacy of the methods which had been pursued. Men had sought to create a world from their own conceptions, to draw from their own minds all the materials they employed; but if, on the contrary, they had consulted experience and obser-vation, they would have had facts and not opinions for the ground-work of their reasoning, and might ultimately have attained to a knowledge of the laws that govern the material world.   What was necessary Bacon defined to be, that men should be slow to generalise, going from particular things to those which are but a single step more general, rising from those to others of a broader scope, and so on until they come to universals.   This is the true and untried way (" Aph." xix. *et seq.*.).

He proceeds to dwell upon the distinction between the " idola " or " idols " of the human mind, and the ideas of the Divine.   Of the latter it is said :—" Except ye become as little children, ye shall not enter into the kingdom of heaven."   And, adopting the Apostolic language, he exclaimed : " Little children, keep your-selves from idols."   These " idols," or delusions of the understanding, he divided into—(1) *Idols of the Tribe* (*Idola tribus*), those belonging to mankind as a whole, to man as a race or tribe.   It is falsely asserted that human sense is the measure or standard of things, whereas, on the contrary, all perceptions, whether of the sense or of the mind, are according to the analogy of man, and not according to the analogy of the universe; and the human intellect is to the rays of things as an unequal union, which blends its own nature with the nature of things, and so distorts and injures it.   (2) *Idols of the Cave* (*Idola specus*) are the special weaknesses of the individual, and only too effectual in prejudicing his search after truth.   (3)   *Idols of the Market-place* (*Idola fori*), the creations of prejudice; things not as they are, but as they are represented by the common talk of the market-place, the gossip of the world; and (4) *Idols of the Theatre* (*Idola theatri*), ideas accepted from the dogmatic teachings of philosophers, because as many philosophies as have been received or discovered, so many plays have in truth been acted, creating scenes and unreal worlds.

Having placed the inquirer on his guard against these *idola*, Bacon, in his second book, explains that "inductive method" by which alone truth can be obtained. Everything must be put to the test of experience; no fact must be accepted as such until it has been proved by experiment. In Nature, whatever is, is so under certain conditions, some of which are only accidental, while others are essential. The difference must be carefully ascertained. When this process has been applied to a number of facts, we are in a position by a comparison of the results to determine one of the laws by which Nature is governed. And when we know the laws (*formæ*) and perceive the real unity of Nature in materials apparently dissimilar, we can go on to further experiment. The search after these eternal and immutable laws or forms he describes as constituting "metaphysics;" but the search after the intermediate, and not fundamental laws, he designates "physics."

The study of Nature, therefore, is to be conducted in such wise that it may yield—(*a*) Axioms or laws deduced from experiment; and (*b*) New experiments deduced from these axioms. As the foundation of all knowledge we need a competent "natural and experimental history," which can be obtained only by a "true and legitimate induction." In pursuing our investigations into the laws or *formæ*, we must examine each "nature" or thing in a variety of ways, taking every case as an "instance" (*instantia*), or indication of its possession of certain qualities, and examining them in groups. As, for example, heat; the "instances agreeing" are not as rays of the sun, but vapours, subterranean air, and the like; these must duly be tabulated.   Then we pass on to "negative instances," rays of the sun, in mid air, rays of the moon, cold vapours; all of which are arranged in a second table.   In a third are placed the *instantiæ*, which have more or less of the "nature" under examination, noting the relative increase or decrease in the same subject; this is the Table of Degrees, or Comparative Table.   And so we go on through twenty-seven tables or classes of *instantiæ*, until, by analysis and comparison, we can make from them an induction, and gather in the first harvest of our patient and persevering labours.

Such is a brief outline of Bacon's experimental philosophy,* which threw open the domains of Nature to the enterprise of man.   It was no part of his work to accumulate *results;* his special province was to explain how they might be secured, and to stimulate the mind of man to undertake the task.   "Be strong in hope," he said, "and do not fancy that our 'Instauratio' is something infinite and beyond human reach, when, in truth, it is mindful alike of mortality and humanity.   It does not expect to accomplish its work in the course of a single age, but leaves it to the process of the ages.   Lastly, it seeks for science, not boastfully, within the little cells of the human intellect, but humbly, in the range of the wide, wide world."

---

* For the deficiences of the Baconian method, see Swan's " Principles of Science."

# John Selden.

## 1584-1654.

———◦◇◦———

IN that remarkable portrait-gallery which is known to us as the Earl of Clarendon's "History of the Great Rebellion," * the learned John Selden— perhaps the greatest of our antiquarian lawyers—is thus presented to the critical judgment of posterity.

"He was a person whom no character can flatter, or transmit in any expressions equal to his merit and virtue. He was of so stupendous a learning in all kinds and in all languages (as may appear in his excellent and transcendent writings),that a man would have thought he had been entirely conversant amongst books, and had never spent an hour but in reading and writing; yet his humanity, courtesy, and affability were such, that he would have been thought to have been bred in the best courts; but that his good nature, charity, and delight in doing good, exceeded that breed-ing. His style in all his writings seems harsh, and sometimes obscure, which is not wholly to be imputed to the abstruse subjects of which he commonly treated, not of the paths trod by other men, but to a little undervaluing the beauty of style, and too much propensity to the language of antiquity; but in his conversation he was the most clear discourser, and had the best

---

* No one can deny the vigour and incisiveness with which Claren-don has sketched the " characters " of his contemporaries ; and though no longer of much value as a record of events, for these it must always be valued and consulted.

faculty of making hard things easy, and presenting them to the
understanding, that hath ever been known.  Mr. Hyde was wont
to say that he valued himself upon nothing more than upon
having had Mr. Selden's acquaintance from the time he was very
young, and held it with great delight as long as they were
suffered to continue together in London; and he was much
troubled always when he heard him blamed, censured, and
reproached for staying in London, and in the Parliament, after
they were in rebellion, and in the worst times, which his age
obliged him to do ; and how wicked soever the actions were which
were every day done, he was confident he had not given his consent to them, but would have hindered them if he could with
his own safety, to which he was always enough indulgent.  If he
had some infirmities with other men, they were weighed down
with wonderful and prodigious abilities and excellencies in the
other scale."

This man of " wonderful and prodigious abilities and
excellencies " was born at Salvington, near Tarring, in
Sussex, on the 16th of December, 1584.  On his mother's
side he was well-born, for she came of the knightly family
of Baker ; but his father appears to have been of low
estate.   His early education he obtained at the Free
Grammar School of Chichester, and he made such admirable use of his opportunities and natural gifts that, at
the age of fourteen, he was admitted of Hart Hall, in the
University of Oxford.  Four years later, he removed to
London, and, according to a custom of the time, which
required that a student at law should enter at one of the
inner inns of court before joining the greater societies,
became a member of Clifford's Inn.  In May, 1604, he
was admitted of the Inner Temple, and soon afterwards
was called to the bar.

Of his favourite studies, and the various stages of his
intellectual growth, biography, up to this date, records

but few particulars. It is clear, however, that he was an assiduous student, and that his inclination led him to investigate antiquarian subjects. He seldom or never appeared at the bar; " but sometimes gave chamber counsel, and was good at conveyancing," thus securing the means and the leisure for the prosecution of his learned pursuits. Having made the acquaintance of Camden, Spelman, and Cotton, to whose painstaking labours the English antiquary is so greatly indebted, he joined them in their researches into the national antiquities; and the first fruits of his industry were garnered up in his " Analecton Anglo-Britannicon Libri Duo," a volume of collections relative to early English history, which he compiled before he was twenty-three years old (1607). It was not published, however, until 1615. Meanwhile, he applied himself to the general study of jurisprudence, and this with such success that, " in a few years," says Anthony à Wood, " his name was wonderfully advanced, not only at home, but in foreign countries, and he was usually styled the great dictator of learning of the English nation."

In 1610, appeared his " England's Epinomis," and " Jani Anglorum Facies Altera," both of them bearing upon points of early English history. In the same year he published his erudite essay on " The Duello, or Single Combat," a minute investigation into the Norman custom of " judicial combat," which is still an authority on the subject. His circle of friends now included Ben Jonson, and Browne, the poet of " Britannia's Pastorals," and Michael Drayton, to the first eighteen songs of whose " Poly-Olbion " he furnished historical and topographical notes.

So far, however, he had not done justice to his capacity

or his learning; but when, in 1614, he gave to the world his elaborate treatise upon "Titles of Honour," the full measure of his erudition was at once perceived. It contains an extraordinary amount of curious information respecting the degrees of nobility and gentry in England, and similar distinctions in other countries, all carefully systematised, and illustrated with judicious comments. Archbishop Usher thought it "Selden's best book;" it is, I think, always excepting the "Table-Talk," his most readable.

With indefatigable industry and keen intellectual acumen Selden went on his laborious way, groping in the dusty by-paths of history and law; and collecting facts, precedents, and evidences of usage, with all the zeal of a constitutional reformer, who found in the Past his landmarks for the guidance of the Present. He looked on, by no means unconcerned, though not directly involved, at the great struggle which had already begun between authority and right, between the prerogatives of the crown and the privileges of the people, and patiently elucidated the principles upon which, as he conceived, it might justly and pacifically be settled. Meanwhile, quietly waiting the further development of a contention which was to expand far beyond any limits at that time conceived of by the boldest, he continued his antiquarian labours, and constantly gained in reputation and influence. We find him, in 1616, editing Sir John Fortescue's famous treatise, " De laudibus Legum Angliæ " (written between 1461 and 1470), and Hengham's " Summæ," with elaborate annotations; and addressing to Sir Francis Bacon, on whom the great seal had just been conferred, a " Brief Discourse " upon the office of Lord Chancellor of England.

We cannot but be struck with the amazing energy and application of the man, who, still plying his learned and judicious pen, found time in 1617 to furnish Purchas (he was then publishing his "Pilgrimes") with a short account "of the Jews sometimes living in England." For in this same year he gave to the world his celebrated work, "De Diis Syriis," a Latin treatise on Syrian idolatry in general, and the heathen deities mentioned in the Old Testament in particular. It made him known to the scholars of the Continent, where, in 1627, it was reprinted by the Elzevirs, under the superintendence of De Dieu, one of the professors in the Walloon College at Leyden, and of Daniel Heinsius, to whom Selden dedicated the edition. The high estimation in which it was held, is proved by the fact that it was reprinted in 1662, and again in 1680.

In the following year appeared his "History of Tithes," from the publication of which may be dated his career as a constitutional reformer. In its learned and ingenious pages he set forth the rise and progress of that onerous ecclesiastical tax, and while admitting its legality, overthrowing the claim for its Divine origin maintained by the Church. As such a claim would not now-a-days be put forward, a refutation of it would not excite any angry feelings; but in 1618 it gave huge offence both to the clergy and the Court. It was a blow at the very foundation on which the advocates of the absolute power of the Crown and the Church rested their pretensions; and both Crown and Church prepared to chastise the audacious offender. In December he was summoned to appear before James I. at his palace of Theobalds. He was introduced into the royal presence by his friends Ben Jonson and Edward Hayward, and subjected to a lecture by the royal theologian, who indicated the objectionable passages, and required him to re-write them or explain them away. Selden was forced to assent; but his submission did not save him from further humiliation. The Court of High Commission pounced upon him, and though they did not extort from him a retractation, they compelled him to sign an ignominious. declaration :—

"My good lords, I must humbly acknowledge the error I have committed in publishing the "History of Tithes ;" and especially in that I have at all, by showing any interpretation of Holy Scriptures, by meddling with councils, fathers, or canons, or by what else soever occurs in it, afford any occasion of argument against any right of maintenance, *jure divino*, of the ministers of the Gospel ; beseeching your lordships to receive this ingenuous and humble acknowledgment, together with the unfeigned protestation of my grief, for that through it I have so incurred both his Majesty's and your lordships' displeasure, conceived against me on behalf of the Church of England.

"JOHN SELDEN."

One cannot but regret that Selden subscribed this shameful submission, but he was not of the stuff of which martyrs are made. A sensitive and studious scholar, he lacked the nerve and the moral courage to hold his ground steadfastly when authority threatened him with pains and penalties, unless he was sustained by the example and encouragement of others. On this occasion he stood alone. We shall see that he could be braver and more consistent when sustained and inspired by the companionship of bolder spirits.

To his "History of Tithes" numerous answers appeared, written by the zealous champions of the Church with more enthusiasm and learning, and more invective than argument. Selden was not allowed to make any rejoinder. The king trembled at the extent to which a controversy on Divine right might be pushed, and sending for the scholar, forbade him to make any reply to a refutation from the pen of Montagu, one of his chaplains. "If you or any of your friends," said James, "shall write against this confutation, I will throw you into prison!" In such circumstances, Montagu necessarily had it all his own way. One's reasoning can hardly fail to be cogent and conclusive when one's adversary is deprived of the right of reply!

His attack on clerical pretentions had so greatly provoked the royal wrath, that our timid scholar thought it advisable to recant certain opinions on subjects of no great moment, which differed from those of His Majesty. To propitiate him, therefore, Selden published three tracts: "Of the Number 666 in the Revelation," "Of Calvin's Judgment on the Book of Revelation," and "Of the Birthday of our Saviour," in which his later judgments happily conformed with those of the royal theologian. In the mystic number he found new and more recondite meanings; in the judgment of Calvin he failed to discover the good sense and moderation which had formerly characterised it; and in Christmas Day he acknowledged the natural return of the anniversary, which, formerly, he had rashly held as dubious.

But a weak man, when the weakness is rather constitutional than moral, will often show an unexpected strength at a great opportunity; and Selden gradually hardened, as it were, under the influence of events. His nature was elevated and inspired by the struggle between the Commons and the Crown, which every year assumed larger proportions and greater intensity. In

G

1621, the Commons drew up a petition, prepared by Coke, against the growth of Papacy; but James, having information of it, anticipated its receipt by a violent letter to the Speaker, prohibiting the House from interfering in any matter which concerned his Government, or the mysteries of State. He added that he meant not to spare any man's insolent behaviour in Parliament. The Commons temperately replied that their liberty of speech was their ancient and undoubted right and privilege, to which James vehemently rejoined that their privileges were derived from the grace and permission of his ancestors and himself. Against this unguarded declaration of absolutism, the Commons, on the 18th of December, recorded a memorable protest, in which they solemnly affirm that the liberties and jurisdiction of Parliament are the ancient and undoubted birthright and inheritance of the subjects of England ; that the affairs of the king and the State, of the defence of the realm, and of the Church of England, the making of laws and the redress of grievances, are fit subjects of debate in Parliament ; that in handling such business, any member of the House had, and of right ought to have, freedom of speech; and that every member had like freedom from all impeachment, imprisonment, and molestation, except by the censure of the House itself.

Before making this protest the Commons had consulted Selden, and obtained from him a long, learned, and lucid exposition of the rights of Parliament and the limits of the prerogative. His share in the business was so obnoxious to the Court that he was arrested, and placed in charge of the Sheriffs of London; but, through the good offices of Bishop Williams, he was released after a few weeks' imprisonment. Thenceforward he was committed to the advocacy of the cause of constitutional reform. Perhaps it would not be extravagant to represent him as an exponent of those political principles which are now identified with Whiggism.

Selden's pen was next employed by the House of Lords on a knotty question of constitutional law, and his work on "The Privilege of the Baronage" was first printed in 1642. He also wrote a short and not very complete treatise on "The Judicature of Parliament." In 1623, he edited and annotated the "Historia Novorum" of Eadmer, the monk of Canterbury.

Entering public life as one of the members for Lancaster, in the Parliament which assembled in February, 1624, Selden ranged himself on the popular side. He took part in the impeachment of Cranfield, Earl of Middlesex, for bribery, and joined in the debates which terminated in the abolition of monopolies. In the First Parliament of Charles I. he sat for Great Bedwin. Associated with Coke, and Pym, and Eliot, he gained immeasurably in self-respect and self-reliance, displaying a courage of which he had never before been considered capable. In each great constitutional debate he played a worthy part ; and his learning proved of immense value to the cause, by showing that the claims of the Commons were founded upon indisputable precedent, and that they contended only for the restoration of their "ancient and undoubted birthright and inheritance." The change which had come over his temper is best appreciated by reference to the fact that he was one of the eight members whom the Commons appointed to present their articles of impeachment against the Duke of Buckingham (1626). Charles interfered to save his favourite by summarily dissolving Parliament.

The Third Parliament of Charles I. was opened on the
17th of March, 1628, and Selden again took his seat
among the leaders of the constitutional party.  He spoke
frequently, and although no orator, he always secured the
attention of the House by his learning, gravity, and
moderation.  His influence was powerfully felt in the
debates upon the "Petition of Right," which reasserted
the ancient liberties of England, and their glorious success was not a little due to his strenuous effort.

The Petition, after stirring vicissitudes, received the
royal assent on the 7th of June; but Charles was as
resolute as ever to maintain the arbitrary prerogatives he
had inherited from the Tudors, and his assent was a
shadow and a mockery.  To keep men in prison without
bringing them to trial, so that they might prove their
innocence, was the kingly privilege he valued most
highly, and the judges assured him that his assent to the
petition did not involve its abandonment.  Therefore
the contention between king and Parliament was not at
an end; it had only begun.  Flushed with the consciousness of their strength, the Commons, however, with
much assistance from Selden, proceeded to discuss the
reforms that were necessary in Church and State, and
especially the need of limiting the power of the Crown to
impose taxation at will.  So long as it could raise money
of its own volition, so long would it remain independent
of Parliamentary control.  In earnest about the full
performance of their task, the Commons drew up two
energetic remonstrances—one against the Duke of
Buckingham, the other declaring that "tonnage and
poundage," like every tax, could be levied only in virtue
of the law (21st June).  Then Charles lost patience.
Having obtained sufficient subsidies to supply his needs,

he thought he was free to go his own course. Hurrying down to the Lord's House he prorogued Parliament until the 20th of October, and thus abruptly closed a session rendered famous by that Petition of Right to which in later times the people always appealed ; to which, as Dr. Lingard says, the Crown was eventually compelled to submit.

During the recess, Selden addressed himself with eagerness to his old avocations, and prepared and published his "*Marmorea Arundeliana*," a learned description of the valuable relics of ancient art which the Earl of Arundel had recently brought to England. He also composed two ecclesiastical and legal treatises, " Of the Original of Ecclesiastical Jurisdiction of Testaments," and " Of the Disposition or Administration of Intestate's Goods."

He was recalled to the stir and stress of political controversy when Parliament had reassembled on the 20th of January, 1629. In the interval, Buckingham had fallen, stricken to death by an assassin's knife ; but the grounds of quarrel between king and Commons had undergone no alteration. The debates soon acquired a tone of indignant bitterness, and religious questions added fresh fuel to the gradually spreading fire. Charles endeavoured to check them, and on the 28th of February, sent down a message commanding the House to adjourn until the 10th of March. But understanding that this adjournment was a prelude to a dissolution, Eliot, Selden, Holles, and others, resolved to put forward a formal declaration of the House, recording for the edification of the people the result of its debates on the illegal levy of taxation, and the encouragement given to Popery and Arminianism. After delivering the royal message, the Speaker made a movement to leave the chair, but Denzil Holles and Benjamin Valentine, probably by a preconcerted arrangement, sprang forward, laid hold of his arm on either side, and firmly held him down. The suddenness of the surprise discomfited Finch, and Sir John Eliot, taking advantage of the pause, addressed the House, which listened to him without interruption, but in a state of growing excitement :—

"You know," he cried, " how our religion is attempted; how Arminianism like a secret pioneer undermines it; how Popery like a strong enemy comes on openly ! Among the enemies of true religion, and the authors of their troubles were some prelates of the Church. I denounce them," he continued, "as enemies to His Majesty. Whoever have occasioned these public breaches in Parliament for their private interests and respects, the felicity has not lasted to a perpetuity of that power. None have gone about to break Parliaments but in the end Parliaments have broken them. . . . It is fit for us," he added, "as true Englishmen, in discharge of our duties, to show the affection that we have to the honour and safety of our sovereign, to show our affection to religion, and to the rights and interest of the subject. It befits us to declare our purpose to maintain them, and our resolution to live and die in their defence. That so, like our fathers, we may preserve ourselves as free men, and by that freedom keep ability for the supply and support of His Majesty, when our services may be needful. To which end this paper which I hold was conceived, and has this scope and meaning."

A storm of voices broke forth, and members started from their seats either to defend or menace the dismayed Speaker, or to seek a hearing amid the tumult. Twice was the Speaker bidden to put the declaration to the vote; twice, with tears, he protested that the king had otherwise ordered him. He made a second effort to leave the chair, but was again held down by Holles, Valentine, and Long—Holles stoutly swearing "by God's wounds" that he should sit there so long as it was their pleasure. A third appeal was made to him, and Selden gravely warned him that such obstinacy must not go unpunished, lest it should be made an evil precedent; while Hayman disowned him for a Kentishman, hotly denounced him as a disgrace to his family and a reproach to his country, and proposed that a new Speaker be chosen in his place. The stir and turmoil continued to increase, until fierce blows were exchanged; force met force, and ready hands sought their sword-hilts. " Let all," exclaimed William Strode, " who desire this declaration read and put to the vote stand up." With a fierce " Aye, aye ! " the great body of members instantly rose, and Eliot flung his paper into the midst of them on the floor of the House.

Soon afterwards, the Serjeant-at-Arms attempted to lift the mace from the table, which in itself would have involved a suspension of the proceedings; but Sir Miles Hobart wrested it from him, and also shut and locked the door of the House, putting the key into his pocket. At this moment Sir John Eliot came forward with a shorter declaration, which he read amid a tumult of applause ; and thereafter Denzil Holles, while Black Rod was knocking at the door, produced the following resolutions, and standing close to the chair, in which, sullen and silent, still sat the Speaker, cried out in a loud voice that he there and then put it to the question :—

*First,* " Whoever shall bring in innovation in religion, or by favour seek to extend or introduce Popery or Arminianism, or other opinions disagreeing from the true and orthodox Church, shall be reputed a capital enemy to this kingdom and commonwealth."

With repeated "Aye, aye !" the Commons signified
their assent.

*Second,* "Whoever shall advise the levying of the
subsidies of tonnage and poundage, not being granted by
Parliament, or shall be an actor or instrument therein,
shall be likewise reputed an innovator in the government,
and a capital enemy to the kingdom and commonwealth."

This too was ratified by general acclamation.

And *third,* "If any merchant or other person whatsoever,
shall voluntarily yield or pay the said subsidies, not being
granted by Parliament, he shall likewise be reputed a
betrayer of the liberty of England."

For a third time the House rang with approving cries
of "Aye, aye !" and Hobart, having flung open the door,
the members swept forth pell mell, carrying with them a
king's officer, who, with a guard of pensioners, had been
despatched by Charles to force an entrance.

Thus came to a close the Third Parliament of Charles
I. ; and for upwards of eleven years no Parliament met in
England.

Charles proceeded to inflict his vengeance on the
leaders of the Opposition. Sir John Eliot, Holles,
Selden, Hayman, Hobart, Langton, Valentine, Strode,
and Long, were examined before the Privy Council, on
the 13th of March, and committed to the Tower, because
they refused to answer out of Parliament for what they
had done under its protection. For more than three
months they were detained in rigid confinement, being
denied even the use of books and writing materials.
Eventually, all but Sir John Eliot sued out their writs of
*habeas corpus.* They were then brought before the
King's Bench, and in accordance with one of the provisions of the Bill of Rights, the cause of their commit-

ment was specified. Littleton, their counsel, pointed out that the offence alleged against them was bailable ; but the judges, through the influence of the Crown, fixed the bail upon terms which the patriots declined to accept. They next took up the ground that no court had a right to interfere with actions done in Parliament. To this the judges assented, but decided that the members had been charged with sedition and taking part in a riot, and that riot and sedition could not be regarded as parliamentary proceedings. Eliot and his companions still held firm, and sentence was finally pronounced against them, to the effect that they should be imprisoned during the king's pleasure, that none should be released without giving security for good behaviour and making submission and acknowledgment of their offence.

After an imprisonment of eight months, the patriots were again offered their liberty on their giving sureties for their good behaviour ; and again, through Selden, who acted as their mouthpiece, they refused. The rigour of their confinement, however, was somewhat relaxed ; and Selden, on application, was transferred by *habeas corpus* to the Marshalsea, and subsequently to the Gatehouse. Here his imprisonment was almost nominal, and he was even allowed to visit his friend the Earl of Kent, at his country-seat. When this incident came to the knowledge of his judges, he was remanded to the Marshalsea ; but, ultimately, at the intercession of the Earls of Arundel and Pembroke, was released upon bail. In 1634, he received his full discharge.

Selden then returned to his literary and antiquarian pursuits ; and in 1636, produced his famous work, the *Mare Clausum*, which, originally designed only as an answer to the *Mare Liberum* of Grotius, had expanded

into a full and elaborate demonstration of England's claim
to the sovereignty of the seas. It had been written
some nineteen years before, and submitted in MS. to
James I. Disputes on the question of maritime supremacy arising with the Dutch in 1635, Selden's treatise
seems to have been brought to the notice of Charles,
who immediately ordered its publication. It was dedicated to the king, and by him was so highly esteemed
that he gave directions for copies of it to be preserved in
the council-chest, in the Court of Exchequer, and in the
Court of Admiralty. In 1652, it was translated into
English by Marchmont Needham, and also by J. H.,
probably James Howell (the author of the quaint
*Epistola Ho-Elianæ*).

To the famous Long Parliament, which assembled on
the 3rd of November, 1640, Selden was returned as
one of the members for the University of Oxford; a
proof that, notwithstanding his former career in the
House, he was not regarded as hostile to the royal cause.
He behaved, however, with perfect consistency; and cast
in his lot with the popular party so long as they kept
within the lines of constitutional action. He sat and
acted on the committee for inquiring into the arbitrary
proceedings of the Earl Marshal's court; as also on the
committee for preparing the remonstrance on the state of
the nation. In this conduct he was countenanced, however, by Lord Falkland and Lord Digby, who afterwards
became the most loyal of the king's followers; and in truth,
opinion in the Lower House was as yet almost unanimous,
and all parties were agreed in resisting the encroachments of the Crown. He joined in the proceedings
which led to the impeachment of Strafford, because he
believed him to have violated the law; but when the

majority in the Commons dropped the impeachment and introduced a bill of attainder, Selden strongly opposed it, because that too was, in his opinion, illegal and arbitrary. The measure of Selden's attachment to the popular cause can easily be attained : he was prepared to support it only so long as it respected the ancient usages ; and we can therefore understand that, sooner or later, a time must come when the swift expansion of reform into revolution would separate him from the party of progress.

That time had not come as yet ; Selden sat on the committee appointed to examine into the unconstitutional decision of the Court of Exchequer on the subject of ship-money ; and though, as a friend of the Church of England, he opposed the abolition of Episcopacy, he was appointed a member of the committee which drew up articles of impeachment against Archbishop Laud. It was, perhaps, with the view of detaching from the popular party a man of so much weight and learning that Charles proposed, when Sir Thomas Littleton was unwell, to confer the Great Seal upon Selden ; but he was dissuaded from making the offer by Lords Falkland and Clarendon, who assured him that it would be rejected. "They concluded," says Clarendon, "that he would absolutely refuse the place if it were offered to him. He was in years, and of a tender constitution ; he had for many years enjoyed his ease, which he loved ; he was rich, and would not have made a journey to York, or have come out of his bed for any preferment which he had never affected." It is probable, however, that he would have been actuated also by higher motives, for of the sincerity of his attachment to the principle of constitutional reform there can be no question.

Selden was one of the majority which carried the

General Remonstrance, but he saw with alarm the rapid drifting of both parties towards the stern arbitrament of war. He regarded with disapproval the action of the House of Commons (February, 1642) in nominating the lord-lieutenants of the counties, for here it obviously encroached upon the royal prerogative ; but, on the other hand, he denounced as equally unconstitutional the commissions of arms issued by the king. His speech on this subject produced a powerful effect, both in Parliament and the country, while it so disturbed the king that, with his consent and at his instigation, Lord Falkland addressed to him a letter inquiring into the grounds of his opposition. In reply, Selden repeated the arguments he had used in his speech, and added that he disputed in the same manner the legality of the ordinance of Parliament for appointing the lieutenants, stigmatising it as "without shadow of law or pretence of precedent."

In the crisis of a great revolution, moderate men are nowhere. Both parties feel that he who is not with them is against them, and cannot brook the implied or spoken rebuke of the man who stands aside and refuses to cast in his lot with either. They resent his conduct, moreover, as indicating a consciousness of superior wisdom. When Edmund Waller's plot to arm the London citizens and seize the persons of the parliamentary leaders was discovered (31st May, 1643), Selden was suspected, along with Whitelocke and Pierpoint, of being implicated in it. The House, however, was satisfied with Waller's explanation, "that he did come one evening to Selden's study, where Pierpoint and Whitclocke then were with Selden, to propose to impart it to them all, and speaking of such a thing in general terms, these gentle-

men did so inveigh against any such thing as treachery
and baseness, and that which might be the occasion
of shedding much blood, that he durst not, for the respect
he had for Selden and the rest, communicate any of the
particulars to them, but was almost disheartened himself
to proceed in it." That Selden would have taken part in
such a conspiracy was very improbable; but no doubt
his want of ardour led to a suspicion of his faithlessness.
The House, however, in acknowledgment of his scholarship, appointed him to the office of Keeper of the Records
in the Tower; and he on his part proved his fidelity to the
popular cause by subscribing with his colleagues, in St.
Margaret's Church, Westminster, on the 28th of September, 1644, the Solemn League and Covenant, by which,
as the price of the Scotch Alliance, it was agreed to
bring the Churches of God in the three kingdoms "to
the nearest conjunction and conformity in religion, confession of faith, form of Church government, direction
for worship, and catechising, that we, and our posterity
after us, may as brethren live in faith and love, and the
Lord may delight to live in the midst of us." After
undertaking to extirpate Popery, Prelacy, superstition,
and schism, and to preserve the rights and privileges of the
Parliament, and the liberties of the kingdom, the subscribers
declared it to be their "true unfeigned purpose, desire,
and endeavour, both in public and private, in all duties
they owed to God and man to amend their lives, and
each to go before another in the example of a real reformation." To Selden, as a Churchman, it must have been
bitterness itself to have subscribed a document which
provided for the abolition of Episcopacy, but events had
proved too powerful for him. Thenceforward, however,
he seem gradually to have abandoned the political stage.

It is certain that he had no sympathy with the vehement action of the party led by Vane, and Cromwell, Fairfax, Ludlow, and Ireton ; the execution of Charles I., and the downfall of the monarchy must have been a death-blow to all his views and hopes of constitutional reform. He made no protest against these measures, nor did he join the king's party, whose violent proceedings were not less distasteful to him ; but he retired from the din and fury of the conflict, to find peace and consolation in his beloved studies.

Even in the press of political duties he had not wholly deserted them. His pen had never ceased its activity. In 1640, he had published a wonderfully learned discourse on the Hebrew polity, civil and religious, under the title of "*De Jure Naturali et Gentium, juxta Disciplinam Hebræorum, libri septem;*" and in 1642, had translated into Latin from the Arabic, a tract of the Patriarch Eutychius upon certain disputed questions of ecclesiastical antiquities. To continue the catalogue of his contributions, which, however, can have but little interest for the general reader, in 1644, he published "*De Anno Civili Veteris Ecclesiæ, seu Reipublicæ Judaicæ Dissertatio*" ("On the Civil Year of the Ancient Church, or a Dissertation on the Jewish Commonwealth") ; and in 1646, his "*Uxor Hebraica, seu de Nuptiis et Divortiis ex Jure Civili, id est Divino et Talmudico, Veterum Ebræorum, libri tres.*" In the following year he published an edition of William de Brampton's "*Fleta,*" with an elaborate preliminary dissertation. His great work, "*De Synedriis et Præfecturis juridicis veterum Hebræorum,*" was given to the world in 1650 ; and in 1652 he terminated his long literary labours with the "*Vindicia Maris Clausi,*" a reply to attacks upon the "*Mare Clausum.*"

The closing years of his life Selden spent under the roof of the Dowager-Countess of Kent, whose legal adviser he was, and to whom, it is said, he was privately married. In the summer of 1654, his constitution, never very robust, began to give way ; and feeling that his end was near, he sent for two of his old friends, Archbishop Ussher and Dr. Langbaine, with whom he held many discussions upon religious matters. His faith in the promises of Christianity was strong and deep. He said "that he had his study full of books and papers on most subjects in the world ; yet at that time he could not recollect any passage wherein he could rest his soul, save out of the Holy Scriptures, wherein the most remarkable passage that lay most upon his spirit was Titus ii. 11, 12, 13, 14. His friend Whitelocke visited him to take his directions relative to his temporal affairs, but Selden was then too weak. He expired on the last day of November, 1654, and on the 14th of December, was buried in the Temple Church, London, the Master of the Temple reading the service, and Archbishop Ussher preaching the funeral sermon.

Selden left a considerable fortune, principally acquired, it is said, through his connection with the family of the Earl of Kent. His valuable library he had intended to bequeath to the Bodleian ; but having taken umbrage at the refusal of the loan of a MS., because he had omitted the usual pledge to restore it safely, he left his books to his executors, Edward Hayward, John Vaughan, and Sir Matthew Hale, who, wisely regarding themselves as "the executors not of his anger, but of his will," carried out his original design, and removed them to the Bodleian. There they were arranged by Anthony à Ward, who tells us that he "laboured several weeks with Mr. Thomas

Barlow and others in sorting them, carrying them upstairs, and placing them. In opening some of the books they found several pair of spectacles, which Mr. Selden had put in and forgotten to take out. Wood records that on the title or first page of all his books Selden was accustomed to write his favourite motto—περι παντος την ελευθεριαν.

Though Selden was, as Ben Jonson wittily said, "the law-book of the judges," and though his legal and antiquarian works are written in the driest and crabbedest style that was ever called English, he was something more than a Dryasdust and a lawyer. We have seen that he was an enlightened politician, and, notwithstanding his constitutional timidity, on the whole a steadfast and consistent one. The principle which governed his political conduct was sound and safe : that all reforms should be the natural developments or applications of the ancient laws of England. Thus he became, to use Professor Arber's expression, the "Champion of Human Law," and it is to his immortal honour that, in a time of convulsion and unrest, he adhered, without change or hesitation, to the "law of the kingdom," which embodied the rights and privileges won by generations of Englishmen. He advocated the supremacy of the constitution over the so-called doctrine of Divine right. Against ecclesiastical pretensions he opposed the civil power, and, exalting it to the highest position in the State, denied the existence of any co-ordinate authority. So strongly did he maintain the supreme power of the nation, that, for the purpose of his argument, he reduced religion almost to a habit of thought, which might be assumed or cast off at pleasure. "So religion," he says, "was brought into the kingdom, so it has been continued, and so it may be cast out, when the State pleases." Again, "The clergy tell the prince they have physic good for the souls of his people. Upon that he admits them ; but when he finds by experience they both trouble him and his people, he will have no more to do with them. What is that to them, or any one else, if a king will not go to heaven?" The supremacy of the civil power has seldom been more uncompromisingly asserted ; but such an assertion of it was not more welcome to the leaders of the popular party than to High Churchmen themselves.

It must not be supposed, from the breadth of Selden's views on the vexed question of Church and State, that he was other than a man of earnest religious feeling. On this point the testimony of Sir Matthew Hale will satisfy everybody ; and Baxter has preserved that testimony for us—" I think it meet to remember that because many Hobbists do report that Mr. Selden was at the heart an infidel, and inclined to the opinions of Hobbes, I desired him to tell me the truth herein.; and he oft professed to me that Mr. Selden was a resolved, serious Christian, and that he was a great adversary to Hobbes' errors, and that he had seen him openly oppose him so earnestly, as either to depart from him, or drive him out of the room." Baxter adds, though the statement is contradicted by Aubrey, that Selden would not have his friend in his chamber, where he lay on his deathbed, exclaiming, "No atheists !"

Whitelocke says of Selden, that "his mind was as great as his learning ; that he was as hospitable and generous as any man, and as good company to those whom he liked." There is evidence of the liberal assistance he gave to Meric Casaubon. As a conversationalist he shone supreme. Over the walnuts and the wine he poured out profuse stores of wit and wisdom. Happily for posterity he had his

H

Boswell; so that we know the author of " Titles of Honour "
under his brightest and most genial aspect.   Is it the
same person ?  inquires James Hannay ;  one scarcely
believes it.   " Dry, grave, and almost crabbed in his
writings, his conversation is homely, humorous, shrewd,
vivid, even delightful !   He is still the great scholar and
the tough Parliamentarian, but merry, playful, and witty.
The ἀνήριθμον γελασμα is on the sea of his vast intellect.
He writes like the opponent of Grotius ;  he talks like the
friend of Ben Jonson."

Selden's "Table-Talk" was published by his amanuensis,
Richard Milward, in 1689.   Fortunate Milward, in having the opportunity to listen to such talk !  Fortunate
Selden, in having an admirer discriminating and industrious enough to record it !   Dr. Johnson preferred this
small but precious volume to all the French *Ana*.   Coleridge found " more weighty hollow sense " in it " than in
the same number of pages of any uninspired writer."   And
as a matter of fact it does not contain one weak or worth-
less line.   We find it a store of " good things," wise or
witty, or both witty and wise.   It includes the happy
illustration that libels and pasquils are like straws, which
serve to show how the wind sets.   And that forcible suggestion, so much admired by Coleridge, that " Transub-
stantiation is only rhetoric turned into logic."   His friends
seem to have been much impressed by the care and
spontaneity of his familiar analogies and comparisons.   As
in his remark on the necessary connection between faith
and works :—" Though in my intellect I may divide them,
just as in the candle I know there is both light and
heat, but yet put out the candle and they are both gone ;
one remains not without the other—so 'tis betwixt faith
and works."   Here is another " happy thought " :—" We

measure the excellency of other men by some excellence we conceive to be in ourselves. Nash, a poet poor enough, as poets used to be, seeing an alderman with his gold chain upon his great horse, by way of scorn said to one of his companions, 'Do you see yon fellow, how goodly, how big he looks? Why, that fellow cannot make a blank verse!'"

To induce any of my readers who may unfortunately be ignorant of Selden's "Table Talk" to make immediate acquaintance with it, I shall subjoin a brief selection of striking passages :—

### "On Equality, and its Advocates.

"This is the juggling trick of the parity; they would have nobody above them, but they do not tell you they would have nobody under them."

[Borrowed by Dr. Johnson when he said to Boswell, "Your levellers wish to level *down* as far as themselves; but they cannot bear levelling *up* to themselves. They would all have some people under them; why not then have some people above them?"]

### "Sermons.

"First, in your sermons use your logic, and then your rhetoric; rhetoric without logic is like a tree with leaves and blossoms, but no root.

"Nothing is true but what is spoken of in the Bible, and meant there for person and place; the rest is application, which a discreet man may do well; but 'tis *his* Scripture, not the Holy Ghost's."

### "Learning and Wisdom.

"No man is wiser for his learning; it may administer matter to work in, or objects to work upon; but wit and wisdom are born with a man."

### " *Oracles.*

" Oracles ceased presently after Christ, as soon as nobody believed them ; just as we have no fortune-tellers, nor wise men, when nobody cares for them. Sometimes you have a season for them, when people believe them ; and neither of them, I conceive, wrought by the devil."

### " *Evil speaking.*

" Speak not ill of a great enemy, but rather give him good words, that he may use you the better if you chance to fall into his hands. The Spaniard did this when he was dying ; his confessor told him, to work him to repentance, how the devil tormented the wicked that went to hell ; the Spaniard replying, called the devil 'my lord'—'I hope my lord the devil is not so cruel.' His confessor reproved him. 'Excuse me,' said the Don, ' for calling him so ; I know not into what hands I may fall ; and if I happen into his, I hope he will use me the better for giving him good words.' "

### " *Ill Words.*

" A gallant man is above ill words. An example we have in the old Lord of Salisbury, who was a great wise man. Stone had called some lord about court 'fool ;' the lord complains, and has Stone whipped ; Stone cries, ' I might have called my Lord of Salisbury fool often enough, before he would have had me whipped.'

" He that speaks ill of another, commonly before he is aware, makes himself such a one as he speaks against ; for if he had civility or breeding, he would forbear such kind of language."

### " *Humility.*

" There is *humilitas quâdam in vitio* [a humility pushed to an excess, until it becomes a vice]. If a man does not take notice of that excellency and perfection that is in himself, how can he be thankful to God, who is the author of all excellency and perfection ? Nay, if a man hath too mean an opinion of himself, it will render him unserviceable both to God and man."

*" Pride.*

" Pride may be allowed to this or that degree, else a man cannot keep up his dignity. In gluttons there must be eating, in drunkenness there must be drinking ; it is not the eating, nor it is not the drinking that is to blame, but the excess. So in pride."

*" Gentlemen.*

" What a gentleman is, 'tis hard with us to define ; in other countries he is known by his privileges ; in Westminster Hall he is one that is reputed one ; in the Court of Honour, he that hath arms. The king cannot make a gentleman of blood, nor God Almighty, but he çan make a gentleman by creation. If you ask which is the better of these two—civilly, the gentleman of blood ; morally, the gentleman by creation may be the better, for the other may be a debauched man, this a person of worth."

*" Patience.*

" Patience is the chiefest fruit of study. A man that strives to make himself a different thing from other men by much reading, gains this chiefest good, that in all future he hath something to entertain and comfort himself withal."

*" Money.*

" Money makes a man laugh. A blind fiddler playing to a company, and playing but saucily, the company laughed at him ; his boy that led him perceiving it, said, ' Father let us begone, they do nothing but laugh at you.' 'Hold thy peace, boy,' said the fiddler, ' we shall have their money presently, and then we will laugh at them.' "

*" Difference of Men.*

" The difference of men is very great ; you would scarce think them to be of the same species ; and yet it consists more in the affection than in the intellect. For as in the strength of body, two men shall be of an equal strength, yet one shall appear stronger than the other, because he exercises and puts out his strength,

the other will not stir nor strain himself. So 'tis in the strength
of the brain; the one endeavours, and strains, and labours, and
studies, the other sits still and is idle, and takes no pains, and
therefore he appears so much the inferior.

### " Marriage.

"1. Of all actions of a man's life, his marriage does least concern
other people, yet of all actions of our life 'tis most meddled with
by other people.

"2. Marriage is a desperate thing. The frogs in Æsop were
extremely wise; they had a great mind to some water, but they
would not leap into the well because they could not get out
again."

### " Measure of Things.

"1. We measure from ourselves, and as things are for our use
and purpose, so we approve them; bring a pear to the table that
is rotten, we cry it down, 'tis naught; but bring a medlar to the
table that is rotten, and 'tis a fine thing, and yet I'll warrant
you the pear thinks as well of itself as the medlar does.

"2. Nay, we measure the goodness of God from ourselves;
we measure his goodness, his justice, his wisdom, by something
we call just, good, or wise in ourselves; and in so doing we
judge proportionally to the country fellow in the play, who
said if he were a king he would live like a lord, and have peas
and bacon every day, and a whip that cried 'slash.'"

### " Friends.

"Old friends are best. King James used to call for his old
shoes; they were easiest for his feet."

### " Self-Denial.

"'Tis much the doctrine of the times that men should not
please themselves, but deny themselves everything they take delight in; not look upon beauty, wear no good clothes, eat no good
meat, &c., which seems the greatest accusation that can be upon

the Maker of all good things. If they be not to be used, why did God make them? The truth is, they that preach against them cannot make use of them their selves, and then again they get esteem by seeming to contemn them. But mark it while you live, if they do not please themselves as much as they can."

### " Proverbs.

" The proverbs of several nations were much studied by Bishop Andrews, and the reason he gave was, because by them he knew the minds of several nations, which is a brave thing ; as we count him a wise man that knows the minds and insides of men, which is done by knowing what is habitual to them. Proverbs are habitual to a nation, being transmitted from father to son."

### " Reverence.

" 'Tis sometimes unreasonable to look after respect and reverence, either from a man's own servant or other inferiors. A great lord and a gentleman talking together, there came a boy by leading a calf with both his hands. Says the lord to the gentleman, 'You shall see me make the boy let go his calf.' With that he came towards him, thinking the boy would have put off his hat, but the boy took no notice of him. The lord seeing that, ' Sirrah,' says he, ' do you not know me that you are no reverence.' ' Yes,' says the boy, ' if your lordship will hold my calf, I will put off my hat.' "

### " Prayer.

" We take care what we speak to men, but to God we may say any thing."

# John, Earl Somers.

## 1650-1716.

I

THE greatest lawyer of his generation, one of the most distinguished men of his age, and foremost in the ranks of our great English statesmen, upon the career and character of John, Earl Somers, it is possible to look with almost unalloyed satisfaction.

I shall begin my sketch of this illustrious man—who may almost be called the founder of our constitutional monarchy; who at any rate laid, broad and firm, the substructure on which that admirable edifice has been raised—by bringing together the worthiest and most notable of the eulogiums that have been heaped upon his memory. For the convenience of space, I shall sometimes have to condense them, but, so far as possible, I shall give them in their original form.

Sir James Mackintosh will be regarded as a competent critic, and in his opinion, Lord Somers nearly realised the perfect model of a wise statesman in a free community. "His wish was public liberty; he employed every talent and resource which was necessary for his end, and not prohibited by the rules of morality. His regulating principle was usefulness. His quiet and refined mind rather shrunk from popular applause. He preserved the most intrepid steadiness, with a disposition so mild, that his friends thought its mildness exces- sive, and his enemies supposed that it could be scarcely natural.*

Earl Russell, as a Whig leader, and a strenuous advo- cate of civil and religious freedom, deserves a respectful hearing. " Somers," he says,† " is a bright example of a statesman who could live in times of revolution without rancour; who could hold the highest posts in a court without meanness; and who could unite mildness and charity to his opponents with the firmest attachment to the great principles of liberty, civil and religious, which he had early expressed, long promoted, and never aban- doned."

The historian Smollett, as a Tory, was not disposed to overrate the merits of a Whig statesman; but he says :‡ " He was well skilled in the law, as in many other branches of polite and useful literature. He possessed a remarkable talent for business, in which he exerted great patience and assiduity; was gentle, candid, and equitable; a Whig in principles, yet moderate, pacific, and conciliating."

Dean Swift had many reasons for not loving him; but in drawing his character, he handles, so to speak, a *Balaam pen*, and when he fain would curse, is forced to bless :§—

* " Life of Sir James Mackintosh."
† Earl Russell, Introduction to the " History of Europe."
‡ Smollett, " History of England, " i. 166.
§ Dean Swift, " History of the Last Years of Queen Anne's Reign."

"The Lord Somers may very deservedly be reputed the head and oracle of that party. He has raised himself, by the concurrence of many circumstances, to the greatest employments of the State, without the least support from birth or fortune; he has constantly, and with great steadiness, cultivated those principles under which he grew. That accident which first produced him to the world, of pleading for the bishops whom King James had sent to the Tower, might have proved a piece of merit as honourable as it was fortunate; but the old republican spirit, which the Revolution had restored, began to teach other lessons: that since we had accepted a new king from a Calvinistical commonwealth, we must also admit new maxims in religion and government. But since the nobility and gentry would probably adhere to the Established Church, and to the right of monarchy as delivered down from their ancestors, it was the practice of these politicians to introduce such men as were perfectly indifferent to any or no religion, and who were not likely to inherit much loyalty from those to whom they owed their birth. Of this number was the person I am now describing. I have hardly known any man with talents more proper to acquire and preserve the favour of a prince; never offending in word or gesture, in the highest degree courteous and complaisant, wherein he set an excellent example to his colleagues, which they did not think fit to follow."

Swift proceeds to speak of two reasons as assigned for this extreme civility: first, that from the consciousness of his humble origin, he kept all familiarity at the utmost distance, lest it should become intrusive; and second, that sensible how subject he was to excitant passions, he avoided all incitement to them, by teaching those he conversed with, from his own example, to keep well within the bounds of decency and respect—a reason, if true, which we are bound to admire. "No man," adds Swift, "is more apt to take fire upon the least appearance of provocation, which temper he strives to subdue with the utmost violence upon himself, so that his breast has been seen to heave and his eyes to sparkle with rage in those very moments when his words and the cadence of his voice were in the humblest and softest manner."

A very fine character of Somers is drawn by his friend Addison in *The Freeholder*. Its length prevents us from quoting it in full. He speaks of him—with justice—as wearing himself out in such studies as made him useful or ornamental to the world, in concerting schemes for the welfare of his country, and in prosecuting such measures as were necessary for making those schemes effectual; but all this was done with a view to the public good that should rise of these generous endeavours, and not to the fame that should accrue to himself. Let the reputation of the action fall where it would, he was satisfied so long as his country reaped the benefit. . . .

" As he was admitted into the secret and most retired thoughts and counsels of his royal master, King William, a great share in the plan of the Protestant succession is universally ascribed to him. And if he did not entirely project the union of the two kingdoms, and the Bill of Regency, which seem to have been the only methods in human policy for securing to us so inestimable a blessing, there is none who will deny him to have been the chief conductor in both these glorious works. For posterity was obliged to allow him that praise after his death which he industriously declined while he was living. . . .

" His life was, in every part of it, set off with that graceful modesty and reserve which made his virtues more beautiful the more they were cast in such agreeable shades.

" His religion was sincere, not ostentatious, and such as inspired him with a universal benevolence towards all his fellow-subjects, not with bitterness against any part of them.

He showed his firm adherence to it as modelled by our national constitution, and was constant to its offices of devotion, both in public and in his family.   He appeared a champion for it, with great reputation, in the cause of the seven bishops, at a time when the Church was really in danger.   To which we may add, that he held a short friendship and correspondence with the great Archbishop Tillotson, being actuated by the same spirit of candour and moderation, and moved rather with pity than indignation towards the persons of those who differed from him in the unessential parts of Christianity.

"His great humanity appeared in the animated circumstances of his conversations.   You found it in the benevolence of his aspect, the complacency of his behaviour, and the tone of his voice. . . . He joined the greatest delicacy of good-breeding to the greatest strength of reason.   By approving the sentiments of a person with whom he conversed, in such particulars as were just, he won him over from those points in which he was mistaken; and had so agreeable a way of conveying knowledge, that whoever conferred with him grew the wiser, without perceiving that he had been instructed."

Addison goes on to say that Somers was not more distinguished as a patriot and statesman, than as a person of universal knowledge and learning.   As by a just division of his time between public affairs and private retirement, he took care to keep up both " the great and good man; " so did he, by the same means, accomplish and perfect himself not only in the knowledge of men and things, but in the skill of the most refined arts and sciences.

"That unwearied diligence which followed him through all the stages of his life, gave him such a thorough insight into the laws of the land, that he passed for one of the greatest masters of his profession at his first appearance in it. . . .
" He enjoyed, in the highest perfection, two talents which do not often meet in the same person—the greatest strength of

good sense, and the most exquisite taste of politeness. Without the first learning is but an incumbrance, and without the last is ungraceful. My Lord Somers was master of these two qualifications in so eminent a degree, that all the parts of knowledge appeared in him with such an additional strength and beauty, as they want in the possession of others. If he delivered his opinion of a piece of poetry, a statue, or a picture, there was something so just and delicate in his observations as naturally produced pleasure and assent in those who heard him.

"His solidity and eloquence, improved by the reading of the finest authors, both of the learned and modern languages, discovered itself in all his productions. His oratory was masculine and persuasive, free from everything trivial and affected. His style in writing was chaste and pure, but at the same time full of spirit and politeness, and fit to convey the most intricate business to the understanding of the reader with the utmost clearness and perspicuity. And here it is to be lamented that this extraordinary person, out of his natural aversion to vainglory, wrote several pieces, as well as performed several actions, which he did not assume the honour of."

The critic concludes with the remark that Somers will undoubtedly make one of the most distinguished figures in the history of his age, though his merit will not appear in all its fulness, because he wrote much to which he did not attach his name; gave privately many excellent counsels; did numerous offices of friendship to persons who never knew their benefactor; performed great services to his country, of which others reaped the glory; and, in a word, made it his endeavour to do worthy actions rather than gain an illustrious character.

Bishop Burnet says * of this great man, that he was very learned in his profession, with a great deal more

---

* Bishop Burnet, "History of Our Own Times," ii. 107.

learning in other professions—in divinity, philosophy, and history. He had a great capacity for business, with an extraordinary temper,—for he was fair and gentle, perhaps to a fault, considering his post,—so that he had all the patience and softness, as well as the justice and equity, becoming a great magistrate.

Horace Walpole generally infuses a flavour of the cynical into his criticisms, but there is neither *arrière pensée* nor insinuation in his character of Somers, whom he calls * one of those divine men, who, like a chapel in a palace, remain unprofaned, while all the rest is tyranny, corruption, and folly. " All the traditional accounts of him, the historians of the last age and its best authors, represent him as the most incorrupt lawyer, and the honestest statesman, as a master orator, a genius of the finest taste, and a patriot of the noblest and most extensive views; as a man who dispensed blessings by his life, and planned them for posterity."

We may sum up these testimonies in the brilliant portrait of the great lawyer-statesman, drawn by Lord Macaulay :—

" He was equally eminent as a jurist and as a politician, as an orator and a writer. His speeches have perished, but his State papers remain, and are models of terse, luminous, and dignified eloquence. . . . He united all the qualities of a great judge—in intellect comprehensive, quick and acute, diligence, integrity, patience, suavity. In council, the calm wisdom which he possessed in a measure rarely found among men of parts so quick and of opinions so decided as his, acquired for him the authority of an oracle. The superiority of his powers appeared not less clearly in private circles. The charm of his conversation was heightened by the frankness with which he poured out

---

* Horace Walpole, " Royal and Noble Authors," Works, i. 430.

his thoughts. His good temper and his good-breeding never failed. His gesture, his look, his tones were expressive of benevolence. His humanity was the more remarkable, because he had received from nature a body such as is generally found united with a peevish and irritable mind. His life was one long malady: his nerves were weak; his complexion was livid; his face was prematurely wrinkled; yet his enemies could not picture that he had ever once, during a long and troubled public life, been goaded, even by sudden provocation, into vehemence inconsistent with the mild dignity of his character."

They asserted, therefore, that by nature he was a man of very strong passions, which he kept under only by the exercise of a very rigid self-control—an assertion which in itself was a panegyric.

"The most accomplished men of those times have told us, that there was scarcely any subject on which Somers was not competent to instruct or delight. He had never travelled, and in that age an Englishman who had not travelled was generally thought unqualified to give an opinion on works of art; but connoisseurs, familiar with the masterpieces of the Vatican and of the Florentine Gallery, allowed that the taste of Somers in painting and sculpture was exquisite. Philology was one of his favourite pursuits. He had learned the whole vast range of polite literature, ancient and modern. He was at once a munificent and a severely judicious patron of genius and learning. Locke owed opulence to Somers. By Somers, Addison was drawn forth from a cell in a college. In distant countries the name of Somers was mentioned with respect and gratitude by great scholars and poets who had never seen his face."

He was the benefactor of Leclerc, and the friend of Filicaja, as he was also the patron of Hickes and Vertue.

"His powers of mind and his acquirements were not denied even by his detractors. The most acrimonious Tories were

forced to admit, with an ungracious snarl which increased the
value of their praise, that he had all the intellectual qualities of
a great man, and that in him alone among his contemporaries
brilliant eloquence and wit were to be found associated with the
quiet and steady prudence which ensures success in life. It is a
remarkable fact, that in the foulest of all the many libels which
were published against him he was slandered under the name of
Cicero. As his abilities could not be questioned, he was charged
with irreligion and immorality. That he was heterodox all the
country vicars and foxhunting squires firmly believed; but as
to the nature and extent of his heterodoxy there were many
different opinions. He seems to have been a Low Churchman
of the school of Tillotson, whom he always loved and honoured;
and he was, like Tillotson, called by bigots a Presbyterian, an
Arian, a Socinian, a Deist, and an Atheist.

"The private life of this great statesman and magistrate was
malignantly scrutinised; and tales were told about his libertin-
ism, which went on growing till they became too absurd for the
credulity even of party spirit. . . . There is, however, reason
to believe that there was a small nucleus of truth round which
this great mass of fiction gathered, and that the wisdom and
self-command which Somers never wanted in the senate, on the
judgment seat, at the council board, or in the society of wits,
scholars, and philosophers, was not always proof against female
attractions." *

John Somers was born, as is supposed, about the 9th
of March, 1650, in the ancient mansion of White Ladies,
which had formerly been a monastery, in the city of
Worcester. He came of a respectable family, which had
long been possessed of the manor of Clifton, in the
parish of Swanstoke, Gloucestershire, and counted
among its kinsmen the celebrated navigator, Sir George

---

* Lord Macaulay, "History of England." chap xx.

Somers, the discoverer of the " still-vext Bermoothes," or Somers Islands. His father, John Somers, was a lawyer—the most eminent in Worcestershire when the great Civil War broke out. Espousing the cause of the Parliament, he levied a troop of horse, rode away to the war, and fought gallantly under Cromwell. Such was his zeal that once, when quartered in the neighbourhood, having vainly sought to persuade the vicar of Swanstoke from delivering harangues in favour of the king, he fired a pistol over his head to check the torrent of his eloquence, as men at sea fire at a water-spout to limit the area of its operations. The mark of the bullet is still shown in the sounding-board.

The mother of Lord Somers was Catherine Ceavern, a lady belonging to a Shropshire family.

His early years were chiefly spent under the charge of an aunt, with whom he resided until he was removed to the University. He received his education at the Worcester College School, where he was well taught in Latin and Greek, and imbibed from his master, Dr. Bright, his enduring love of polite letters. He seems to have been a weakly boy, with no turn for out-of-door sports, but a great passion for reading. When sixteen years old, he was admitted to Trinity College, Oxford; but he appears to have been quickly recalled hence, and placed in his father's office to learn an attorney's business, with the view of becoming his father's successor. It was soon seen that the drudgery of the desk was uncongenial to him; and every leisure hour he could command he spent in severe application to his beloved literary pursuits. The room in which he pored over his books night and day was long afterwards known as Somers's Study. In 1672, he was fortunate enough to

I

form the acquaintance of the Earl of Shrewsbury, who resided for some time at White Ladies; and he also drew upon himself the attention of the great lawyer, Sir Francis Winnington, afterwards Solicitor-General, by whose advice he went to London, and on the 24th of March, 1669, was entered a student of the Middle Temple.

In the following year he began to keep his terms, and, through his friend, the Earl of Shrewsbury, was introduced to Dryden and other literary notabilities. But a brief experience of their society forced upon him a knowledge of his own deficiencies, and to complete his scholastic education he resolved upon returning to the University. In 1674 he resumed his studies at Trinity College. There, says Cooksey, he lived as other students lived; his exercises were no wise remarkable; and nothing is recorded of him, except that in 1675 he gave £5 towards the repair of the chapel—"a proof of the liberality with which his father supported him, few students being in those times enabled to spare a donation, small as this may seem, out of the usual allowance to young men of his rank,"—and a proof, may it not be considered, of his ready munificence?

Most men with a brilliant University career rise to eminence in after-life; but it is also true that many of our English worthies have never worn University honours. At Trinity, Somers does not seem to have distinguished himself by extraordinary scholarship or ability. There is some evidence, however, that his force of character had made itself known and felt. His father, we are told, was accustomed to visit London during the terms, and, on his way, generally left his horse at the George Inn, Acton, where, over his glass, he often boasted of "his hopeful son at the Temple" (Somers continued to keep his terms while studying at Trinity). One day, on a repetition of the usual vaunt, the landlord rejoined, "Why don't you let us see him, sir?" Accordingly, Mr. Somers requested his son to travel with him as far as Acton on his homeward journey; but on their arrival at the George, he took the landlord aside and said, "I have brought him, Cobbett; but you must not talk to him as you do to me; he will not suffer such fellows as you in his company." *

On the 5th of May, 1676, he was called to the bar, having completed his seven years' apprenticeship, but he continued his residence at the University for some four or five years longer. He thus attained to a singularly wide knowledge of modern languages and literature. He was familiar not only with the great French writers, but with those of Italy, from Petrarca to his own contemporary Filicaja, for whom he cherished a very warm admiration; and in all, could speak, read, and write in seven languages. His acquaintance with the civil law was profound. Nor did he fail to devote a considerable portion of his time to the constitutional history of his country. His studies in this direction led him to embrace the political principles of the Whig party, whose leaders— Shaftesbury, Algernon Sydney, and Lord William Russell —eagerly welcomed this young and brilliant recruit. He quickly demonstrated the value of his adhesion. The great question which then engaged public attention was that of the exclusion of James, Duke of York, from the succession to the Crown, on the ground that he was a Papist. The Whigs† contended for the authority of

---

* "Life of Lord Somers" (ed. 1716), p. 11.

† These party names now first came into use; one (Whig) was of Scotch, the other of Irish origin.

Parliament to limit, restrain, or qualify the title to the
succession ; the Tory, or High Church, party and the
Catholics opposed all interference with the principle of
absolute hereditary right.   In support of the Whig
doctrine Somers, in 1680, published a very able tract,
entitled " A Brief History of the Succession, collected out
of the Records and the most Authentic Historians."   It
influenced the opinions of many by its clear exposition of
the thesis it was designed to support.   In the House of
Commons the Exclusion Bill passed by large majorities ;
but it was defeated in the Lords, who found themselves
in taking this step supported by public opinion.   The
nation was not prepared for the extreme measure of
excluding the rightful heir, and was even less disposed to
endorse Shaftesbury's project of legitimatising the Duke
of Monmouth.

Flushed with triumph, the Tory party took to itself
a courageous spirit, and, after the " breaking " of the
Oxford Parliament, in 1681, instigated the issue of a
royal " Declaration," drawn up by Lord Chief Justice
North, in explanation and defence of the prompt dissolution
of the last two Parliaments.   A reply immediately
appeared, under the title of " A Just and Modest Vindication," in which the action taken by these unlucky
Parliaments was maintained with cogency and ease.   It is
possibly true, as alleged, that Sir William Jones, and
perhaps Sydney, had a hand in it ; but the internal
evidence shows that it was mainly composed by Somers.

"To vindicate the proceedings of the last two Parliaments,
by proving the extent and nature of the powers lodged by the
Constitution in the House of Commons, was the design of this
excellent tract ; and if it should be thought that the writer has
argued in support of some privileges conferring too unlimited a

power upon the Commons, it must be remembered, that he wrote at a period when the representatives of the people could ill afford to relinquish any means of withstanding the arbitrary designs of the Court. So broken were the spirits of the Opposition by the triumphs of the Court, that this excellent publication produced very little effect.* It was most creditable to Somers that, at a time when the hopes even of the brave and the good were thus depressed, he ventured to call the nation to a sense of its rights and its danger." †

We have read this tract. It is lucidly and forcibly written, and contains a complete treasury of constitutional aphorisms. To the Court party it must have been unpleasant reading, as when it hints that " kings were instituted for the good of the people, and the government ordained for the sake of those that are to be governed." It is our belief that a judicious selection from the Somers tracts, with such annotations as are necessary for their elucidation or illustration, would be acceptable to a large circle of readers, and tend to advance and broaden their political education.

In the intoxication of victory, the Government aimed a blow at one of the most eloquent and powerful of their adversaries, and resolved that the Earl of Shaftesbury should be brought to trial for his life. Evidence was collected for the purpose of sustaining a charge of high treason ; but when the bill came before the grand jury of London, they threw it out, in spite of the threats and remonstrances of the two chief justices, Pemberton and North. Enraged at their defeat, the king's advisers flung opprobrium on the grand jurors, declaring them

---

* Such is the statement of Bishop Burnet ; but unquestionably it added largely to the reputation of Somers.

† Roscoe, p. 144.

perjured and dishonest. Somers again leaped into the arena with ready pen, and defended with equal vigour and success the institution of the grand jury in general, and the action of the Old Bailey grand jury in particular, in his pamphlet, "The Security of Englishmen's Lives; or, the Trust, Power, and Duty of the Grand Juries of England Explained, according to the Fundamentals of the English Government, and the Declaration of the same made in Parliament by many statutes." As in all Somers's tracts, constitutional maxims, forcibly put, are very numerous. Here is a specimen :—

"The king's interest is more concerned in the protection of the innocent than in the punishment of the guilty."

And again :—

"Every design of changing the constitution ought to be most warily observed and timely opposed; nor is it only the interest of the people that such fundamentals should be duly guarded, for whose benefit they are at first so carefully laid, and whom the judges are sworn to serve, but of the king too, for whose sake those pretend to act who would subvert them."

Somers did not allow his energies to be wholly absorbed by political contention. He found or made time to gratify his ardent love of letters; and in 1681, gave a proof of the versatility of his powers and the extent of his acquirements, by his translation into English of Ovid's Epistles from "Dido to Æneas," and "Ariadne to Theseus." No one will suppose that Somers thought himself a worthy rival of Dryden. Poetry is a jealous mistress, and he who would gain the smiles of the muse, must devote himself wholly to her service. But the writing of verse is an elegant accomplishment, with which a statesman or a jurist may profitably grace his learned leisure. Somers did not write better than the mob of gentlemen who write with ease, but he rendered his original with spirit and accuracy, and if not a good poet, was far from being a bad translator. The following passage is a fair specimen of his merits :—

"With cruel haste, to distant lands you fly,
  You know not where they are nor where they lie ;
  On Carthage and its rising walls you frown,
  And shun a sceptre which is now your own.
  All you have gained you proudly do contemn,
  And fondly seek a favor'd diadem ;
  And should you reach at last this promised land,
  Who'll give its power into a stranger's hand ?
  Another easy Dido do you seek,
  And new occasions new-made vows to break ?
  When can you walls like ours of Carthage build,
  And see your streets with crowds of subjects filled ?
  But though all this succeeded to your mind,
  So true a wife no search could ever find.

"Scorched up with love's fierce fire, my life does waste,
  Like incense on the flaming altar cast ;
  All day Æneas walks before my sight,
  In all my dreams I see him every night,
  But see him still ungrateful as before,
  And such as, if I could, I should abhor.
  But the strong flame burns on against my will ;
  I call him false, but love the traitor still."

A further proof of his scholarship was his version of "The Life of Alcibiades," which he contributed to the translation of Plutarch by "various hands," published in the same year. The evidence which connects him with the authorship of the strong and vigorous, but coarse invective, "Dryden's Satire to his Muse," a reply to glorious John's "Absalom and Ahitophel," is far from satisfactory. Dr.

Johnson says it was ascribed to Somers, but in Pope's opinion, "falsely." He adds:—"The poem, whosesoever it was, has much virulence and some sprightliness. The writer tells all the ill that he can collect of Dryden and his friends." Horace Walpole remarks, that "the gross ribaldry of it cannot be supposed to have flowed from so humane and polished a nature as Lord Somers's." This, however, cannot count for much, as, in the heat of political warfare, a satirist will allow himself an exceptional license; but more weight may be allowed to the fact that Somers himself positively disavowed the authorship.[*]

The generous patronage which he extended to men of letters and to literary enterprises is a matter beyond doubt. It was at his instigation that the first folio edition of Milton was printed, and he encouraged the rising genius of the author of "The Rape of the Lock."

> "The courtly Talbot, Somers, Sheffield read."

Blackmore refers to him as an acknowledged *arbiter elegantiarum.*

> "'Twill Somers' scales and Talbot's test abide,
> And with their mark please all the world beside."

He was the friend of Addison and the correspondent of Tillotson. Talent or scholarship never appealed to his sympathies in vain.

Soon after the death of his father in 1681, Somers bade farewell to the classic shades of Oxford, and having taken his bachelor's degree, finally removed to London, where he began to practise at the bar. A competent authority observes that—

---

Sir Walter Scott, "Life of Dryden," p. 257.

" Probably no man ever commenced practice as an advocate in England with such high and varied qualifications.   He was consummately skilled as a lawyer—from the practice of commencing an action, which he had learned when a lad in his father's office, to the most abstruse doctrines of real property, which he had imbibed from Winnington, and the most enlarged views of general jurisprudence, with which he had become familiar from his civil law studies at Oxford.   He was moreover deeply versed in all constitutional learning, and besides being a fine classical scholar, he was familiarly acquainted with the languages and the literature of all the polished nations on the continent of Europe.   Above all, he had steady habits of application, and he could not only make the necessary active exertion, but undergo the necessary drudgery, and submit to the necessary sacrifices, to ensure success at the English bar."

Success he immediately obtained, and success so complete, that his professional income in the reign of James II. amounted to £700 per annum, an exceptionally large sum at that period.   He had scarcely been a year at the bar when he was employed as one of the counsel in the then famous case of Pilkington and Shute, the sheriffs of London, who with others were indicted for a riot on Midsummer Day, 1681, caused by the attempt of the Crown to influence the election.   But it was in a far more important trial that his reputation as a constitutional lawyer was solidly established.   When James II. asserted the " dispensing power" of the Crown, and, in April, 1688, published a Declaration of Indulgence which suspended the operation of the penal laws against both Nonconformists and Roman Catholics, and of all acts imposing a test as a qualification for office in Church or State, he ordered that every clergyman should read it during divine service on two successive Sundays.   " Little time," says Mr. Green, " was given for deliberation; but

little time was needed.    The clergy refused almost to a
man to be the instruments of their own humiliation.
The declaration was read in only four of the London
churches, and in these the congregation flocked out of
church at the first words of it.    Nearly all the country
parsons refused to obey the royal orders, and the bishops
went with the rest of the clergy."    The Archbishop of
Canterbury, with six of his suffragans, humbly petitioned
the king to be absolved from it.    When their protest
was laid before James, he exclaimed, " It is a standard
of rebellion !" and, impelled by the fate which was
driving him on to destruction, directed an information to
be filed against them for publishing a seditious libel
against the king and his government.

On the 15th of June, 1688, they were brought to
trial in the Court of King's Bench.    Their counsel were
Sir Robert Sawyer, Mr. Finch, Mr. Pollexfen, Sir George
Treby, Mr. Pemberton, Sergeant Levaig, and Mr. Somers.
To the last the bishops had at first objected on the
ostensible grounds of his youth and want of practice ;
more probably, because he was a Whig in politics, and a
known opponent of the doctrines of " divine right " and
" passive obedience," which they had so zealously and
unwisely advocated ; but Pollexfen, insisting on his
profound constitutional learning, and his thorough knowledge of " precedents and records," declared that unless
he was retained he himself would abandon the defence.
His services proved to be invaluable.    He supplied his
brother-counsel with the facts gleaned by his wide and
laborious research ; while his own speeches were distinguished by the force and clearness of their arguments.
His closing address was remarkably impressive, and,
assisted as it was by the popular feeling, led to the

acquittal of the Seven Bishops—an event which may justly be regarded as the first stage of the Revolution.

In its subsequent stages he played a not less weighty part. The Whig leaders, in their bold effort to establish a constitutional system of government, were guided by his sound and sage advice. He was admitted into "the most secret councils of the Prince of Orange;" and was certainly concerned in drawing up the celebrated "Invitation" to him to intervene by force of arms for the restoration of English liberty and the protection of the Protestant religion.

James fled from England on the 23rd of December, and a month afterwards a convention of both Houses of Parliament was summoned by the Prince to settle the government of the country. In this convention Somers represented the city of Worcester. In the debates of the Lower House he seems at once to have taken the lead; his "luminous eloquence" and "varied stores of knowledge" making a deep impression upon his fellow-members. He drew up the famous Resolution with which the debate terminated—"That King James II., having endeavoured to subvert the constitution of the kingdom by breaking the original contract between king and people, and by the advice of Jesuits and other wicked persons having violated the fundamental laws, and having withdrawn himself out of this kingdom, has abdicated the government, and that the throne is thereby become vacant." The House of Lords having adopted certain amendments, Somers was one of the committee which the Commons appointed to confer with them upon the subject. The principal objection made by the peers was to the word "abdicate," for which they proposed to substitute "deserted," and at the same time to omit the concluding clause. Somers supported the resolution with ingenuity and learning, quoting Grotius and Brissonius, Spilevius and Bartolus, and referring to the precedent of 1399. Eventually the Lords yielded, and having adopted the resolution, immediately afterwards proposed and carried another, that the Prince and Princess of Orange should be declared King and Queen of England.

This resolution was, of course, affirmed by the Commons, and the theme being thus supplied, the convention applied their energies to the great subject of constitutional reform. A committee was appointed, which, under the guidance of Somers, set forth the necessary conditions for " the better securing our religion, liberty, and laws," and embodied them in the famous " Declaration of Rights," which, with some amendments, was accepted by both Houses. The Declaration recited the misgovernment of James, his abdication, and the firm purpose of the Lords and Commons to maintain the ancient rights and liberties of Englishmen. It condemned as illegal his establishment of an ecclesiastical commission, and his levying an army without the sanction of Parliament. It denied the right of any king to suspend or dispense with laws, as they had been suspended or dispensed with of late, or to exact money save by consent of Parliament. It asserted the right of the subject to petition, to a free choice of representatives in Parliament, and to a pure and merciful administration of justice. It maintained the right of both Houses to liberty of debate. It demanded securities for the free exercise of the Protestant religion, while it bound the new sovereign to maintain together the laws and liberties of the people. All these things it claimed as the undoubted inheritance of Englishmen.

Having thus vindicated the principles of the constitution, the Lords and Commons, in full confidence that his Highness the Prince would perfect the deliverance he had begun, and preserve their rights against all further injury, resolved that William and Mary, Prince and Princess of Orange, should be declared King of England for their joint and separate lives, and that during their joint lives the administration of the government should be in the Prince alone.

The Declaration was presented to William and Mary on the 13th of February by the two Houses, and accepted by William in his own name, and in that of his wife.    It was in a large measure through the sagacity, skill, and moderation of Somers, that this settlement of the nation was effected, and the foundation laid deep and strong of the constitutional government of Great Britain.

It was impossible that services such as his should go without reward, and William III. hastened to appoint him Solicitor-General and to confer on him the honour of knighthood (May, 1691).    His first official speech was made in defence of the Bill for declaring the Convention a Parliament.    To those who disputed its legality, because it was not summoned by royal writ, he replied * :—

" ' If this were not a legal Parliament, they who had taken the oaths which it had prescribed were guilty of high treason ; the laws repealed by it were still in force ; all concerned in levying, collecting, or paying taxes under its statutes were highly criminal, and the whole nation must presently return to King James.'  He spoke with much zeal, and such an ascendant of authority, that none was prepared to answer; so the bill

---

* Bishop Burnet, " History of Our Own Times," iii. 57.

passed without any more opposition. This was a great service done in a very critical time, and contributed not a little to raise Somers's character."

His next important labour was to carry through the House the Toleration Act, by which the Protestant dissenters of England were for the first time permitted by law to worship God according to the dictates of their conscience; and he also assisted in the establishment of the Presbyterian religion in Scotland. It was he who was selected to draw up the Declaration of War against France (May 15th). In truth, the difficulty experienced in compressing within concise limits a memoir of this great man arises from the fact that his advice and his assistance were sought in all the important measures of the time. His biography for some years is closely inter-mixed with the history of his country—a history which he helped to make or influence—and can hardly be given without involving a narrative of historical events that lies altogether beyond our scope. The reader, therefore, must turn from these pages when he feels the need of fuller information, to the great work of Lord Macaulay, or the popular and picturesque volumes of Mr. Green, or the earlier authorities of Burnet, Tindal, and Bishop Kennett.

On the 2nd of May, 1692, he was raised to the post of Attorney-General, in which capacity he conducted the prosecution of Lord Mohun for the murder of Mountford, the comedian. The titled bravo was acquitted by a majority of sixty-nine to fourteen. The rapid increase of Somers's reputation, and of his influence both in Parliament and the country, led to his appointment, in March, 1693, to the high office of Lord Keeper of the Great Seal. The promotion gave general satisfaction, which Garth

the author of " The Dispensary," echoed in his mediocre
rhymes :—

"Haste, and the matchless Atticus address !
From Heaven and great Nassau he has the mace;
The oppressed to his asylum still repair,
Arts he supports, and learning is his care.
He softens the harsh rigour of the laws,
Blunts their keen edge and cuts their harpy claws,
And graciously he casts a pitying eye,
On the sad state of virtuous poverty.
Whene'er he speaks, Heavens ! how the listening throng
Dwells on the melting music of his tongue ;
And when the power of eloquence he'd try,
Here, lightning strikes you—there, soft breezes sigh."

As a judge the merits of Somers have been almost
unanimously admired, and his contemporaries have
recorded in eulogistic language the favourable opinions
called forth by his industry, patience, clear-sightedness,
and urbanity. His temper was as gentle as his intelligence was keen, and there was about him such a charm
of manner that it robbed even an adverse judgment of
its sting. The great debt of gratitude we owe to him as
an equity judge is said to be due to his having " introduced and established the principles and doctrines of the
civil law on the subjects of legacies, trusts, and charities,
and all others to which they were properly applicable."
It was Somers, too, who established the practice of a
Parliamentary dissolution of marriage on account of the
adultery of the wife ; and for students of English literature it is interesting to remember that the first case of
this kind was that of the notorious Countess of Maccles-
field, the mother of Richard Savage.

In 1695, during William's absence from England,

Somers served as one of the lords justices, as he did also
in 1697 and 1698.  In 1697 he was appointed Lord
High Chancellor, and was raised to the peerage by the
style and title of Baron Somers of Evesham.  In the
debates of the House of Lords he actively interposed, and
it was his eloquence and authority that prevented a
renewal of the Licensing Act, and gave England the
inestimable boon of a free press.  Always on the side of
freedom, he advised the king to veto the "Place Bill,"
which prohibited any person holding a place of profit
under the Crown from sitting in the House of Commons.
On the other hand, it was in deference to his arguments
that William gave his assent to the Bill for Triennial
Parliaments, which he had formerly vetoed.  After his
elevation to the peerage, he strongly opposed the Property
Qualification Bill, which required property in land as a
qualification for a member of the Lower House, contending that the people might reasonably be left to their freedom in choosing their representatives in Parliament; that
it would be cruel and unjust if a poor man had so fair a
reputation as to be chosen, notwithstanding his poverty,
by those who were willing to pay him wages, to brand
him with an incapacity because of his small estate; that
corruption in elections was to be dreaded from the rich
rather than the poor; and that, at all events, it was
absurd that land should be the only property recognised
as a qualification.

I think we may agree with Lord Campbell that our
brilliant lawyer-statesman had now reached the climax
of his splendid career, "his highest pitch of worldly
prosperity."  The services he had rendered to his country
had assured him of an immortal name; he himself must
have rejoiced in the knowledge that he had successfully

reared the fabric of constitutional liberty. He was held in high esteem by the king; his influence was very great in both Houses of Parliament; by the nation he was loved and revered. The commercial classes were grateful to the only Lord Chancellor who had understood questions of trade and finance; the lawyers admired his vast legal knowledge, and were proud of the new dignity he had conferred on their profession; while men of letters were never weary of repeating the praises of the accomplished scholar whose patronage of literature was so discriminating and generous. Among those unbribed panegyrists was Joseph Addison, who dedicated to him his "Epistle in Praise of King William," in terms of melodious flattery :—

> "If yet your thoughts are loose from State affairs,
>   Nor feel the burden of a nation's cares,—
> If yet your time and actions are your own,
>   Receive the present of a Muse unknown:
> A Muse that in adventurous numbers sings
>   The rout of armies and the fall of kings,
> Britain advanced, and Europe's peace restored,
>   By Somers' counsels and by Nassau's sword.

> "To you, my lord, these daring thoughts belong,
>   Who helped to raise the subject of my song;
> To you the hero of my verse reveals
>   His great designs, to you in council tells
> His inmost thoughts, determining the doom
>   Of towns unstormed, and battles yet to come.
> And well could you in your immortal strains,
>   Describe his conduct and reward his pains;
> But since the State has all your cares engrossed,
>   And poetry in higher thoughts is lost,
> Attend to what a lesser muse indites,
>   Pardon her faults and countenance her flights."

K

Addison found in Somers a liberal patron. Both he
and Montague, the accomplished Chancellor of the Exchequer, were favourably disposed towards the young
man of letters, who was also a firm though moderate
Whig. They were anxious to employ him in the service
of the Crown abroad; and that he might obtain that
intimate knowledge of the French language, then indispensable to a diplomatist, Somers procured him a pension
of three hundred pounds a-year, which enabled him to
visit the Continent.

For some years England had enjoyed peace at home
and credit abroad under the direction of the Whig
Administration, the leading members of which—Somers,
Russell, Charles Montague, and Lord Shrewsbury—were
known as "the Junto," from their close union in thought
and action. In both Houses they had a majority, and
the majority did but reflect the national feeling of confidence. But after the Treaty of Ryswick a change came
over the spirit of the country. The new Parliament
returned at the close of 1698 showed the existence of a
Tory majority indifferent to foreign policy, and pledged
to a reduction of taxation. Somers recognised at once
the insecurity of the position. "There is nothing to
support the Whigs," he wrote, "but the difficulty of the
king's posing with the other party, and the almost
impossibility of finding a set of Tories who will unite; so
that in the end I conclude it will be a pieced business,
which will fall asunder immediately." The unpopularity
of the Ministry was farther increased by their share in
the Partition Treaties, though the policy which dictated
them was capable of effective justification. In our own
times a ministry that has lost the confidence of both
Houses, or even of the House of Commons alone, imme-

diately resigns; but this theory of ministerial responsibility was not as yet accepted by English statesmen, and
Montague and Somers continued to hold office in the
face of a preponderant Opposition. At length William
called for the resignation of Russell and Montague, the
two ministers most obnoxious to the Tories, in the hope
that this concession would satisfy the House. But the
animosity of the Opposition leaders was then concentrated
on a single object, "the great magistrate who still held
the highest civil post in the realm, and of whose authority and influence with the king they were bitterly
jealous."

"It was not so easy to get rid of him," says Macaulay, "as it
had been to drive his colleagues from office. His abilities the
most intolerant Tories were forced grudgingly to acknowledge.
His integrity might be questioned in nameless libels and coffee-
house tattle, but was certain to come forth bright and pure from
the most severe Parliamentary investigation. . . . His serenity,
his modesty, his self-command, proof even against the most
sudden surprises of passion; his self-respect, which forced the
proudest grandees of the kingdom to respect him; his urbanity,
which won the hearts of the youngest lawyers of the Chancery
Bar, gained for him many private friends and admirers among
the most respectable members of the Opposition. But such men
as Howe and Seymour hated him implacably: they hated his
commanding genius much; they hated the mild majesty of his
virtue still more."

In the House of Commons they preferred various charges
against the great Chancellor, of which the chief seems to
have been that, after the discovery, in 1696, of a plot for
assassinating the king, he had arbitrarily removed several
gentlemen from the commission of the peace who had
refused to subscribe to a voluntary association then formed

for His Majesty's protection. And on the 10th of April, 1700, they moved that an humble address should be presented to the king, praying him to remove " John, Lord Somers, Lord Chancellor of England, from his presence and councils for ever." Somers was so powerfully defended, and the admiration for his character was so widely felt, that even in a Tory House of Commons this motion was defeated by a majority of 167 votes against 106. But the repeated attempts of the Chancellor's enemies made such an impression on the king, that he resolved to offer him up as a sacrifice. Somers at the time was lying at Tunbridge Wells, suffering severely from an illness induced by his patriotic labours. As soon as he recovered sufficiently to make his appearance at Court, William told him it seemed necessary for his service that he should part with the seals, and that it was desirable that his delivery of them should appear to be his own act. To this cowardly proposition Somers replied, that he would not voluntarily resign his office, or his enemies would say that he had been actuated by fear or the consciousness of guilt; but that whenever His Majesty should send a warrant, under his hand, demanding the seals, he would immediately give them up. On the 17th of April the warrant was brought by Lord Jersey, and Somers surrendered the insignia of the office which, for seven years, he had held with so much honour.*

---

* " Thus," says Tindal, " the Lord Somers was discharged from this great office, which he had held seven years with a high reputation for capacity, integrity, and diligence. His being thus removed was much censured by all but those who procured it. Our princes used not to dismiss ministers who served them well, unless they were pressed to it by a House of Commons that refused to give money till they were laid aside. But here a minister, who was always vindicated by a large majority in the House of Commons when he was charged there,

The conduct of William in thus dismissing the ablest and most faithful of his ministers, to gratify the spleen of faction, was very generally reprobated. In Westminster Hall it produced something like a panic of consternation; "the courts were immediately deserted, the laws silent, and all proceedings at a stand," for no one thought himself worthy to succeed so great a man. Somers himself preserved his usual serenity. His removal, says Bishop Kennet, though it displeased many people, yet seemed not to affect his lordship, who retired with content and temper, and upon all occasions in Parliament served the king and the interest of the public with the same zeal as if he had not lost a place.

But his enemies were not yet satisfied. They had secured his dismissal, but not his disgrace. And after a fierce debate on the Partition Treaties, they made a proposal in the House of Commons (14th April, 1701) that he should be impeached for his share in these Treaties, and for other high crimes and misdemeanours. He immediately sent a message to the House that, having heard that complaint had been made of him, he begged,

and who had served both with fidelity and success, and was indeed censured with nothing so much as for his being complete with the king's humour and motives, or, at least, for being too soft or too feeble in representing his errors to him, was removed without the shadow of complaint against him. This was done with so much haste, that those who had prevailed with the king to do it, had not yet concerted who should succeed him. They thought that all the great men of the law were aspiring to that high post, so that any one to whom it should be offered would certainly accept it. But they soon found they were mistaken; for what by reason of the instability of the Court, what by reason of the just apprehensions men might have of succeeding so great a man, both the Lord Chief Justice Holt and the Attorney-General Trevor, to whom the seals were offered, excused themselves."— Tindal, "Continuation of Rapin, xiv. 515."

out of his high respect for the Commons of England, that he might have permission to be heard before them in his own defence.    This was granted; but of the speech made by the great statesman we have, unfortunately, only a most imperfect report, from which it appears that he pleaded in vindication of his conduct that he had simply obeyed the sovereign's orders.    As a Privy Councillor, he had stated to his Majesty the objections he felt to many portions of the Treaties; as a Chancellor, he had affixed to them the Great Seal, by command of the king.    His speech produced a powerful impression; but his enemies succeeded in carrying, though only by a majority of 10 (198 to 188), a resolution to the effect—" That John, Lord Somers, by advising his Majesty in the year 1698 to the Treaty for Partition of the Spanish monarchy, whereby large territories of the king of Spain's dominions were to be delivered up to France, was guilty of a high crime and misdemeanour."    And his impeachment before the House of Lords was ordered in due form.

Having also resolved to impeach Russell, Earl of Oxford, the Earl of Portland, and Montague, Lord Halifax, they presented an address to the king, praying him to remove all four noblemen from his councils and presence for ever.    The lords, on the other hand, presented a counter-address, in which his Majesty was solicited " not to pass any censure upon the accused Lords until they were tried upon their impeachments, and judgment had been given according to the usage of Parliament and the laws of the land."    The articles of impeachment were exhibited on the 19th of May, and so far as Lord Somers was concerned, accused him of misconduct in connection with the Partition Treaties, in passing certain grants under the Great Seal to himself and others, and in granting a

commission to Captain Kidd, the notorious buccaneer.
To these charges it seems to us that the reply of Lord
Somers was complete. He had acted as the king's servant
in the matter of the Partition Treaties,—to the policy
of which he had not been favourably inclined,—and
though this answer would not hold good with our
present view of ministerial responsibility, which requires
a minister to resign office if he differs in opinion on
important questions from his colleagues in the Crown, it
was sufficient in the reign of William. He proved that
the moneys and rents given to him by the king had not
been procured by his own solicitation. And as to Captain
Kidd, he had granted him, at the request of the American
colonists, a commission to act as a privateer; but had no
knowledge that he would end by becoming a pirate. To
Lord Somers' "Answer" the Commons delayed putting in
a "replication;" and conscious of the weakness of their
case, interposed other obstacles to the prosecution of the
impeachment. At length the Lords ordered that the
trial should positively commence on Friday, the 13th of
June; and, on that day, no one appearing for the prosecution, they decided that "the defendant should be
acquitted, and the impeachment dismissed."

During these proceedings, Lord Somers behaved with
great dignity and moderation. Addison remarks that,
for the wide extent of his knowledge and capacity, he
had often been compared with Lord Bacon. But, he
adds, the conduct of these extraordinary persons under
the same circumstances was very different.

"They were both impeached by a House of Commons. One
of them, as he had given just occasion for it, sunk under it; and
was reduced to such an abject submission as very much
diminished the lustre of so exalted a character. But, my Lord

Somers was too well fortified in his integrity to fear the impotence of an attempt upon his reputation; and though his accusers would gladly have dropped their impeachment, he was instant with them for the prosecution of it, and would not let that matter rest until it was brought to an issue. For the same virtue and greatness of mind which made him disregard fame, made him impatient of an undeserved reproach."

Towards the end of the session, Sunderland entered into a correspondence with Lord Somers for the purpose of effecting a reconciliation between King William and the Whig leaders. Somers prepared the noble speech with which William opened his last Parliament (31st December), and arrangements were in progress for the formation of a Whig Ministry when the aspect of affairs was completely changed by the king's death, 8th March, 1702. To Queen Anne, Somers was for various reasons obnoxious; and he abandoned, if he had ever entertained, his hopes of being recalled to office. In the House of Lords his influence was exerted in support of the foreign policy, which was based upon Whig principles, of Godolphin and Marlborough; and he strongly advocated every measure for the development or confirmation of the rights of the subject—civil and religious. His leisure was gracefully occupied in literary and philosophical pursuits. For five years he acted as President of the Royal Society, regularly attending its meetings, and taking part in its discussions. He greatly coveted the society of learned men, who were warmly welcomed to his house in town and his country residence, Brookmans, in Hertfordshire. I shall not here enumerate his legislative reforms, with the exception of his Act, passed in 1706, for the amendment of the law and the better advancement of justice. But special reference must be made to his labours in accomplishing the union of England and Scotland, which, in truth, it was his sagacity, firmness, and authority that crowned with success; and to his wisdom in afterwards insisting upon the abolition of the Scottish Privy Council, which otherwise would have effectually kept apart the sympathies and interests of the two nations. He was also actively concerned in that settlement of the succession which, on the death of Anne, called the House of Brunswick to the throne.

In Queen Anne's second Parliament, the Whigs secured a large majority; and thereupon Somers was induced to strengthen the administration by becoming Lord President of the Council.

"The great capacity and inflexible integrity of this lord," says Burnet,* "would have made his promotion to this post very acceptable to the Whigs at any juncture, but it was more particularly so at this time; for it was expected that the pro positions for a general peace would be quickly made; and so they reckoned that the management of that upon which not only the safety of the nation, but of all Europe depended, was in sure hands when he was set at the head of the councils, upon whom neither ill practices nor false colours were like to make any impression. Thus the minds of all those who were truly zealous for the present Constitution were much quieted by this promotion; though their jealousies had a deep root, and were not easily removed."

In 1710, the Tories again came into power; and from that date Lord Somers ceased, through his severe physical infirmities, to take any active part in public life. On the accession of George I. he was made one of the Privy Council, and a seat in the Cabinet was assigned to him;† but

* "History of Our Own Times," iv. 247-8.
† He also received an additional pension of £2000 a-year.

these were nominal honours.   A paralytic affection had enfeebled his faculties, and incapacitated him for public affairs.   Only at intervals a spark of his former fire flashed forth; as when he expressed to Lord Townshend his warm approval of the Septennial Bill.   His decline was very rapid; and a fit of apoplexy striking him in his shattered condition, he passed away on the 26th of April, 1716, aged 66 years.

# William, Earl of Mansfield.

THE most cursory examination of the biography of
our great lawyers discloses an interesting fact,
that nearly all have "risen from the ranks," and
have attained to fortune and fame in spite of the
obstacles thrown in their way by low birth and poverty.
In the law, more than in any other profession in England,
is "the career open to talent" (*la carrière ouverte aux
talens*)—is it possible for the son of the peasant or the
artisan to rise to an equality of rank with the son of the
peer of bluest blood and most ancient descent. The
reason is not far to seek; it is a profession in which
eminence cannot be obtained, except by indomitable
energy, perseverance and patience, and intellectual
power. It is a profession, therefore, seldom chosen by
young men who are fain to trust for their advancement
in life to exterior influences. Again, though its prizes
are numerous and splendid, they cannot be won until after
an arduous and generally a prolonged competition; hence
it possesses small attraction for quick and impetuous
temperaments, which weary of a pursuit that offers no
immediate result to their labours. And thus it comes to
pass that, to men who can work and wait, it presents a
fair field and an ample scope in which "patronage" and

139

" interest " avail but little, if at all—in which the course
is well defined, and, as a rule, the competition honestly
undertaken ; in which whosoever will may reasonably
hope to come to the front in virtue of his personal
qualifications, and without being heavily handicapped by
adventitious circumstances.    It was this which led an
eminent judge, when asked to explain the secret of success in the legal profession, to reply :  " Some succeed  by
great talent, some by high connections, some  by miracle,
but the majority by beginning without a shilling."

There is no rule, however, without an exception.
Among the illustrious names which adorn the annals of
English jurisprudence, none are more illustrious than that
of William Murray, Earl of Mansfield ; and Murray was
a man of high birth, a scion of one of the oldest of Scotch
families.    The fourth son of Andrew, Viscount Stormont,
he was born at Perth, on the 2nd of March, 1705.
According to one authority, he was removed to London at
the early age of three ; but Lord Campbell, on the
authority of family papers, asserts that he was educated
at the Grammar School at Perth, where he was taught
the practice of English composition very thoroughly, and
obtained a good knowledge of Horace and Sallust, until
his fourteenth year.*    He was then sent to Westminster,
with the view of being educated for the bar.    As the son
of a Jacobite peer, he would have had little chance of
promotion in the army, and in the Scotch Church the
livings were too poor to offer any attraction to ambitious

---

* Among the Stormont accounts are entries of : " 1715, May 27,—
Sent to Scone per Lady's letter for Mr. William, *Cæsaris Commentarius*,
£1, 4s." (Scotch money, equal to 2s. English) ; and, " 1717, August
8,—At order, bought of Mr. Freebairn for Mr. William, my Lord's son
*Titus Livius*, in a great folio and large print, for 20s. sterling."

youth. The legal profession was, therefore, his sole resource.

The story was, that he departed for London on a Galloway pony, taking leave of his parents at Cumlongan, in Dumfriesshire, and thence proceeding by way of Gretna Green and Carlisle, arrived in the English capital on the 8th of May, 1718. There he was received by one John Wemyss, a Scotch apothecary, who had been born on the Stormont estate, and was eager to be of service to a son of the laird. He assisted him to sell his pony, and invested the proceeds to the best advantage; conducted him to Westminster School, and finally lodged him at a dame's in Dean Yard. An extract from the statement of account which he afterwards presented to Lady Stormont, will be of interest in connection with the manners and customs of the times :—

|  | Lib. | sh. | d. |
|---|---|---|---|
| " 1718, May 8.—ffor ye carriadge Mr. William's Box and bringing it home, | – | 09 | – |
| ffor his horse before he was sold, | – | 08 | 7 |
| To Dr. Ffriend* for entrance, | 1 | 01 | – |
| ffor a Trunk to him ffor his cloaths, | – | 13 | – |
| To his Landlady where he Boards, for Entry money, | 5 | 05 | – |
| 20.—ffor a sword to him, | 1 | 01 | – |
| ffor a belt, | – | 2 | – |
| ffor pocket-money to him, | – | 3 | – |
| June 5.—ffor pocket money, | – | 1 | – |
| ffor two wigs as per receit, | 4 | 4 | – |
| „ 18.—ffor a double letter and pocket-money to him, | – | 2 | – |
| Aug. 16.—To Mr. William who went to the country, | – | 6 | – |

---

* Dr. Friend, Headmaster of the School.

|  |  | Lib. | sh. | d. |
|---|---|---|---|---|
| Dec. 17.—Three guineas to the master and a double letter, . . . . | | 3 | 4 | – |
| 1719, Jany. 4.—ffor pocket-money 5 shil. ; and the ij to Dr. Friend, 3 guineas, . | | 3 | 8 | – |
| „ 21.—To Mr. Wm. to Treat with before the Elections began, . . . | | 1 | 1 | – |
| Pay'd the Taylor as pr. bill, . . | | 1 | 1 | – |
| Pay'd Mrs. Tollet for ¾ years Board and for things laid out for him as pr. bill, . . . . | | 20 | 10 | – |

Thus bewigged and besworded, the lank, high cheek-boned Scotch youth entered Westminster School, and started on his adventurous career. His north country dialect at first excited some ridicule, but it soon ceased when it was found that there was muscle in his arm and courage in his soul. His classical acquirements commanded respect, and that grace of manner which afterwards won so many hearts soon told in his favour. He had been nearly a year at the school before he was elected a King's scholar. Bishop Newton, one of his contemporaries and comrades, tells us that he gave early proof of his uncommon abilities, not so much in his poetry as in his other exercises, and particularly in his declamations. We have only one anecdote, however, of this period of his life, and it does not throw much light upon his character.* Lady Kinnoul, in one of his vacations, observing him with a pen in his hand, and seemingly thoughtful, asked him if he were writing his Latin theme, and what, in plain English, was the subject of it. He answered smartly, "What is that to you?" She replied, "How can you be so rude? I asked you civilly a plain question, and did not expect from a schoolboy so pert an answer."

---

* Holliday, "Life of William Earl of Mansfield," p. 2.

"Indeed, my lady," said Murray, " I can only answer once more, *What is that to you ?* "  The explanation is, that the theme was headed, " *Quid ad te pertinet.*"

In May, 1728, Murray stood first on the list of the king's scholars to be sent to Oxford, and was entered of Christ Church on the 18th of June in that year.  In 1724, through the generosity of a friend—a son of Lord Foley — he was enabled to become a member of the Honourable Society of Lincoln's Inn, though he remained at Oxford for three years longer, sedulously pursuing those studies which were best adapted to facilitate his success in the profession he had adopted, and, in particular, cultivating with untiring perseverence the art of oratory.  He read Cicero constantly and assiduously, translating the great master into English, and re-translating into Latin.  Quinctilian was also consulted, while to the speeches of Demosthenes he gave the most critical attention.  He also practised original composition in both Latin and English, acquiring an elegant and exact style.  We may quote a specimen of his Latin prose, because it contains a panegyric on the oratorical excellences of that great Greek orator, whose resistless eloquence

> " Wielded at will that fierce democracy,
> Shook the arsenal, and fulmined over Greece."

" Qua solemnitate exordii animos auditorum incitat !  Deosque deasque omnes benevolentiæ suæ in civitatem testes adhibet !  Quam sibi modesta meritorum in cives suos commemoratione ad se audiendum munivit viam ! . . . Quis flexanimam Demosthenis potentiam digne explicaverit, qua summissio placidoque principio in animos omnium, velut in accensos agros taciturno roris imbre leniter fluentis incendium quod reliquerit Æschines extinguit, populique furorem placat.  Mox vehemens et acer viquadem incredibili auditores extra se, contra Æschinem calumniatorem odio, mercenarium Philippi contemptu proditorem patriæ ira rapit."

[ " With what solemnity his exordium appeals to the minds of his hearers ! He calls all the gods and goddesses to witness to his love for his country. With how modest an allusion to his own services does he preface the way for a favourable hearing ! . . . Who shall ever be able to explain the power of Demosthenes over the human affections. Beginning in a mild and subdued tone, like dew descending gently on the parched fields, he extinguishes the flame which Æschines had raised, and soothes the popular fury. But soon afterwards, growing vehement and bitter, with what incredible force he controls his hearers, and holds up Æschines to their contempt and hatred as a calumniator, as the mercenary of Philip, and the betrayer of his native land."]

In 1727 Murray gained the Latin prize poem " On the Death of George I." The versification is correct, but feeble ; the imagery poor, and the poet's spirit is nowhere present. Murray had no imagination ; but if he had had, we may doubt whether the subject was one to have stimulated it. The most noticeable fact about the competition is that the elder Pitt, the " Great Commoner," was a candidate ; and it has absurdly been alleged that his defeat embittered him against the more fortunate Murray, and was the primary cause of his keen hostility to the latter in their after strife as leaders of the State. There was a deeper reason for that hostility, however, than the disappointment arising from a failure in a boyish struggle.

Having taken his degree of B.A., Murray removed to London, and began his course of study at Lincoln's Inn. It would seem to have been regulated by broad and sound principles. Murray aimed at being something more than a lawyer ; he was fired by a lofty ambition, and already aspired to succeed as an advocate and a politician, a scholar and a wit. He began by acquiring a thorough knowledge of the great historians, rightly conceiving that a knowledge of the past is essential to a just and accurate understanding of the present. Next he took up the study of ethics, and he appears to have set a special value on the philosophical works of Cicero. The Roman civil law engaged his close attention; he traced in it the elements of modern jurisprudence, and acknowledged its permanent influence on European polity. He read with care the works of Grotius, which form the foundation of international law; and those of Craig, which expound the traditions and effects of feudalism. English municipal law he studied in the erudite compositions of Bracton and Littleton; and with "precedents" and old "usages" he did not fail to make himself acquainted, in the text-books and reports which the old school of lawyers regarded with so blind a veneration. Scotch law, with its characteristics, he read up in the pages, always clear and precise, of Mackenzie and Stair; and he laboured with zeal to gain a complete mastery of the jurisprudence of France, and of her celebrated commercial code, which was then far in advance of anything that England possessed. To gain practical experience, and understand the application of the theories he had so conscientiously made his own, he regularly attended the Courts at Westminster, and analysed the decisions of the judges.

His day's work at an end, " he drank champagne with the wits."* At Will's or Button's Coffeehouse he met the leaders of literature and society, and discussed with them the merits of the last new play or poem, toasted

---

* Dr. Johnson's statement to Boswell.

L

the newest beauty, and pointed the sharpest epigram.
His rank and his university reputation gave him at once
a position which his grace of manner and force of character justified and confirmed.   An acquaintance with Pope,
begun at Westminster, now ripened into a steady friendship; the famous poet took a special interest in the
brilliant young advocate, which the latter repaid by a strong
and genuine admiration.   " Mr. Pope," says Bishop Warburton, " had all the warmth of affection for this great
lawyer; and indeed," he adds, "no man ever more
deserved to have a poet for his friend, in the obtaining of
which, as neither vanity, party, nor fear had a share, so
he supported his title to it by all the offices of a generous
and true friendship."   A pleasant story is told by one of
Mansfield's biographers,* to the effect that, " One day he
was suprised by a gentleman of Lincoln's Inn, who took
the liberty of entering his room without the ceremonious
introduction of a servant, in the singular act of practising
the graces of a speaker at a glass, while Pope sate by, in
the character of a friendly preceptor."   The anecdote is
interesting, as showing with what care and attention to
details the young lawyer prepared himself for the great
part he intended to play.

On the 24th of June, 1730, Murray took his degree
of M.A.   He then went on a long-vacation tour through
France and Italy, and on his return was called to the bar
in Lincoln's Inn Hall (November 23).   For two years
and more he failed to obtain a brief; but his strong
resolution did not desert him, and he would not allow his
want of success to quench his ambition or divert his
intellectual energies into any other channel of advance-

---

* Holliday, p. 24.

ment. He knew exactly the limit of his powers, and felt that by the law he must rise or fall. So, in his chambers, at 5 King's Bench Walk, in the Temple, he steadily waited for the clients that never came,—for the opportunity of distinction that, however long deferred, he was sure would one day be his; and in the interval he widened his knowledge of classical and contemporary literature, and compiled two letters "On the Study of Ancient and Modern History," which prove that in historical composition he might have attained to no ordinary excellence.

It is said that he never knew the difference between total destitution and an income of £2000 a-year.[*] There would seem to be some exaggeration in this statement, though it is ascribed to Lord Mansfield himself; but in his case, as in the case of so many eminent lawyers, it is certainly true that his rise into distinction was sudden. As early as 1732 he was engaged in an important appeal, in which both the Attorney and Solicitor General were employed, and in the two following years he was frequently retained in similar cases before the House of Lords; but it was his appearance as counsel, in 1737, against a bill introduced to disfranchise the city of Edinburgh on account of the Porteous riots, which first attached celebrity to his name. The measure was defeated; and Edinburgh conferred the honour of her freedom upon the successful advocate, who, it was freely predicted, was destined to increase the fame of his native land by the splendour of his abilities. By this time his reputation was so great that Pope selected him to receive the dedication of his "Imitations of Horace,"[†] and addressed him in a passage of the most elegant flattery, in

---

[*] Mr. Buller, in Seward's "Anecdotes," iv. 492.
[†] Sixth Epistle of the First Book.

which he alludes, it is said, to his friend's having unsuc-
cessfully solicited the hand of a lady of large fortune and
great beauty* :—

> " Go, then, and if you can admire the state
> Of beaming diamonds and reflected plate,
> Procure a taste to double the surprise,
> And gaze on Parian charms with learned eyes ;
> Be struck with bright brocade or Tyrian dye,
> Our birth-day nobles' splendid livery.
> If not so pleased, at council-board rejoice
> To see their judgments hang upon thy voice ;
> From morn to night, at Senate, Rolls, and Hall,
> Plead much, read more, dine late, or not at all.
> But wherefore all this labour, all this strife—
> For fame, for riches, for a noble wife ?
> Shall one whom nature, learning, birth, conspired
> To form, not to admire, but be admired,
> Sigh while his Chloe, blind to wit and worth,
> Weds the rich dulness of some son of earth ?
> Yet, time ennobles or degrades each line :
> It brightened Craggs's, and may darken thine.
> And what is fame ?  The meanest have their day ;
> The greatest can but blaze and pass away.
> Grand as thou art, with all the power of words,
> So known, so honoured in the House of Lords †—
> Conspicuous scene !—another yet is nigh,
> More silent far, where kings and poets lie ;
> Where Murray, long enough his country's pride,
> Shall be no more than Tully or than Hyde."

Murray at this time retired to a small cottage on the
banks of the Thames, near Twickenham ; not, as Lord

---

* The rejection came from the lady's family, not from the lady,
and was based on his narrowness of income.

† An unfortunate instance of bathos, which Colley Cibber happily
ridiculed :—

> " Persuasion tips his tongue whene'er he talks ;
> And he has chambers in the King's Bench Walks."

Campbell suggests, " that he might nourish his regrets," bnt that he might spend his vacation in the enjoyment of rural pleasures. This incident inspired his poet-friend to apply to him, in graceful style, Horace's " Ode to Venus" :*—

> " Again ? new tumults in my breast ?
> Ah, spare me, Venus !—let me, let me rest !
> I am not now, alas ! the man
> As in the gentle reign of my Queen Anne.
> Oh, sound no more thy soft alarms,
> Nor circle sober fifty with thy charms.
> Mother too fierce of dear desires,
> Turn, turn to willing hearts your wanton fires ;
> To *number five* direct your doves,
> There spread round Murray all your blooming loves,
> Noble and young, who strikes the heart
> With every sprightly, every decent part ;
> Equal the injured to defend,
> To charm the mistress or to fire the friend ;
> He, with a hundred hearts refined,
> Shall stretch thy conquests over half the kind.
> To him each rival shall submit,
>   Make but his riches equal to his wit.
> Then shall thy form the marble grace—
> Thy Grecian form—and Chloe lend the face ;
> His house, embosomed in the grove,
> Sacred to social life and social love,
> Shall glitter in the pendent green,
> Where Thames reflects the visionary scene :
> Thither the silver-sounding lyres
> Shall call the smiling Loves and young Desires ;
> There every Grace and Muse shall throng,
> Exalt the dance, or animate the song ;
> There youths and nymphs, in consort gay,
> Shall hail the rising, close the parting day."

I shall not apologise for the length of my quotation ;

---

* Odes, Vol. IV., Ode i.

the reader will be delighted at the opportunity of perusing verses so elegant and so polished.

The seal was set upon Murray's professional reputation by his successful defence of Mrs. Cibber, the celebrated actress, in the action brought against her by her husband, Theophilus, the scoundrel son of Colley Cibber, for adultery with a Colonel Sloper. That Mrs. Cibber was not immaculate need hardly be said; but her husband was an infamous wretch, and the willing instrument of his own dishonour. Murray's speech for the defence was a marvel of forensic eloquence. He had found his opportunity, and he made the most of it. The next day he was the most famous advocate in England; "henceforth," he says, "business poured in upon me from all quarters, and from a few hundred pounds in the year, I fortunately found myself in the receipt of thousands."

Among others, the Duchess of Marlborough was eager to secure his services, and sent him a general retainer, with a fee of one thousand guineas. With superb self-denial, he returned her nine hundred and ninety-five, remarking that "the professional fee, with a general retainer, will neither be less nor more than five guineas." She was a very inconsiderate client, and expected him to be at her call on all occasions. Late one night, returning to his chambers, he found a handsome equipage at the door, and the pavement thronged with footmen and pages holding lighted torches in their hands. The Duchess was seated in the advocate's own chair, and, on his entrance, greeted him with the characteristic reproach, "Young man, if you mean to rise in the world, you must not sup out."

Another night she called when he was not at home, and after waiting for some hours, left in great dudgeon. Said his clerk to him next morning—"I could not make out, sir, who she was, for she would not give me her name; but she swore so dreadfully that she must be a lady of quality."

When, in 1738, the London merchants, in a spirit of unpatriotic greed, endeavoured to force Walpole into a war with Spain, because the Spaniards attempted to check the smuggling that was carried on with the Spanish Colonies under the English flag, they petitioned the House of Commons for a redress of grievances, and employed Murray to support their complaints at the bar. Every oratorical resource was employed by the great advocate to exaggerate the insolence and cruelty of the Spaniards, and to brand as cowardice Walpole's sagacious and enlightened policy of peace. It was asserted that the prisoners taken from English merchant vessels had been not merely plundered of their property, but tortured in their persons, thrown into dungeons, or forced to labour in the Spanish dockyards upon scant and unwholesome food, their legs cramped with irons, and their bodies overrun with vermin. In support of these statements Murray made dexterous use of what Burke has called "the fable of Jenkins's ears," the said Jenkins being the master of a trading sloop which had been boarded and searched by a Spanish guarda-costa. Before the House of Commons he said:—"The Spanish captain had torn off one of his ears, bidding him carry it to the King, and tell His Majesty that were he present he should be similarly served." A member asked him what his feelings were when he found himself in the hands of such barbarians. Probably the question had been pre-arranged, for one can hardly believe that the reply was impromptu:—"I recommended my soul to

God, and my cause to my country." These words were eagerly caught up by the populace, and, traversing all England, kindled into a flame the latent fires of indignant patriotism, never slow to break forth in England. It is true, indeed, that Jenkins had lost an ear, which he carried about with him, wrapped in cotton, to excite sympathy; but it is true also that he had lost it in the pillory. Murray's device, however, was entirely successful; the merchants gained their object, and a Declaration of War against Spain was issued on the 19th of October, 1739. It was received by a credulous and excited people with extravagant manifestations of joy. A triumphal procession paraded the streets of London, as if victory had already been won. From all the metropolitan steeples the bells sent forth merry peals. "Let them ring," said Walpole moodily; "by-and-bye there will be ringing of hands."

A few months previously Murray had ensured his domestic happiness by a fortunate marriage, which at the same time strengthened both his social and political position. His choice fell upon the Lady Elizabeth Finch, a daughter of the Earl of Winchelsea, and a woman of many graces of person and character. In every respect she was fitted to preside over the household of an active and ambitious lawyer.

Murray wanted neither energy nor courage; but a predominant element in his character was prudence. With rare self-command he avoided any prominent part in the intrigues which marked the last days of Walpole. When the great minister was at last overthrown, and the Newcastle faction rose into power, he still refused to take any political office, though pressed to do so by his father-in-law, who had become first Lord of the

Admiralty. He adhered to his resolution to trust for advancement to his own profession. An opening was at last provided by the resignation, in 1742, of Sir John Strange, the Solicitor-General. Murray was immediately appointed to the vacancy, and without delay returned to the House of Commons for Boroughbridge.

The sentiments with which his promotion filled his mind are expressed in a letter which, at this time, he addressed to a Scotch friend :—

"Dear Sir,—Give me leave to acknowledge your very obliging letter ; your partiality flatters me extremely, because I am persuaded it proceeds from goodwill, and there is nothing I covet so much as the goodwill of those I value and esteem. The office I have accepted came unasked, and recommended by many circumstances to make it agreeable, else I could have liked very well to continue as I was ; my ambition is not so much to aspire to high things, as to act my part, whatever it is, as well as I can. In my way of thinking, I cannot condole with you upon the loss of that office to which you did honour while you filled it, though I was heartily concerned when I heard of it. I could condole with those who took it from you ; the enjoyment of it could not add much to your figure or character, the loss of it can take nothing from either ; and I am convinced that, in making the change, no part of the motive was personal to you."

Busy in law and politics, and much courted by the highest society for his charming conversation and gracious manners, Murray found it difficult to maintain his old literary tastes ; and Pope, in his new edition of the " Dunciad," introduces him among those who had been lost to literature through the urgent demands of more active but less honourable pursuits. " We ply," exclaims the poet,—

" We ply the memory, we load the brain,
  Bind rebel wit, and double chain on chain ;
  Confine the thought to exercise the breath,
  And keep them in the pale of words till death.
  Whate'er the talents, or howe'er designed,
  We hang one jingling padlock on the mind :
  A poet the first day he dips his quill,—
  And what the last ? a very poet still.
  Pity ! the charm works only in one wall,
  Lost, lost too soon in yonder house or hall.
  There truant Wyndham every muse gave o'er,
  There Talbot sunk, and was a wit no more !
  How sweet an Ovid, Murray, was our boast ! "

Pope, however, kept up his friendship with the great
lawyer to the last, and a few days before his death caused
himself, weak and infirm as he was, to be conveyed from
Twickenham to Lincoln's Inn Fields, to dine with Murray,
Warburton, and Bolingbroke.    " Oh !" exclaims Lord
Campbell, " Oh, for a Boswell to have given us their conversation !    But, perhaps, it is better that their confidence
has not been betrayed, for, amidst the gratification arising
from their lively sallies, we might have found Bolingbroke
scoffing at religion, Warburton irreverently anathematis-
ing all who differed with him on questions of criticism,
Pope vindicating himself from the charge of Roman
Catholic bigotry by denying divine revelation, and Murray
softening the misconduct of those who had been, or were,
in the service of the Pretender, by admitting that he
himself had had a hankering after the doctrine of the
divine right of kings."    Well, one would wish to have
had the men as they were, with their blemishes as well
as their excellences ; and the more faithful the transcript of their conversation, the more valuable would it
have been to us.

In the House of Commons, through his superiority as a debater, Murray virtually became the ministerial leader, and though not in the Cabinet, expounded its measures and defended its policy. He professed a judicious ignorance of Cabinet secrets, yet it was plain enough that he was brought acquainted with them. He spoke always in a tone of great modesty; yet his manner was that of a man who knew his authority and the value of his position. In many points his oratorical style seems to have borne a marked resemblance to that of Mr. Gladstone; he lacked the passion, the enthusiasm, the force of conviction, of our great Liberal stateman, but he was not less mellifluous in tone or copious in explanation, or fluent of speech, or polished in diction, or methodical in argument. Though on the opposite bench sat the mighty Commoner, prepared to harass and toss and trample him, he generally managed to hold his own, and at all times commanded the attention of the House. Walpole has drawn a parallel, or rather a contrast, between him, Pitt, and Henry Fox [*] :—

"Murray," he says, "who at the beginning of the session was awed by Pitt, finding himself supported by Fox, [†] surmounted his fears, and convinced the House, and Pitt too, of his superior abilities. He grew most uneasy to the latter. Pitt could only attack; Murray only defend. Fox, the boldest and ablest champion, was still more formed to worry; but the keenness of his sabre was blunted by the difficulty with which he drew it from the scabbard; I mean, the hesitation and ungracefulness of his delivery took off from the force of his arguments. Murray, the brightest genius of the House, had too much and too little

---

[*] Walpole, "Memoirs," i. 358.
[†] Henry Fox, afterwards first Lord Holland, the father of Charles James Fox.

of the lawyer: he refined too much, and could wrangle too little, for a popular assembly. Pitt's figure was commanding; Murray's engaging, from a decent openness; Fox's dark and troubled; yet the latter was the only agreeable man. Pitt could not unbend; Murray in private was inelegant; Fox was cheerful, social, communicative. In conversation none of them had wit: Murray never had; Fox had in his speeches, from clearness of head and asperity of argument. Pitt's wit was genuine; not tortured into the service, like the quaintnesses of my Lord Chesterfield."

Walpole's criticism is obviously biassed by his personal antipathies; but one of the most curious facts in our political history is the vehement hostility which the elder Pitt displayed against Murray. There was no doubt a strong opposition of character between the impetuous, passionate, and imperious English orator and the calm, plausible, and graceful Scotch lawyer, but it hardly explains the matter. Their difference of character was apparent in their oratory. Murray excelled in lucidity of statement and force of argument, but was incapable of those bursts of fiery eloquence with which his great rival awed or charmed the House of Commons. Lord Shelbourne says of him, that[*]—

"His eloquence was of an argumentative, metaphysical cast; and his great art always appeared to me to be to watch his opportunity to introduce a proposition unperceived, when his cause was ever so bad, afterwards found a true argument upon it, of which nobody could be more capable, and then give way to his imagination, in which he was by no means wanting, nor in scholarship, particularly classical learning, thanks to Westminster. His oratory resembled a full and tranquil river which rolls onward with even current, always transparent, and never

---

[*] "Life of Earl of Shelbourne," by Lord E. Fitzmaurice, i. 88.

chafed by rock or tempest; Pitt's was like a mighty torrent, which was sometimes turbid and obscure, sometimes spent itself in wayward digressions, but, where it poured forth all its strength, was irresistible."

Whatever the secret cause, if such there were, certain it is that Pitt never ceased his invectives against Murray. "He undertook," says Lord Waldegrave,* "the difficult task of silencing Murray, the ablest man, as well as the ablest debater in the House of Commons." Lord Holland, referring to Pitt's attacks, says :—"In both Mr. Pitt's speeches, every word was Murray, yet so managed that neither he nor anybody else could, or did take public notice of it, or in any degree reprehend him. I sate near Murray, who suffered for an hour." It was, perhaps, on the same occasion that Pitt used an expression which became almost proverbial :—

"After Murray had suffered for some time, Pitt stopped, threw his eyes around, then, fixing their whole power on Murray, said :—'I must now address a few words to Mr. Solicitor; they shall be few, but they shall be daggers.' Murray was agitated.    The look was continued; the agitation increased.   'Judge Festus trembles!' exclaimed Pitt; 'he shall hear me some other day.' He sate down; Murray made no reply; and a languid debate is said to have shown the paralysis of the House." †

The contest between the two rivals has been emphasised by Lord Macaulay :— ‡

"Murray far surpassed Pitt in correctness of taste, in power of reasoning, in depth and variety of knowledge.   His Parlia-

---

* "Earl Waldegrave's" Memoirs, p. 31.
† Buller's Reminiscences, in "Seward's Anecdotes," i. p. 154.
‡ Lord Macaulay, "Critical and Historical Essays—William Pitt."

mentary eloquence never blazed into sudden flashes of dazzling brilliancy; but its clear, placid, and mellow splendour was never for an instant overclouded. Intellectually, he was, we believe, fully equal to Pitt; but he was deficient in the moral qualities to which Pitt owed most of his success. Murray wanted the energy, the courage, the all-grasping and all-risking ambition which makes men great in stirring times. His heart was a little cold; his temper cautious even to timidity; his manners decorous even to formality. He never exposed his fortunes or his fame to any risk which he could avoid."

If we may be allowed yet another quotation, we will place before the reader Lord Chesterfield's opinion :—

"Your fate," he says, writing to his son, "depends upon your success as a speaker; and take my word for it that success turns more upon man than matter. Mr. Pitt and Mr. Murray, the Solicitor-General, are, beyond comparison, the best speakers. Why? Only because they are the best orators. They alone can influence or quiet the House; they alone are attended to in that numerous and noisy assembly, that you might hear a pin fall while either of them is speaking. Is it that their matter is better or their arguments stronger than other people's? Does the House expect extraordinary information from them? Not in the least; but the House expects pleasure from them, and therefore attends; finds it, and therefore approves."

In December, 1743, Pitt brought forward a motion for an address to the Crown, praying that the 18,000 Hanoverian troops then in the pay of the British Government might be dismissed. His speech was a good example of that "manner" to which Chesterfield refers, but it is not without "matter," clearly put and vividly enforced :—

"It does not appear," he said, "that either justice or policy required us to engage in the quarrels of the Continent; that there was any need of forming an army in the Low Countries; or that, in order to form an army, auxiliaries were necessary.

"But, not to dwell upon disputable points, I think it may justly be concluded that the measures of our Ministry have been ill-concerted, because it is undoubtedly wrong to squander the public money without effect; to pay armies only to be a show to our friends and a scorn to our enemies.

"The troops of Hanover, whom we are now expected to pay, marched into the Low Countries, where they still remain. They marched to the place most distant from the enemy, least in danger of an attack, and most strongly fortified, if any attack had been designed. They have, therefore, no other claim to be paid than that they left their own country for a place of greater security. It is always reasonable to judge of the future by the past; and therefore it is probable that, next year, the services of these troops will not be of equal importance with those for which they are now to be paid. And I shall not be surprised if, after another such glorious campaign, the opponents of the Ministry should be challenged to propose better men, and be told that the money of this nation cannot be more properly employed than in hiring Hanoverians to cut and slay. . . .

"That we should inviolably observe our treaties, and observe them though every other nation should disregard them; that we should show an example of fidelity to mankind, and stand firm in the practice of virtue, though we stand alone, I readily allow. I am, therefore, far from advising that we should recede from our stipulations, whatever we may suffer by adhering to them; or that we should neglect the support of the Pragmatic Sanction, however we may be at present embarrassed, or however disadvantageous may be its assertion. . . .

"It is now too apparent that this powerful, this great, this formidable nation is considered only as a province to a despicable electorate; and that, in consequence of a plan formed long ago, and universally pursued, these troops are hired only to drain

us of our money. That they have hitherto been of no use to
Great Britain or to Austria is evident beyond a doubt; and
therefore it is plain that they are retained only for the purpose
of Hanover. . . .

"To dwell upon all the instances of partiality which have
been shown, and the yearly visits which have been paid to that
delightful country—to reckon up all the sums that have been
spent to aggrandise and enrich it, would be an irksome and
invidious task—invidious to those who are afraid to be told
the truth, and irksome to those who are unwilling to hear of the
dishonour and injuries of their country. I shall dwell no longer
upon this unpleasing subject than to express my hope that we
shall no longer suffer ourselves to be deceived and oppressed;
that we shall at length perform our duty as representatives of
the people; and, by refusing to ratify this contract, show that,
however the interests of Hanover have been preferred by the
Ministers, the Parliament pays no regard but to the interests of
Great Britain."

To this spirited attack, Murray replied as follows :—

"The motion now under our consideration is of such a new
and extraordinary nature, and is such a direct attack on the first
prerogatives of the Crown, that I should think myself very little
deserving of the honour which His Majesty has been pleased to
confer upon me, if I did not rise to oppose it. There are certain
powers vested in the king, as there are certain privileges
belonging to the people; and an infringement of either would
lead to the overthrow of our happy constitution. As the
guardians of the liberties of the people, we are bound to respect
the royal prerogative. But if there be anything certain, it is
this—that to the king alone it belongs, not only to declare war,
but to determine how the war, when declared, shall be carried
on. He is to direct what forces are to be raised; when
armies are to march; when squadrons are to sail; when his
commanders are to act, and when they are to keep upon the
defensive. If this motion were carried, I should expect to see

a venerable member moving an address that a general engagement shall be immediately ordered in Flanders, although the
mover has never been out of England, nor the 'division of a
battle knows more than a spinster.'. . . .

"On every side the most happy effects have been produced
by the method his Majesty has chosen for assisting the Queen of
Hungary. I hope it will not be said that we ought to assist
her with our own troops alone. To raise by recruiting at home
the army which would be necessary must be injurious to our
industry, and injurious to our Constitution. We must, therefore, have foreign troops in our pay; and where shall we find
any to be preferred to the Hanoverians?" . . .

In conclusion :—

"I will not say that upon no occasion would this House
interfere with its advice as to the exercise of the prerogatives of the Crown. If wicked or incapable ministers were
bringing disgrace on the British arms, degrading the national
honour, and hazarding the national safety, we might be called
upon to advise the king to change his measures and his advisers.
But our allies have been effectually protected, and the interests
of England, in every part of the world, have been vindicated.
It is insinuated, indeed, that all our measures are scarcely
calculated for the benefit of the Electorate of Hanover. This is
an insinuation of a most dangerous nature, and it ought not
to be resorted to for mere party purposes, because it tends not
only to wean the affections of the people from the sovereign
on the throne, but from the Protestant succession in the Hanoverian line, and to bring about a counter-revolution which would
be fatal to religion and liberty. Whether the republican
faction or Jacobitish faction, which are now united, shall prevail
when the split comes, destruction alike awaits constitutional
freedom. What ground is there for the danger? I do not
pretend to be in the secrets of the Cabinet, and I am unable to
dive into the hidden reasons of the human mind to analyse
the true motives of action; but when the measures of the

M

Government are wisely calculated to promote the dignity and prosperity of England, and have actually produced the happy results which might have been expected from them, why should you say that their hidden and sole object is to enrich Hanover and add a few patches to its territory?"

The year 1745 was distinguished by the last Jacobite rebellion, that romantic episode of history which reads more like an old chivalric legend than a sober eighteenth-century narrative. Prince Charles Edward at first seemed destined to recover the crown of his ancestors. After defeating the royal army at Prestonpans and capturing Carlisle, he pushed his way unopposed into the very heart of the kingdom, and halted not until he reached Derby. There his good fortune deserted him. Alarmed at the apathy of the people, and dreading lest they should be surrounded by superior forces, the Highland chiefs insisted on a retreat; and the baffled Prince, dispirited and ashamed, recrossed the Borders, pursued by the Duke of Cumberland.

Murray came of a Jacobite family, and had himself been accused of Jacobite sympathies; but his political prudence held him firm to the cause of the reigning sovereign, and it does not seem that any suspicion attached to him of collusion with the young Stuart prince. But when the rebellion was quenched in blood on Drummossie Moor, and the rebel lords were brought to trial on charges of high treason, he must have felt it a painful duty to conduct their prosecution. The only one of these cases which it is necessary to notice is that of Lord Lovat; and probably towards that cruel, treacherous, and tyrannical old man, whose whole life had been one of infamy, he felt no special tenderness or compassion. As Lord Lovat had not actually taken up arms—withdrawing to his castle in Inverness-shire, while he sent his son and retainers to join the standard of Prince Charles Edward—he could not be proceeded against by the presentment of an English grand jury, but could be brought to trial only by impeachment. Upon Murray, as one of the managers appointed to conduct his prosecution before the Peers, fell no light or agreeable task; but he performed it with ability and moderation. The trial began on the 9th of March, 1746, and ended in a verdict of "Guilty." When the prisoner was asked if he could show any cause why sentence of death should not be passed upon him, he said :—

"My Lords, I am very sorry I gave your Lordships so much trouble in my trial, and I give you a million of thanks for your being so good in your patience and attendance while it lasted. I thought myself much loaded by one Mr. Murray,* who, your Lordships know, was the bitterest witness there was against me. I have since suffered by another Mr. Murray, who, I must say with pleasure, is one known to his country, and whose eloquence and learning are much beyond what is to be expected by an ignorant man like me. I heard him with pleasure, though it was against me. I have the honour to be his relation, though, perhaps, he neither knows it nor values it. I wish that his being born in the North may not hinder him from the preferment that his merit entitles him to. Till that gentleman spoke, your Lordships were inclined to grant my earnest request, and allow me further time to bring up witnesses to prove my innocence; but, it seems, that has been overruled. All now that I have to say is a little in vindication of my own character."

Having attempted this Herculean labour—not with any surprising measure of success—he concluded : " I

---

* John Murray of Broughton, who had been secretary to Charles Edward, and one of his most trusted but not wariest advisers.

beg your Lordships' pardon for this long and rude
discourse. I had great need of my cousin Murray's
eloquence for half-an-hour, and then it would have
been more agreeable."

It is not often that one hears of a prisoner undertaking to panegyrise the prosecuting counsel. I suppose it was the influence of blood, and of that fervid
Scottish nationality, which finds so many unexpected
ways of asserting itself. On the night before his execution he remembered his eloquent and accomplished
cousin. "Mr. Solicitor," he said, "is a great man, and
he will meet with high promotion if he is not too far
north."

As Pitt was at this time in office (Paymaster of the
Forces), Murray's Parliamentary life was tolerably free
from disturbing influences; and it was not until the
death of Frederick Prince of Wales, in 1751, that he was
brought conspicuously before the public. In that year
he had to conduct a Regency Bill through the Lower
House. Shortly afterwards, the cry of favouritism was
revived against him. In early life he had been closely
acquainted with two gentlemen, his contemporaries at
Westminster, named Fawcett and Stone, and with Dr.
Johnson, afterwards Bishop of Gloucester. In the course
of years the young men were separated by differences of
pursuit and character. Fawcett became a provincial
barrister and recorder of Newcastle; Stone was sub-
governor to young Prince George. At a dinner given
by the Dean of Durham, Fawcett was one of the company; and the conversation turning on the preferment
of Dr. Johnson (who held a Durham prebend), he remarked that he was glad Johnson was so well off. He
remembered him a Jacobite several years ago, and then

he used to be with a relation of his who was very disaffected, Vernon, a mercer, where the Pretender's health was frequently drunk.    Among the guests was a Lord Ravensworth, who foolishly repeated these idle words to Mr. Pelham, the Prime Minister.    An inquiry was then instituted; and Fawcett, in the course of it, stated that, though he could not recollect positively whether Johnson drank the disloyal health, he was certain that Murray and Stone had done so several times, and down so late as the year 1732.    The matter was then referred to the Privy Council, before whom the accused appeared and made their defence.

Murray spoke with his customary skill, but perhaps with less than his usual candour.    He declared that, ever since he had been able to form his own opinions, he had been well affected to the present establishment.    That when he went to Oxford he had taken the oaths to the Government, and had done so seriously and sincerely. That when he pleaded at the bar of the Commons, it was with entire fidelity to the principles by which the Government was supported.    That he had determined never to enter the House of Commons but upon Whig principles, and that when at last he accepted a seat, it was under the auspices of a noble Duke who for forty years had been a loyal adherent of the Hanoverian line. With regard to office, it was not to be supposed that a man of Sir John Strange's well-known loyalty would have resigned in his favour, if he had not been thoroughly convinced of his sincerity.    That ever since he had been in the king's service, he had got nothing by his employment (he spoke not by way of complaint) but the ordinary perquisites of office, and had never recommended any friend of his own to preferment.    That he had not been able to learn any objection to his conduct without doors, except that, in prosecuting the rebel lords, he had refrained from loading them with reproachful epithets, as if epithets would have added to their guilt.   That he did not think such language would be agreeable to his royal master; and that had he been employed for the Crown against Sir Walter Raleigh, and that unfortunate person had been as guilty of high treason as the rebels, he would not have made Sir Edward Coke's speech against him for his estate.   After analysing Fawcett's evidence, he concluded by acknowledging the indulgence of the lords in hearing him, and the justice and goodness of the king, who would not suffer his servants to be stabbed in the dark, but gave them an opportunity of vindicating their innocence.*

He then took a voluntary oath† to that effect, and gave a particular answer to every charge, denying that he had ever been present at Mr. Vernon's when treasonable oaths were drunk, and stating his belief that Mr. Vernon was incapable of countenancing such conduct.   The Lords of the Council unanimously reported to the king that the accusation appeared to be without foundation, and that it ought not to cast a stain on the character of the Bishop, or of any gentleman included in it.   The Duke of Bedford, however, thought proper to bring the affair before the House of Lords, and moved an address to the king that he would be pleased to lay a copy of the proceedings of the Council before the House; but the motion was negatived by a large majority.

---

* For fuller particulars see Halliday; see also Bubb Doddington's Diary, pp. 211-235.

† Lord Campbell doubts that he took this oath, but the evidence seems incontrovertible.

Suspicion of his sincerity, nevertheless, long adhered to Murray, on the principle that where there is smoke there must be fire; and the reproach of early Jacobitism continued to be levelled at him with merciless effect. Pitt had again gone into Opposition, and with eagerness availed himself of so powerful a weapon against his old rival. Having occasion to denounce the Jacobite tendencies of the University of Oxford, he dexterously introduced a telling personal allusion :—

"The body he was describing," he said, " was learned and respectable ; so much the more dangerous ! He would mention what had happened to himself the last summer on a party of pleasure thither. They were at the window of the Angel Inn ; a lady was desired to sing ' God save great George, our King.' The chorus was re-echoed by a set of young lads drinking at a college over the way, but with the addition of rank treason. He hoped, as they were boys, he should be excused for not taking more notice of them. Perhaps some of them might hereafter zealously fill the office of Attorney or Solicitor-General to a Brunswick sovereign. After this, walking down the High Street, in a bookseller's shop he observed a print of a young Highlander with a blue ribbon. The bookseller, thinking he wanted it, held it out to him. But what was the motto? *Hunc saltem everso juvenem !* This was the prayer of that learned body. Yet, if they are disappointed in their plots, the most zealous of them, when leader of the Government party in this House, may assure you that he always approved of the Protestant succession, and that he refused to enter Parliament, except upon Whig principles."

We owe a record of this speech to Horace Walpole, who adds * : " Colours, much less words, could not paint the confusion and agitation that worked in

---

* Walpole, " Memorials of the Reign of George II." i. 358.

Murray's face during this almost apostrophe.   His countenance spoke everything that Fawcett had been terrified
to prevaricate away."

And yet it could hardly be imputed as a crime to a
man whom every one acknowledged to have done loyal
service as an officer of the Crown, that in his youth he
had drank a foolish toast or two over a cup of wine !


## II.

On March 6, 1754, died Henry Pelham, who, for
eight years, had presided over the Ministry with a prudence and a skill not always acknowledged by historians.
As an administrator he displayed considerable ability;
but much of the success of his Government was due to
the eagerness with which, unlike Sir Robert Walpole, he
endeavoured to secure the co-operation of the ablest.
He gave reason to none to attach themselves to the
Opposition.   He had no cause to fear that any of them
would supplant him; he knew that their mutual
jealousies constituted a sufficient safe-guard.     Thus,
Henry Fox, Pitt, and Murray, though differing widely in
feeling and sentiment, readily acted under his supremacy
while neither would have acknowledged or allowed the
supremacy of any other.

But his death dissolved the long truce which had thus
been maintained between rival politicians.   By virtue of
his immense parliamentary influence, the Duke of Newcastle, incapable as he was, succeeded to the Treasury;
but who was to lead the House of Commons ?   Unlike
his brother, the Duke distrusted every man of genius,
and was so greedy of office and patronage that he was
unwilling to share them even with the staunchest sup-

porter. What he wanted was a man who would do the
work and covet none of the power—a man who would
consent to be, and to act as, an agent and a subordinate.
Newcastle was well aware that he durst not hint at such
a position to William Pitt. It was useless to apply to
Murray ; for, though he would have been acceptable to
the king, and not unpopular with the nation, he steadfastly refused political advancement. His ambition was
bound up with his profession. In this difficulty Newcastle applied to Henry Fox, one of the most unscrupulous
of politicians, and, after some discussion, the high
contracting parties agreed to the following conditions :

Fox was to be Secretary of State, with the lead of the
House of Commons; but the disposal of the secret
service money, that is, the bribery of members of Parliament, was to be left to Newcastle, though Fox was to be
made acquainted with the details of expenditure. This
agreement was concluded on the 12th of March. Next
morning the Duke overturned it. "My brother," he
said, "when he was at the Treasury, never told anybody
what he did with the secret service money ; no more
will I." But, then, Pelham was not only First Lord of
the Treasury, but leader of the Commons ; and it was
unnecessary for him to take any person into his confidence. "How," said Fox, "how can I talk to gentlemen when I do not know which of them have received
qualifications, and which have not?" "And who," he
added, "is to have the disposal of places?"

"I myself," returned the Duke.

"How, then, am I to manage the House of
Commons?"

"Oh, let the members of the House of Commons
come to me."

It was impossible for Fox to accept such humiliating terms; and the leadership of the House was finally placed in the hands of one of the dullest of men, Sir Thomas Robinson. "Sir Thomas Robinson lead us!" exclaimed Pitt, "the Duke might as well send his jack-boot to lead us." The result was exactly what New-castle had aimed at. "He is alone and all-powerful," writes Horace Walpole, "and, I suppose, smiles at those who thought that we must be governed by a succession of geniuses. Which of the Popes was it, who, being chosen for his insufficiency, said, 'I could not have believed that it was so easy to govern?'"

Under the new arrangement Murray became Attorney General, on the elevation of Sir Dudley Ryder to the Bench. For twelve years he had held the Solicitorship, combining with it the anomalous duty of defending the Government policy. His elevation to the higher office still left him charged with this responsibility, which, it may be, he would have declined had he known that Pitt was going into Opposition, and would renew his vehement attacks. The political horizon was loaded with storm-clouds, which appalled his cautious and some-what timorous disposition. The war in which England had been rashly involved brought her neither fame nor fortune. Minorca was captured by the Duke of Richelieu, and Admiral Byng, who had been despatched to relieve Port Mahon, falling in with the French fleet, declined to engage it. The country was moved to a paroxysm of indignation by the disgrace that had befallen its arms. Men went about lamenting the degeneracy of the race, and protesting that they and their brothers were cowards, fit only to be enslaved. Caricatures and libels, in which the king and his ministers were treated with the utmost freedom, passed from hand to hand. The walls were covered with furious placards. The great cities and the counties sent up addresses of remonstrance to the Throne. The Ministers quailed before this outburst of contempt and rage, and Newcastle began to tremble not only for his place, but his neck. He had made up his quarrel with Fox in the previous year; but Fox, too, deserted him, fearing lest he should be made a scapegoat to save "the old intriguer who, imbecile as he seemed, never wanted dexterity where danger was to be avoided." In his despair Newcastle went to Murray, but at last the prize for which the ambitious Scotchman so long had waited was within his reach ; the office of Chief-Justice of the King's Bench was vacant, and Murray was sick to death of Parliamentary turmoil. Newcastle offered him any terms—the Chancellorship of the Duchy of Lancaster for life, a Tellership of the Exchequer, and as large a pension as he chose to stipulate for—£2000, £4000, £6000 a-year. When Newcastle perceived that Murray's resolution was unalterable, he begged him to wait out the session, and, if not the session, a month or a week ; but to no purpose. Would he speak in support of the Address? Not a word ; he would have the Chief-Justice-ship, or he would go into Opposition.*

On the 8th of November, 1756, Murray became Lord Chief-Justice, and he was immediately raised to the peerage by the title of Baron Mansfield of Mansfield, in the

---

* " He knew," says Horace Walpole, " that it was safer to expound laws than to be exposed to them ; and, exclaiming, ' Good God ! what merit have I that you should load this country, for which so little is done with spirit, with the additional burthen of £6000 a-year?' at last peremptorily declared that if he was not to be Chief-Justice, neither would he any longer be Attorney-General."

county of Nottingham.   Contrary to usage, he received
a seat in the Cabinet, though how long he held it does
not seem very accurately known.   Lord Temple, in
1806, stated that the noble and learned lord had
attended every council from 1760 to 1763 ; that in the
latter year he left off attending, not because he considered it incompatible with his judicial position, but
because he would not sit with the Duke of Bedford, of
whose measures he disapproved.   In 1765 he resumed
his attendances, and was named as one of the council
of inquiry in the bill passed by Sir Fletcher Norton ;
but after the formation of the Rockingham Ministry he
finally withdrew.

On the occasion of his taking leave of the society of
Lincoln's Inn, the usual complimentary speech was
delivered with more than usual warmth by the Honourable
Charles Yorke, son of Lord Chancellor Hardwicke.   Lord
Mansfield, in reply, said :—

"I am too sensible, sir, of my being undeserving of the praises
which you have so elegantly bestowed upon me to suffer com-
mendations so delicate as yours to insinuate themselves into my
mind ; but I have pleasure in that kind of partiality which is
the occasion of them.   To deserve such praises is a worthy
object of ambition, and from such a tongue flattery itself is
pleasing.

"If I have had in any measure success in my profession, it is
owing to the great man who has presided in our highest courts
of judicature the whole time I have attended the Bar.   It was
impossible to attend him, to sit under him every day, without
catching some beams from his light.   The disciples of Socrates,
whom I will take the liberty to call the great lawyer of antiquity,
since the first principles of all law are derived from his philosophy,
owe their reputation to their having been the reporters of the
sayings of their master.   If we can arrogate nothing to ourselves,

we can boast the school we were brought up in; the scholar may glory in his master, and we may challenge past ages to show us his equal.

"My Lord Bacon had the same extent of thought, and the same strength of language and expression; but his life had a stain.

"My Lord Clarendon had the same ability and the same zeal for the constitution of his country; but the civil war prevented his laying deep the foundations of law, and the avocations of politics interrupted the business of the Chancellor.

"My Lord Somers came the nearest to his character; but his time was short, and envy and faction sullied the lustre of his glory.

"It is the peculiar felicity of the great man I am speaking of to have presided very near twenty years, and to have shone with a splendour that has risen superior to faction and that has subdued envy.

"I did not intend to have said—I should not have said—so much on this occasion, but that, in this situation with all that hear me, what I say must carry the weight of testimony rather than appear the voice of panegyric.

"For you, sir, you have given great pledges to your country; and large as the expectations of the country are concerning you, I dare say you will answer them.

"For the society, I shall always think myself honoured by every mark of their esteem, affection, and friendship; and shall desire the continuance of it no longer than while I remain zealous for the constitution of this country, and a friend to the interests of virtue."

The appointment of Lord Mansfield as Chief Justice was almost simultaneous with the resignation of Newcastle, who was succeeded by a ministry of which Pitt was the guiding spirit. It lasted, however, for barely five months. Early in April, 1757, Pitt and his colleagues retired. In the intrigues that followed Mansfield played an important part. The seals of the Chancellor of the Exchequer were temporarily placed in his hands, and when Lord Waldegrave, " an honest and sensible man, but unpractised in affairs," was empowered to form a Government, he was employed to negotiate with his old friend Newcastle and his old rival Mr. Pitt, for their accession. " The negotiation, however," says Lord Waldegrave, " did not long remain in his hands ; some thinking him too able, others that he was not enough their friend," and Lord Hardwicke was selected to act as intermediary. Not long afterwards Lord Hardwicke resigned the Great Seal, and it was offered to Mansfield ; but no pressure would induce him to accept it. He had obtained the great object of his ambition, and sought no farther advancement.

His remarkable powers were first displayed in the House of Lords on the occasion of the introduction of a bill to amend the Habeas Corpus Act, in the direction of extending its provisions. There was nothing unreasonable or unconstitutional in the bill, which had readily passed the Lower House, but it was opposed by Lord Mansfield in a spirit of the blindest conservatism, though with forcible and impressive eloquence, and its rejection was due to his brilliant exertions. Says Horace Walpole :—

" The fate of the bill, which could not be procured by the sanction of the judges, Lord Mansfield was forced to take upon himself. He spoke for two hours and a-half ; his voice and manner, composed of harmonious solemnity, were the least graces of his speech. I am not averse to own that I never heard so much argument, so much sense, so much oratory united. His deviations into the abstruse minutiæ of the law served but as a foil to the luminous parts of the oration. Perhaps it was the only speech which, in my time at least, had real effect; that is, convinced many persons; nor did I ever know how true a votary I was to liberty, till I found that I was not one of the number staggered by that speech. I took as many notes of it as I possibly could; and, prolix as they would be, I would give them to the reader, if it would not be injustice to Lord Mansfield to curtail and mangle, as I should, by the want of connection, so beautiful a thread of argumentation."

The incident says more for Lord Mansfield's oratorical powers than for his political sagacity. In the long and unhappy contention between England and her American colonies, he showed an equal insensibility to the claims of freedom; and from first to last was on the side of arbitrary force and coercion. He supported the right of the mother country to tax the colonies without their consent, in disregard of the great principle that taxation and representation must go hand in hand. In a debate which took place in February, 1766, he annunciated the old, arbitrary, and inconsistent doctrine of virtual representation :—

"There can be no doubt but that the inhabitants of the colonies are represented in parliament, as the greatest part of the people of England are represented; among nine millions of whom there are eight who have no votes in electing members of parliament. Every objection, therefore, to the dependency of the colonies upon parliament, which arises to it upon the ground of representation, goes to the whole present constitution of Great Britain; and, I suppose, it is not meant to new-model that too. People may form their own speculative ideas of perfection, and indulge their own fancies, or those of other men. Every man in this country has his particular notions of liberty; but perfection never did, and never can, exist in any human institution. For what purpose, then, are arguments drawn from a distinction, in which there is no actual difference, of a virtual and actual representation ? A member of parliament, chosen for any borough, represents not only the constituents and inhabitants of that particular place, but he represents the inhabitants of every other borough in Great Britain. He represents the city of London, and all other the commons of this land, and the inhabitants of all the colonies and dominions of Great Britain; and is in duty and conscience bound to take care of their interests."

Any schoolboy, now-a-days, would point out the gross fallacy of this specious argument. Lord Mansfield's speeches in the House of Lords, with few exceptions, make us regret that, on becoming Chief Justice he did not abstain from all intervention in parliamentary debates. He showed an altogether narrower and more obstinate mind in the Upper Chamber than he did on the Bench. In February, 1775, he again spoke upon American affairs, and asserted that England must either adopt coercive measures or for ever relinquish her claim of sovereignty over the colonies. In November, 1778, we find him bitterly opposing all measures of conciliation as "furnishing America with grounds to erect new claims on, or to hold out terms of pretended obedience and submission." Again, in the following month, he called for the employment of force :—" What a Swedish general said to his men in the reign of Gustavus Adolphus is extremely applicable to us at present. Pointing to the enemy, who was marching down to engage them, said he, ' My lads, you see those men yonder : if you do not kill them, they will kill you.' If we do not, my Lords, get the better of America, America will get the better of us."

In religious matters Mansfield displayed a more liberal spirit, and was ever the advocate of an enlightened toleration. A case coming before him respecting the admissibility of a Quaker's affirmation in an action of debt on the statute against bribery, he laid down the following broad rule for the construction of the Act of Toleration :—

"I think it of the utmost importance that all the consequences of this Act should be pursued with the greatest liberality, in case of the scrupulous consciences of dissenters on the one hand ; but so as those scruples of conscience should not be prejudicial to the rest of the king's subjects ; for a scruple of conscience entitles a party to indulgence and protection, so far as not to suffer for it; but it is of consequence that the subject should not suffer too."

In 1767 a Roman Catholic priest was tried before him, on the prosecution of a common informer, for saying mass contrary to the provisions of William III.'s statute. He charged the jury strongly in the prisoner's favour, employing a subtlety of argument which was scarcely justifiable. Of the penal laws against the Roman Catholics, he thus spoke :—

"In the beginning of the Protestant religion, in order to establish it, they thought it in some manner necessary to enact these penal laws ; for then the Pope had great power, and they thought that they could not take too effectual means to prevent him exercising any part of it in these dominions; and the Jesuits were then a very formidable body ; and, apprehending great danger from them, knowing their close connections with the Pope, the penal laws were chiefly designed against them. But now the case is quite altered: the Pope has very little power, and seems to grow less and less daily. As for the Jesuits, they are now banished out of most kingdoms in Europe, so that there is now nothing to fear from either of these quarters ; neither was it ever the design of the legislators to have these laws enforced by every common informer, but only at proper times and seasons, when they saw a necessity for it, and by proper persons appointed by themselves for that purpose ;

N

and yet, more properly speaking, they were never designed to be enforced at all, but were only made *in terorem.*"

In the same year the broad principles of religious freedom were very distinctly enunciated by Lord Mansfield, in a speech in the House of Lords. A bye-law of the Corporation of London imposed a fine upon persons refusing the office of sheriff, while what was known as the Corporation Act required that every holder of such an office must take the sacrament according to the forms of the Church of England. At length, a dissenter, named Evans, was elected. He refused to serve, because he could not conscientiously take the sacrament, and he also refused to pay the fine. An action for the amount was then brought against him by the Chamberlain of London, in the Sheriff's-Court, and the judgment was given for the plaintiff. On the defendant appealing to the Court of Hustings, the judgment was affirmed ; but on an appeal being carried before the Judges Delegates, he proved successful. The city then brought a writ of error in the House of Lords, and the judges were directed to give their opinion. Lord Mansfield's was as follows :—

"The defendant in the present case pleads that he is a Dissenter within the description of the Toleration Act; that he hath not taken the sacrament in the Church of England within one year preceding the time of his supposed election, nor even in his whole life ; and that he cannot in conscience do it.

" Conscience is not controllable by human laws, nor answerable to human tribunals. Persecution, or attempts to force conscience, will never produce conviction, and are only calculated to make hypocrites or martyrs.

" My Lords, there never was a single instance, from the Saxon times down to our own, in which a man was ever punished for erroneous opinions concerning rites or modes of worship, but upon some positive law. The common law of England, which is only common reason or usage, knows of no persecution for mere opinions. For atheism, blasphemy, and reviling the Christian religion, there have been instances of persons prosecuted and punished upon the common law; but bare Nonconformity is no sin by the common law; and all positive laws inflicting any pains or penalties for nonconformity to the established rites or modes are repealed by the Act of Toleration; and Dissenters are thereby exempted from all ecclesiastical censures.

" What bloodshed and confusion have been occasioned, from the reign of Henry IV., when the first penal statutes were enacted, down to the Revolution in this kingdom, by laws made to force conscience ! There is nothing, certainly, more unreasonable, more inconsistent with the rights of human nature, more contrary to the spirit and precepts of the Christian religion, more iniquitous and unjust, more impolitic, than persecution. It is against natural religion, revealed religion, and sound policy.

" Sad experience and a large mind taught that great man, the President de Thou, this doctrine. Let any man read the many admirable things which, though a Papist, he hath dared to advance on this subject, in the dedication of his History to Henry IV. of France (which I never read without rapture), and he will be fully convinced, not only how cruel, but how impolitic it is to persecute for religious opinions. . . .

" There was no occasion to revoke the Edict of Nantes. The Jesuits needed only to have advised a plan similar to that which is contended for in the present case—make a law to render them incapable of office ; make another to punish them for not serving. If they accept, punish them (for it is admitted on all hands that the defendant, in the cause before your Lordships, is persecutable for taking the office upon him)—if they accept, punish them ; if they refuse, punish them : if they say yes, punish them ; if they say no, punish them. My Lords, this is a most exquisite dilemma, from which there is no escaping ; it is a trap a man cannot get out of ; it is as bad persecution as that of Procrastes—if they are too short, stretch them ; if they are too long, lop them."

The peers immediately affirmed the judgment of the Delegates, reversing the judgment of the Sheriff's Court and of the Court of Hustings.

To give the lay reader an accurate conception of Lord Mansfield's pre-eminent merits as a judge is almost impossible, for a detailed history of cases and decisions would only perplex and weary him ; and yet, without such a history, some of his highest qualities must pass unobserved.

That he was a great judge we may infer from the significant circumstance that, though he presided in the Court of King's Bench for upwards of thirty years, his opinions were unanimously adopted by his brethren— men of profound learning and indisputable ability—in all his cases.   Again, in so long a period he necessarily pronounced many thousand judgments, yet only two were reversed.

"And what," says Lord Campbell, "will appear to my professional brethren a more striking fact still—strongly evincing the confidence reposed in his professional candour and ability by such men as Dunning and Erskine, opposed to him in politics, who practised before him—in all his time there never was a bill of exceptions tendered to his direction, the counsel against whom he decided either acquiescing in his ruling, or being perfectly satisfied that the question would afterwards be fully brought before the court, and satisfactorily determined upon a motion for a new trial."

Lord Campbell adds that the whole community of England, from their first experience of him on the bench, with the exception of occasional displays of party hostility, concurred in doing homage to his extraordinary merits as a judge. When he was expected to pronounce an important judgment, crowds thronged the court to listen to his silvery voice and graceful, yet never feeble, fluency. To gratify the curiosity of the public, his addresses to juries were reported in the newspapers; and thus began the practice of reporting, which has since expanded to such formidable proportions. His reputation drew so many suitors to the Court of King's Bench that the business of the other courts " dwindled away almost to nothing." Knowing the loyalty with which Scotchmen stand by one another, and the very fervid character of their nationality, we can well believe that in his native country he was regarded with veneration; and certainly, if his countrymen had reason to be proud of him for the fresh splendour he threw on the name of Scotchman, they had not less reason to be thankful to him "for the admirable manner in which, as a law lord in the House of Peers, he revised and corrected the decisions of their supreme court, giving new consistency and certainty both to their feudal and commercial code.

How did he attain to this exalted repute? Why was he so great a judge? It is easy to enumerate his intellectual qualifications, his logical understanding, his keenness of perception, his scientific acquaintance with jurisprudence, his firmness of will, his tenacity of purpose, his unrivalled power of application; and to say that, thus endowed, he could not fail to be—what he was—one of the greatest of English judges; but there is a vagueness about the statement which will not satisfy the reader. Other judges have been not less richly gifted, and yet have not made the mark that Mansfield did. Well, then, something must be allowed for his admirable *manner*. While firm, he was patient; while decided in the formation and expression of his opinions, he never refused to listen with respect and courtesy to those of others. His rectitude was unassailable; and timid as he was in political life, on the bench he was nobly courageous—neither deferring to the influence of the Court nor the voice of the multitude.* Again, he loved his work profoundly. He was a born judge, and was never so happy as when seated in his place in court. And he had a lofty ambition to bequeath his name to posterity as that of one who had greatly served his country by improving the administration of justice, and establishing its legal system on broad and stable principles.

There was an aristocratic fibre in Mansfield's character which made the arts of the demagogue repulsive to him, and strengthened his intellectual contempt of the applause of the mob. Besides, no man possessed as he was with a lofty and fervent ambition, will suffer himself to be deceived by the illusion of popularity.

---

* In his famous speech (in 1770) in support of a bill for curtailing the privileges of Parliament, his contempt for what is called popularity was forcibly and clearly expressed. "It has been said," he remarked, "by a noble lord on my left hand, that I likewise am running the race of popularity. If the noble lord means by popularity that applause bestowed by after times on good and virtuous actions, I have long been struggling in that race, to what purpose all-trying time can alone determine; but if the noble lord means that mushroom popularity that is raised without merit, and lost without a crime, he is much mistaken in his opinion. I defy the noble lord to point out a single action in my life where the popularity of the times ever had the smallest influence on my determina

A very fair and discriminating critic, Mr. Roscoe, has summed up the judicial merits of Lord Mansfield in language which we shall adopt with little alteration. He says :—

"No judge ever impressed so forcibly upon the jurisprudence of this country, the peculiar qualities of his mind. In scarcely any other instance can the influence of a judge be traced by any marked improvement in the principles of law or in the practice of the courts. With Lord Mansfield it was widely different, and many of the most important branches of modern law derive their character and almost their existence from his genius. The law of insurance has frequently been mentioned as an instance of the admirable facility with which his strong, clear intellect created a system of law adapted to all the exigencies of society. When he was raised to the Bench, the contract of insurance was little known, and a few unimportant 'nisi prius decisions' were all that existed on the subject. Yet, under his sagacious administration, this branch of law was developed into a system, remarkable for the excellence of its principles and the intelligibility and good sense of its practice. In many other branches of law his interposition was

---

tion. I thank God I have a more permanent and steady rule for my conduct—the dictates of my own breast. Those that have foregone that pleasing adviser, and given up their minds to be the slave of every popular impulse, I sincerely pity. I pity them still more if their vanity leads them to mistake the shouts of a mob for the trumpet of fame. Experience might inform them that many who have been saluted with the huzzas of a crowd one day, have received their execrations the next; and many who, by the popularity of their times, have been held up as spotless patriots, have, nevertheless, appeared upon the historian's page, when truth has triumphed over delusion, the assassins of liberty. Why, then, can the noble lord think that I am ambitious of present popularity—that relic of folly and shadow of renown—I am at a loss to determine."—" Parliamentary History," vol. xxiv. p. 977.

not less needed, and not less successful. It has, indeed, been said, that Lord Mansfield leaned too much in his decisions to equitable principles; and certainly in some instances his opinions have been reversed and overruled on this ground; yet, considering the anomalous scheme of the English law, and the expense and injustice which frequently arise from compelling a party who is clearly entitled to redress to seek it in another form at the expense of infinite delay and vexation, it is difficult to say whether the preservation of the exact boundaries between the tribunals of the common law and of equity are easily preserved at such a cost. The learning of Lord Mansfield has also been questioned, and perhaps his mind was not deeply imbued with the most recondite knowledge of his profession. So great, however, was the grasp of his intellect, and so lively and quick his powers of apprehension, that, on subjects where abstruse and recondite learning was required, he was always enabled to make with small preparation a brilliant display. He excelled particularly in the statement of a case, arranging the facts in an order so lucid, and with so wise a reference to the conclusions to be founded on them, that the hearer felt inclined to be convinced before he was in possession of the arguments." *

Like every great man, Mansfield was fortunate in his opportunity. He took his seat as Chief-Justice at a critical period in the annals of English jurisprudence, when the rapid developement of commerce, the changed relations of the individual to society, the expansion of the rights of property, had originated new necessities, and it was indispensable that the law should be adapted to meet them. This was a task for which Mansfield's genius was eminently fitted, and he did it so well and so thoroughly as to leave little in the same direction to be done by his successors. The principles which he laid

---

* H. Roscoe, "Eminent British Lawyers," 217.

down, and the precedents which he established, are the principles and the precedents that, in the main, govern the practice of our courts to the present day. It was certainly a singular good fortune for him that he should find a sphere in which his eminently creative and formative intellect could successfully labour, and it was not less a stroke of good fortune for this country that such an intellect should be at her command, exactly when it was urgently needed and could be most beneficial.

In his own time the nature of his work was justly appreciated, and happily defined, by one of the greatest of his contemporaries, Edmund Burke :—

"His ideas go," he said, " to the growing inclination of the law, by making its liberality keep pace with the demands of justice and the actual concerns of the world, not restricting the infinitely diversified occasions of men, and the rules of natural justice, within artificial circumscriptions, but conforming our jurisprudence to the growth of our commerce and our empire."

One of the most conspicuous trials in which Mansfield's dignified impartiality was proved arose out of the famous Wilkes affair.

John Wilkes, Member of Parliament for Aylesbury, was proprietor of a weekly paper called the *North Briton*. He was a man of some parts and no character, and his journal faithfully reflected him; it was lively, but unscrupulous. Started while Lord Bute was at the head of the Government, it had run through forty-five numbers when he resigned, and though almost every issue had contained grossly libellous matter, the Government had wisely refrained from prosecuting it. But as soon as George Grenville assumed the reins of administration, its impunity ceased. The forty-fifth number, published on the

23rd of April, 1767, was selected for prosecution. Wilkes was arrested on a " general warrant," from Earl Halifax, the Secretary of State—that is, a warrant not naming the person to be arrested—and flung into the Tower. His papers were seized and placed in the hands of Halifax. Proceedings so arbitrary excited a storm of indignation, and the Member for Aylesbury became a popular hero. A writ of *habeas corpus* released him from prison, and Chief-Justice Pratt (afterwards Lord Camden) declared general warrants illegal. The King, perplexed and disturbed by the confusion which raged around him, then made an effort to obtain Pitt's assistance ; but the great Commoner insisted on the recall to office of the leaders of the Whig party, and no agreement was concluded. The Granville government went on its imperious way, and carried in the House of Commons (November 15th), by **273** votes against **111**, a resolution to the effect that the forty-fifth number of the *North Briton* was a false, scandalous, and malicious libel. Wilkes then threw himself upon his privilege as a Member of Parliament. The House immediately declared that this privilege did not extend to the case of writing and publishing seditious libels, though Pitt pointed out that such a surrender of its privileges was highly dangerous to Parliament, and an infringment on the rights of the people. On the 25th of January, 1768, Wilkes was expelled from the House.

While Wilkes was absent in France, two criminal informations were filed against him ; one for writing and publishing No. 45 of the *North Briton,* and the other, for writing a coarse and profane poem called " An Essay on Woman ;" and on both of these he was found " guilty." Process of outlawry was then issued against him, and, as he did not appear to receive sentence, he was formerly declared an outlaw. In the spring of 1768, however, when the writs were out for a general election, he suddenly returned, proposed himself as a candidate for Middlesex, and was elected amidst exuberant manifestations of popular rejoicing. On the 20th of April, being the first day of term, Wilkes, according to a promise he had made, surrendered to his outlawry, and was committed to custody. A violent mob delivered him from the hands of the officers ; but he contrived to elude the attentions of his admirers, and prudently gave himself up at the King's Bench Prison. He then applied in due form for the reversal of his outlawry, and on the 8th of June, Lord Mansfield delivered judgment.

In his exordium he reviewed the various arguments which had been put forward by Wilkes' counsel ; they were entirely technical, and he easily showed that they carried no valid force. He then proceeded, in one of his most eloquent outbursts, to say :—

"These are the errors which have been objected ; and, for the reasons I have given, I cannot allow any of them. It was our duty, as well as our inclination, sedulously to consider whether upon any other ground, or in any other light, we could find an informality which we might allow with satisfaction to our own minds, and avow to the world.

"But here let me pause ! It is fit to take some notice of the various terms being held out : the numerous crowds which have attended and now attend in and about the hall, out of all reach of hearing what passes in court ; and the tumults which, in other places, have shamefully insulted all order and government. Audacious addresses in private dictate to us, from those they call the people, the judgment to be given now, and afterwards upon the conviction. Reasons of policy are urged, from danger to the kingdom by commotions and general confusion.

"Give me leave to take the opportunity of this great and respectable audience, to let the whole world know that all such attempts are vain. Unless we have been able to find an error which will bear us out to reverse the outlawry, it must be affirmed. The constitution does not allow reasons of state to influence our judgments. God forbid it should! We must not regard political consequences, how formidable soever they might be; if rebellion was the certain consequence, we are bound to say '*Fiat justitia, ruat cœlum.*' The constitution trusts to the king with reasons of state and policy; he may stop prosecutions; he may pardon offences; it is his to judge whether the law or the criminal should yield. We have no election. None of us encouraged or approved the commission of either of the crimes of which the defendant is convicted; none of us had any hand in his being prosecuted. As to myself, I took no part in another place in the addresses for that prosecution. We did not advise or assist the defendant to fly from justice; it was his own act, and he must take the consequences. None of us have been consulted, or had anything to do with the present prosecution. It is not in our power to stop it; it was not in our power to bring it on. We cannot pardon. We are to say what we take the law to be; if we do not speak our real opinions, we prevaricate with God and our own consciences.

"I pass over many anonymous letters which I have received. Those in print are public; and some of them have been brought judicially before the court. Whoever the writers are, they take the wrong way. I will do my duty unawed. What am I to fear? That *mendax infamia* from the press, which daily raises false facts and false motives? The lies of calumny carry no terror to me. I trust that my temper of mind, and the colour and conduct of my life, have given me a suit of armour against these arrows. If, during this king's reign, I have ever supported his government and assisted his measures, I have done it without any other reward than the consciousness of doing what I thought right. If I have ever opposed, I have done it upon the points themselves, without mixing in party or faction, and without any collateral views. I honour the king, and respect the people; but many things required by the favour of either are, in my account, objects not worth ambition. I wish popularity; but it is that popularity which follows, not that which is run after; it is that popularity which, sooner or later, never fails to do justice to the pursuit of noble ends by noble means. I will not do that which my conscience tells me is wrong upon this occasion, to gain the huzzas of thousands, or the daily praise of all the papers which come from the press. I will not avoid doing what I think is right, though it should draw on me the whole artillery of libels; all that falsehood and malice can invent, or the credulity of a deluded populace can swallow. I can say, with a great magistrate, upon an occasion and under circumstances not unlike, '*Ego hoc animo semper fui, ut invidiam virtute partam, gloriam, non invidiam, putarem.*'

"The threats go farther than abuse; personal violence is denounced. I do not believe it; it is not the genius of the worst of men of this country, in the worst of times. But I have set my mind at rest. The last end that can happen to any man never comes too soon, if he falls in support of the law and liberty of his country (for liberty is synonymous to law and government). Such a shock, too, might be productive of public good; it might awake the better part of the kingdom out of that lethargy which seems to have benumbed them; and bring the weak part back to their senses, as men intoxicated are sometimes stunned into sobriety.

"Once for all, let it be understood that no endeavours of this kind will influence any man who at present sits here. If they had any effect, it would be contrary to their intent; leaning against their impression might give a bias the other way. But I hope, and I know, that I have fortitude enough to resist even that weakness. No libels, no threats, nothing that has happened, nothing that can happen, will weigh a feather against allowing the defendant, upon this and every other question, not only the whole advantage he is entitled to from substantial law and justice, but every benefit from the most critical nicety of form, which any other defendant could claim under the like objection. The only effect I feel from such outrages is an anxiety to be able to explain the grounds upon which we proceed; so as to satisfy all mankind that a flaw of form given way to in this case, could not have been got over in any other."

Lord Mansfield then indicated a fatal blunder in the proceedings, which had passed unnoticed by the counsel for Wilkes, and gave judgment in favour of the reversal of the outlawry. It would be difficult, as Lord Brougham says, to overrate the merit of this famous *Concio ad Populum :*—

"Great elegance of composition, force of diction, just and strong, but natural, expression of personal feelings, a commanding attitude of defiance to lawless threats, but so assumed and so tempered with the dignity which was natural to the man, and which here, as on all other measures, he sustained throughout, all under this, one of the most striking productions on record."

The struggle was continued for several years. In 1770 Wilkes was returned for Middlesex ; the House expelled him. He was immediately re-elected, whereupon the House resolved, "That Mr. Wilkes, having been in this session of Parliament expelled the House, was and is incapable of being elected a member to serve in the present Parliament," and the Speaker issued his writ for a new election. This unconstitutional proceeding Middlesex resented by again returning Wilkes; and the House was driven forward to attempt a fresh encroachment on the rights of the electors. It declared that Colonel Luttrell, whom Wilkes had defeated by an immense majority, ought to have been returned, and was legally the representative of Middlesex; a declaration which, in effect, transferred the right of election from the electors to the House, and placed it in the power of the majority to unseat at any time an obnoxious member. In the Peers' Chamber Chatham stood forward to protest against the usurpation of the House of Commons. The liberty of the subject, he said, was invaded not only in the provinces, but at home. The English people were loud in their complaints, they demanded redress; and it was certain that, one way or other, they would have it. They would never return, nor ought they to return, to a state of tranquillity, until their grievances were redressed. In his judgment, it would be better for them to perish in a glorious contention for their rights, than to purchase a slavish tranquillity at the expense of one iota of the constitution. Lord Mansfield, in reply, contended that the proposed amendment was an attack upon the privileges of the other House of Parliament, a contention which provoked from Chatham one of his finest bursts of vehement and indignant eloquence.

Amid this ever-increasing political excitement appeared the celebrated " Letters of Junius ; " letters which have certainly been overrated, but for combined power and virulence are very remarkable. One addressed to the king was so freely and strongly written,* that the Government very foolishly resolved on prosecuting it. Accordingly the necessary proceedings were taken against Woodfall, the original printer and publisher, and against others who in various forms had republished it. The case of Mr. Almon was brought to trial before Lord Mansfield and a special jury, on the 2nd of June, 1770, when, on

---

* Its merits, however, are purely those of style. The argument is feeble, and feebly drawn out ; and the political views are by no means elevated or comprehensive.

behalf of the Crown, proof was adduced that a copy of
the libel had been bought at the defendant's shop, from
a person acting there as his servant.  The defendant's
counsel, Sergeant Glyn, argued that a man could not be
made a criminal by the act of his servant; but Lord
Mansfield ruled that a sale by a servant was evidence
when not contradicted or explained, of a publication by
the master, on the principle, whatever a man does by
another, he does by himself (*qui facit per alium facit
per se*).  The jury then found the defendant guilty.

In the ensuing term motion was made for a new trial,
on the ground that there was no proof whatever of a
*criminal intention* on the defendant's part, nor even
that he knew of the sale of the libel.  The motion was
refused, however, on the ground that the publication at
the defendant's shop was *prima facie* evidence of a guilty
publication *by him*.  This judgment met with severe
censure both within and without the walls of Parliament;
but Lord Campbell considers it was clearly according to
law and reason (which do not always run in couples!)
For were proof required of the master's personal
interference or direct sanction, libels might be published
with absolute impunity; while innocence is sufficiently
protected by the admission of evidence to rebut the
presumption.

On the 13th of June came on the trial of Woodfall,
the printer of the *Morning Advertiser;* and, as the
defendant's liability as publisher could not be disputed,
his counsel sought to persuade the jury that the matter
published was not libellous.  Then arose a great dispute,
whether this was a question for the jury or exclusively
for the Court?  Lord Mansfield directed the jury that all
they had to consider was whether the defendant had

published the letter set out in the information, and
whether the inuendoes imputed a particular meaning to
particular words, as that "the k——" meant His
Majesty King George III.; that it was not for them to
decide whether the publication, as alleged by the counsel
for the Crown, was false and libellous; for whether it
was libellous or innocent was a mere question of law,
upon which the opinion of the Court might be taken
"by a demurrer, or a motion in arrest of judgment."

After a prolonged deliberation, the jury returned a
verdict of "Guilty of the printing and publishing only."
Thereafter, two applications were made to the Court of
King's Bench; the first, by the defendant, to stay judgment; the second, by the Crown, to enter the verdict
according to the legal finding of the jury. After listening to elaborate arguments, Lord Mansfield delivered the
opinion of the Court in favour of a new trial—

"Had the verdict," he said, "been simply 'guilty of printing
and publishing,' we should have thought that it ought to be
entered generally for the Crown; but we cannot exclude the
word 'only,' and this appears to negative something charged in
the information which the jury thought was submitted to them.
Where there are more charges than one, 'guilty of some *only*' is
an acquittal as to the rest; but in this information there is no
charge except for *printing and publishing*; clearly there can be
no judgment of acquittal, because the fact found against the
defendant by the jury is the very crime they had to try. That
the law is as I stated to the jury has been so often unanimously
agreed by the whole Court, upon every report I have made of a
trial for a libel, that it would be improper to make it a question
now in this place. Among those who have concurred, the bar
will recollect the *dead* and the living not now here. And we
all again declare our opinion that the direction was right and
according to law. Can any meaning be affixed to the word 'only'

o

which may affect the verdict? If they meant to say 'they did not find it a libel,' or 'did not find the epithets false and malicious,' it would not affect the verdict, because none of these things were to be proved or found either way. It is impossible to say with certainty what the jury really did mean. Probably they had different meanings. It is possible some of them might mean not to find the whole sense put upon part of the words by the *inuendoes* in the information. If there be a meaning favourable to the defendant which by possibility the words will bear, he ought not to be convicted. Therefore we order the verdict to be set aside, and that there shall be a new trial."

No new trial took place, the Crown lawyers being perfectly well aware that no jury would find the publisher of *Junius* guilty—at least, no jury in the city of London.

In the case of Miller, Mansfield's direction to the jury was couched in the same spirit; laying down the erroneous and pernicious doctrine—long since eliminated from English law—that the juries could decide only the fact of publication and the inuendoes. In laying down this doctrine he did nothing *morally* wrong; he followed the example of his predecessors, and was supported by the unanimous opinion of his fellow-judges; but it is surprising that his enlightened and powerful mind did not see the issues which could not fail to flow from it. As his ruling was favourable to the action of the Government, it was not unnaturally supposed to have been influenced by political motives, and provoked very general censure. In the public press he was bitterly assailed by *Junius*.

" Our language," said the anonymous vituperator, " has no term of reproach, the mind has no idea of detestation, which has not already been happily applied to you, and exhausted. Ample justice has been done by abler pens than mine to the separate merits of your life and character. Let it be *my* humble office to collect the sweets till their united virtue tortures the sense.

"Permit me to begin with paying a just tribute to Scotch sincerity wherever I find it. I own I am not apt to confide in the professions of gentlemen of that country; and when they smile, I feel an involuntary erection to guard myself against mischief. With this general opinion of an ancient nation, I always thought it much to your lordship's honour that in your earlier days you were but little infected with the prudence of your country. You had some original attachments which you took every proper opportunity to acknowledge. The liberal spirit of youth prevailed over your native discretion. Your zeal in the cause of an unhappy prince was expressed with the sincerity of wine and some of the solemnities of religion. This, I conceive, is the most amiable point of view in which your character has appeared. Like an honest man you took that part in politics which might have been expected from your birth, education, country, and connections. There was something generous in your attachment to the House of Stuart. We lament the mistake of a good man, and do not begin to detest him until he affects to renounce his principles. Why did you not adhere to that loyalty you once professed? Why did you not follow the example of your worthy brother? With him you might have shared in the honour of the Pretender's confidence; with him you might have preserved the integrity of your character; and England, I think, might have spared you without regret. Your friends will say, perhaps, that although you deserted the fortunes of your liege lord, you have adhered firmly to the principles which drove his father from the throne; that without openly supporting the person, you have done essential service to the cause, and consoled yourself for the loss of a favourite family by reviving and re-establishing the maxims of their Government. This is the way in which a Scotchman's understanding converts the errors of his heart. My lord, I acknowledge the truth of the defence, and can trace it throughout all your conduct. I see through your whole life one uniform plan to enlarge the power of the Crown at the expense of the liberty of the subject."

It must be confessed that this is brilliant writing, and that there is a deadly ingenuity in the way in which the writer compliments Mansfield on that part of his conduct which he would willingly have had forgotten.

Mansfield suffered much in public estimation from his alliance with Lord Bute, and the influence he exercised, or was supposed to exercise, over the politics of the Cabinet. He laid himself open to attack, moreover, by presiding on the woolsack as Speaker of the House of Lords, and virtually exercising almost all the functions of the Lord Chancellor, while keeping the great seal in commission. To our modern ideas the position of Chief Justice seems incompatible with that of an active member of the Government, and the combination of political partisanship with judicial administration cannot but be productive of unfortunate consequences. Mansfield himself was probably not unconscious of this fact, and refrained from replying to the invectives of *Junius*, because he felt that they were not without justification. The Attorney-General advised a prosecution; but the Chief Justice prudently refused to allow *Junius* another opportunity for inquiring into all the circumstances of his political career.

At this time his hands were fully occupied in defending himself against parliamentary assaults. In the House of Commons, Mr. Sergeant Glyn moved for a committee to inquire into the proceedings of the judges in Westminster Hall, particularly in cases relating to the liberty of the press ; and in the course of the debate, Mansfield's conduct was severely censured by Dunning and Edmund Burke.

In the House of Lords the attack was still more formidable. It was led by the Earl of Chatham, and supported by Lord Camden. The defence was not without dignity :—

" Judges," said Mansfield, " cannot go astray from the express and known law of the land. They are bound by oath punctually to follow the law. I have ever made it the rule of my conduct to do what was just, and, conscious of my own integrity, am able to look with contempt upon libels and libellers. Before the noble lord, therefore, arraigns my judicial character, he should make himself acquainted with facts. The scurrility of a news-paper may be good information for a coffee-house politician, but a peer of Parliament should always speak from higher authority ; though, if my noble accuser is no more acquainted with the principles of law in the present point than in what he advanced to support the motion, when he told us an action would lie against the House of Commons for expelling Mr. Wilkes, I am fearful the highest authorities will not extend his ideas of jurisprudence, nor entitle him to a patient hearing upon a legal question in this assembly."

Lord Chatham rejoined :—

" If I conceive the noble lord on the woolsack right, or have been rightly informed by the public prints—from which, I can-didly confess, I originally derived my information on the subject —the doctrine of the King's Bench is, that a libel or not a libel is a question of law to be decided only by the court, and the sole power of the jury is to determine upon the fact of printing and publishing. This I understand to be the noble lord's opinion, but this I never understood to be the law of England ; on the con-trary, I always understood that the jury were competent judges of the law as well as of the fact, and, indeed, if they are not, I can see no essential benefit arising from their institution to the community. . . . I am therefore desirous—I am earnestly desirous—that a day may be appointed for examining into the conduct of such judges as dare to establish this anti-constitutional practice in our courts. I am well assured from the most respectable authority, that the practice is immediately subversive 'of our dearest rights, our most invaluable liberties; and, profligate as the times may be, there are objects that interest should lead us to defend, even if we are wholly unactuated by principle."

After Lord Camden had spoken, in terms even more bitter and direct, the Duke of Grafton, on behalf of the Government, moved the adjournment of the House, which was carried by a large majority. Here it would have been well for Lord Mansfield to have let the matter rest; but, smarting under the censure which Burke and Dunning had heaped upon him in the Lower Chamber, he next day intimated that he had a matter of importance to submit to the Peers, and moved that they should be summoned for the purpose.

Accordingly, on the 10th of December, their Lordships assembled in large numbers, eagerly expecting " a passage of arms," in which Toryism, as represented by Lord Mansfield, was to lay low the principle of Anarchy, as represented by Lords Chatham and Camden. But in the interval Lord Mansfield's courage had oozed out, and his constitutional timidity had got the better of him. To the intense surprise of the House, he contented himself with saying that he had left with the clerk of the House a copy of the judgment of the Court of King's Bench, in the case of *The King* against *Woodfall*, and that their Lordships might read it and take copies of it if they pleased. On an inquiry from Lord Camden whether he meant to have the paper entered on the

Journals, he replied : " No, no ; only to leave it with the clerk."

On the following day, Lord Camden, addressing the House, said that he considered the paper delivered in by the Chief-Justice as a personal challenge, and he accepted it. In direct contradiction to Lord Mansfield, he maintained that his doctrine was not the law of England. And he proposed four questions to Lord Mansfield, founded on the aforesaid opinion of the Court of King's Bench, to which he desired categorical answers.

" ' I have the highest esteem,' said Lord Mansfield, with manifest uneasiness, ' for the noble and learned lord who thus attacks me, and I have ever courted his esteem in return. From his candour I had not expected this treatment. I have studied the point more than any other in my life, and have consulted all the judges on it, except the noble and learned lord, who appears to view it differently from all others. But this mode of questioning takes me by surprise. It is unfair. I will not answer interrogatories.'

" *Lord Chatham*, sarcastically : ' Interrogatories ! Was ever anything heard so extraordinary ? Can the noble and learned lord be taken by surprise when, as he tells us, he has been considering the point all his life, and has taken the opinions of all the judges upon it ?"

" *Lord Camden :* ' I am willing that the noble and learned lord should have whatever time he deems requisite to prepare himself, but let him name a day when his answers may be given in, and I shall then be ready to meet him.'

" *Lord Mansfield :* ' I am not bound to answer, and I will not answer, the questions which the noble and learned lord has so astutely framed and so irregularly administered ; but I pledge myself that the matter shall be discussed.' "

The Duke of Richmond here congratulated the House

that the Chief-Justice had at least pledged himself to the point.

"*Lord Mansfield*, breaking down: 'My Lords, I did not pledge myself to any particular point. I only said I should hereafter give my opinion. And as to fixing a day, I said, No, I will not fix a day.'"

"The dismay and confusion of Lord Mansfield," says Horace Walpole, "was obvious to the whole audience; nor did one Peer interpose a syllable in his behalf."

After this unfortunate *fiasco*, Lord Mansfield, for some time to come, took little if any part in the debates. Mr. Justice Bathurst was made Lord Chancellor, and Mansfield resigned his post as Speaker of the House of Lords.

In 1775, when the great struggle with the American colonies occupied the thought and energy of the nation, he received the leadership of his party, and became again the chief organ of the Government in the Upper House. We have already alluded to this part of his career, and pass from it with the remark that his services were highly esteemed by the King, who created him a Knight of the Thistle, and afterwards raised him to the dignity of Earl of Mansfield, with remainder to his nephew, Viscount Stormont, and his heirs. In 1777 he was called upon to try Horne Tooke for a libel written in opposition to the American War, and on this occasion he left to the jury not only the question of fact but of law, not only of publication but of criminality. Horne Tooke was found guilty. Mansfield was present in the House on the 7th of April, 1778—the day which witnessed the great Chatham's last appearance on the political stage. Who does not remember the scene—the entrance of the aged statesman, " hanging upon two friends, lapped up in flannel, pale and emaciated "—those friends being his son, William Pitt, and his son-in-law, Lord Mahon. As he passed to his seat with slowness and difficulty, leaning on his crutches, the Peers all rose as a mark of respect. " Within his large wig, little more was to be seen than his aquiline nose and his penetrating eye. He looked like a dying man, yet never was seen a figure of more dignity." *

" I thank God," he said, " that I have been enabled to come here this day to perform my duty, and to speak on a subject which has so deeply impressed my mind. I am old and infirm —have one foot, more than one foot, in the grave. I am risen from my bed, to stand up in the cause of my country—perhaps never again to speak in this House."

He expressed his pleasure that he was still able to protest against the dismemberment of this ancient and most noble monarchy.

" My lords, his Majesty succeeded to an empire as great in extent as its reputation was unsullied. Shall we banish the lustre of this nation by an ignominious surrender of its rights and fairest possessions? Shall this great kingdom, that has survived, whole and entire, the Danish depredations, the Scottish inroads"—and here he looked at Lord Mansfield—" and the Norman Conquest; that has stood the threatened invasion of the Spanish Armada, now fall prostrate before the House of Bourbon? Surely, my lords, this nation is no longer what it was! Shall a people that, seventeen years ago, was the terror of the world, now stoop so low as to tell its ancient inveterate enemy, ' Take all we have, only give us peace?' It is impossible!

" I wage war," he continued, " with no man, or set of men. I wish for none of their employments; nor would I co-operate

* Seward, " Anecdotes," ii. 383.

with men who still persist in unretracted error; or who, instead of acting on a firm decisive line of conduct, halt between two opinions, where there is no middle path. In God's name, if it is absolutely necessary to declare either for peace or war, and the former cannot be preserved with honour, why is not the latter commenced without hesitation? I am not, I confess, well informed of the resources of this kingdom, but I trust it has still sufficient to maintain its just rights, though I know them not. But, my lords, any state is better than despair! Let us at least make one effort; and if we must fall, let us fall like men."

The Duke of Richmond having replied, Chatham made an effort to speak again.

"He fell back npon his seat," says Lord Camden, "and was to all appearance in the agonies of death. This threw the whole House into confusion. Every person rose upon his legs in a moment, hurrying from one place to another—some sending for assistance, others producing salts, and others reviving spirits; many crowding about the Earl to observe his countenance; all affected; most part really unnerved; and even those who might have felt a secret pleasure at the accident, yet put on the appearance of distress, except only the Earl of Mansfield, who sat still, almost as much unmoved as the senseless body itself."

In the "No Popery" riots of 1780, so vividly depicted by Charles Dickens in his "Barnaby Rudge," Lord Mansfield was fated to be a signal sufferer. His judicial decisions, conceived in the most enlightened spirit, had always acknowledged and protected the rights of conscience, and vindicated the liberties of the Protestant Dissenter as of the Roman Catholic. This wise tolerance excited the popular wrath. On the 6th of June, the so-called "Protestant Association," some 60,000 strong, after marching in procession through the City, swept into Palace Yard, and surrounded the Houses of Parliament. Owing to the illness of Thurlow, the Lord Chancellor, Mansfield had to preside that day as Speaker in the Upper Chamber. As he drove through Parliament Street he was recognised by the mob, who broke the windows of his carriage, and assailed him with shouts and execrations as a notorious Papist. With difficulty he reached the door, through which he passed into his retiring-room, and received the protection of the officers of the House against the rabble that pressed close upon his footsteps. With rent robes and dishevelled wig he proceeded to take his seat upon the woolsack, preserving his usual dignity and composure of mien. Other Peers had been still more grossly ill-treated. The Archbishop of York's lawn-sleeves were torn off and thrown in his face; the Bishop of Lincoln, his carriage having been broken in pieces, was carried fainting into a gentleman's house, whence, later on, he went away in disguise; Lords Stormont, Hillsborough, and Townshend had narrowly escaped with their lives; the Duke of Northumberland was forced out of his carriage, robbed of his watch and purse, and almost stripped of his clothes.

The day's business, however, was begun with the usual formalities, and the Duke of Richmond was speaking in support of a bill for annual parliaments and universal suffrage—an infelicitous measure to bring forth at such a crisis—when Lord Montford rushed in, besprinkled with mud and hair-powder, and broke into a torrent of agitated speech. The Duke of Richmond, offended at this interruption, appealed to the woolsack for protection, and Mansfield endeavoured to interfere; but Lord Montford claimed to be heard on a matter of life and death, asserting that Lord Boston, on his way to his duty as a

Peer of Parliament, had been roughly handled, and would certainly be murdered if none hastened to his assistance. At this crisis the House presented an almost grotesque appearance. Some of their lordships moved restlessly about, with their hair loose upon their shoulders; others were bespattered with mud thrown by plebeian hands; most of them as pale as the Ghost in "Hamlet;" and all of them greatly perturbed, and speaking loudly and together. One proposed to send for the Guards, another for the justices or civil magistrates; many vociferated, "Adjourn! Adjourn!;" while the skies resounded with the huzzas, shoutings, hootings, and hissings in Palace Yard.

Lord Townshend at last plucked up courage to volunteer, if joined by others, to attempt Lord Boston's rescue. The Duke of Richmond was fired by his example, but suggested that if they went as "a band," the mace ought to be carried before the noble and learned lord on the woolsack, and that he should go at their head—the conscript fathers of Great Britain, led by their consul, advancing to meet the plebs in all their dignity! Lord Mansfield did not lack physical courage, and expressed himself perfectly willing to take the post of honour—and danger—so courteously provided for him; but the Duke of Gloucester wisely disapproved of a device which would hardly have had other than fatal results. While the perplexed senators continued their discussion, in came Lord Boston, who, by skilfully engaging some of the leaders of the mob in a subtle argument on the question "whether the Pope really was Anti-Christ," had contrived to effect his escape with no other damage than dishevelled hair and a considerable sprinkling of hair-powder over his clothes. Lord Mansfield

then ordered Black Rod to call before them the High
Bailiff of Westminster, who informed them that he had
received no communication from the Secretary of State;
but, attracted by "the disturbance"—a wide euphemism,
surely, for a formidable riot!—had done his utmost to
restore tranquillity. As yet he had been able to collect
only six constables, who were quietly waiting in the
Guildhall until more could be assembled, as no good
could be done with such a handful.

It cannot be said that the High Bailiff's speech was
encouraging; and the Peers, greatly dismayed, insisted on
the adjournment of the House. Thereafter the Assembly
gradually thinned, most of the Lords having either retired
to the coffee-houses or gone off in hackney-carriages;
while others had slunk home under cover of the growing darkness. Thus it came to pass that Lord Mansfield, in his seventy-sixth year, was left alone and
unprotected, except by the officers of the House and his
own servants. There seems to have been a strange want of
chivalry in this desertion of the venerable Chief-Justice;
but, on the other hand, his remaining to the last may
have been a piece of unnecessary Quixotism.

Next day (June 7th), the insurrection, unchecked by
any display of energy and decision on the part of the
authorities, assumed more alarming proportions. Newgate and the other metropolitan prisons were broken
open, and their inmates released. The Inns of Court
were besieged, and preparations made for attacking the
Bank. Having sacked the houses of three of the London
magistrates, the infuriated populace rolled towards Lord
Mansfield's mansion in Bloomsbury Square. Apprehending an attack, Lord Mansfield had sent for Sir
John Hawkins, who arrived with a party of con-

stables, and advised that the military should immediately be summoned. Contrary to Sir John's recommendation, Lord Mansfield insisted that the soldiers should be stationed, not in his house, but in the neighbouring church of St. George's—from a fear, perhaps, that the sight of the red coats might further inflame the temper of the rioters. Scarcely had his order been obeyed before the mob poured into the square, carrying torches and other combustibles, and filling the air with their yells and drunken shouts. When they began to beat at the outer door, Lord Mansfield and his wife retreated by a back passage. The work of destruction went on apace, and before morning there was nothing left of the stately structure but the blackened and mouldering outer walls. The whole of Lord Mansfield's valuable library of printed books and manuscripts, his private papers and correspondence, his pictures, plate, furniture,—all were consumed. The rioters, to prove their disinterestedness, flung into the flames a costly tankard of silver, filled with guineas.

We take from Sir Nathaniel Wroxall's Memoirs a graphic account of his experiences of this memorable scene :—

"About nine o'clock," he says, "accompanied by three other gentlemen—who, as well as myself, were alarmed at the accounts brought in every moment of the outrages committed, and of the still greater acts of violence meditated as soon as darkness should favour and facilitate their further progress—we set out, . . . and drove to Bloomsbury Square, attracted to that spot by a rumour, generally spread, that Lord Mansfield's residence, situate at the north-east corner, was either already burnt or destined for destruction. Hart Street and Great Russell Street presented each to the view as we passed large fires, composed of furniture taken from the houses of magistrates or other obnoxious individuals. Quitting the coach, we crossed the square, and had scarcely got under the wall of Bedford House when we heard the door of Lord Mansfield's house burst open with violence. In a few minutes all the contents of the apartments, being precipitated from the windows, were piled up and wrapt in flames. A file of foot-soldiers arriving, drew up near the blazing pile, but without either attempting to quench the fire or to impede the mob, who were, indeed, far too numerous to admit of their being dispersed, or even intimidated, by a small detachment of infantry. The populace remained masters; while we, after surveying the spectacle for a short time, moved into Holborn."

Lord Mansfield afterwards regretted, and with just reason, that he had not met the attack of the multitude with a greater display of vigour. Erskine tells us that he more than once heard him say that perhaps some blame might attach to himself and others in authority for their forbearance in not directing force to be at the first moment repelled by force : it is the highest humanity to check the infancy of tumults.

The loss which he had sustained in the destruction of his library was irreparable. The loss of furniture and plate might have been repaired; indeed, the House of Commons authorised the payment of adequate compensation, but with lofty generosity he declined it. Nothing could give back to him his valuable MSS., or the books enriched with the autographs of Pope, Swift, Bolingbroke, and the brightest luminaries of the age. All he could do was to summon to his aid the fortitude of a Christian. Perhaps the sympathy which the poet Cowper expressed in some graceful stanzas afforded him as much consolation as, in the circumstances, it was possible for him to receive :—

" So then the Vandals of our isle,
    Sworn foes to men and law,
Have burnt to dust a nobler pile
    Than ever Roman saw.

" Lord Murray sighs o'er Pope and Swift,
    And many a treasure more,
The well-judged purchase and the gift
    That graced his lettered store .

" Their pages mangled, burnt, and torn,
    Their loss was his alone ;
But ages yet to come shall mourn
    The burning of his own.*

" When wit and genius meet their doom
    In all-devouring flame,
They tell us of the fate of Rome,
    And bid us fear the same.

" O'er Murray's loss the Muses wept ;
    They felt the rude alarm ;
Yet blessed the guardian care that kept
    His sacred head from harm.

" There memory, like the bee that's fed
    From Flora's balmy store,
The quintessence of all he read
    Had treasured up before.

" The lawless herd, with fury blind,
    Have done him cruel wrong :
The flowers are gone ; but still we find
    The honey on his tongue."

On the trial of Lord George Gordon for the share
which that mad fanatic had in the outbreak, Erskine,
in the eloquent speech he delivered for the defence,

---

* An allusion to several essays, judicial and historical, which he
had prepared for posthumous publication.

alluded very gracefully to the destruction of Lord Mansfield's house, and deduced from it an argument in favour of his client :—

"Can any man living believe," he exclaimed, "that Lord George Gordon could possibly have excited the mob to destroy the house of that great and venerable magistrate, who has presided so long in this great and high tribunal that the oldest of us do not remember him with any other impression than the awful form and figure of justice ; a magistrate who had always been the friend of the Protestant Dissenters against the ill-timed jealousies of the Establishment ;—his countryman, too ; and, without adverting to the partiality not unjustly imputed to men of that country, a man of whom any country might be proud ? No, gentlemen, it is not credible that a man of noble birth and liberal education (unless agitated by the most implacable personal resentment, which is not imputed to the prisoner) could possibly consent to this burning of the house of Lord Mansfield." *

During the administrations of the Marquis of Rockingham and Lord Shelbourne, the aged Chief-Justice took no part in political warfare, and gradually ceased to intervene in the debates. When he *did* speak, his speeches were scarcely worthy of his reputation. Apparently, advancing years increased his constitutional timidity, so that in most of the measures brought before Parliament, his nervous disposition detected the germs of future evil. This was specially apparent in the last speech which he addressed to the House. He was opposed to the administration formed by the younger Pitt, and when a motion was introduced in the Upper Chamber which tended to give it an indirect support, he met it with an uncompromising negative, while enunciating

---

* Lord Erskine, "Speeches," i. 112.

declarations of wrath and judgment to come that might appropriately have fallen from the lips of a Cassandra :—

"We have no time to spare," he cried; "we are even now at the last hour. The ship sinks while we are deliberating on what course we should steer. . . . Before you render a dissolution of Parliament indispensible, think for a moment of the evils which must ensue. Are you prepared to disband the army, to lay up the navy, to paralyse all the operations of Government, and to expose yourselves to the machinations of rival States which have so recently conspired your destruction? I own I tremble at the precipice on which we stand."

By common consent Lord Mansfield is acknowledged to have been a great judge; if he had not been so bad a politician, he might have been a great man.

In the Court of King's Bench he continued to preside until 1788 without any diminution of intellectual vigour. His increasing physical infirmities then compelled his retirement. On the 4th of June he sent in his formal resignation. The counsel practising in his court immediately assembled, and through Erskine, their leader, presented him with an address, in which they deplored "the loss of a magistrate whose conspicuous and exalted talents conferred dignity upon the profession, whose enlightened and regular administration of justice made its duties less difficult and laborious, and whose manners rendered them pleasant and respectable." In reply, Lord Mansfield said that if he had given satisfaction it was owing to "the learning and candour of the Bar." The liberality and integrity of their practice had freed the judicial investigation of truth and justice from many difficulties. He added—"The memory of the assistance I have received from them, and the deep impression which the extraordinary mark they have now given me of their approbation and affection has made upon my mind, will be a source of perpetual consolation in my decline of life, under the pressure of bodily infirmities which made it my duty to retire."

With mental faculties unimpaired, Lord Mansfield lived for nearly five years after his resignation, enjoying the amenities of his country seat at Kenwood, and dividing his time between rural recreations and the cultivation of letters. Lord Campbell quotes a letter written by one of the aged lawyer's grandnephews, which gives a pleasing picture of him in his declining days :—*

"I first saw Lord Mansfield when I went to Westminster School in 1787, and used occasionally to spend part of my holidays at Kenwood. He was very kind, treating me familiarly as a boy, and always called me *schoolfellow.* He took a great interest in all that was going on in Westminster School, used to talk of his boyish days, and relate anecdotes of what occurred when he was there. I remember one, of his having made a plum-pudding, and, there being no other apparatus for the purpose, it was boiled in his night-cap; he told this with great glee. He always drank claret, and had a small decanter containing a few glasses placed by him at dinner, which he finished.

"He still took pleasure in ornamenting his grounds. Some cedars in the wood opposite his house were planted by his own hand.

"He was a great admirer of Pope, and occasionally selected passages from his poems which he taught me to recite. His voice and modulation were beautiful.

"He told me he had conversed with a man who was present at the execution of the Blessed Martyr. How wonderful it

---

* Lord Campbell, "Lives of the Chief-Justices," ii. 555.

seems that there should be only one person between me and him who saw Charles's head cut off!"

On the 9th of March, 1793, his nephew, Lord Stormont, spent the evening with him, discussing the merits of a cause then before the House of Peers, and observed that his mind was as strong and clear as usual. Next morning, however, he became drowsy at breakfast, and complained of feeling very sleepy. He seemed to suffer no pain, but was put to bed, and his pulse being low, was plied with stimulants and cordials. On Monday, the 11th, he was somewhat better, and on Tuesday, the 12th, expressed a wish to be taken up and carried to his chair. He soon expressed a desire, however, to be carried back to bed, saying, " Let me sleep; let me sleep." These were his last words. He lingered for several days, but did not recover consciousness, and on Wednesday night, the 20th, passed away without a struggle or a sigh, in the eighty-ninth year of his age. *O fortunatè senex!* A long life of honour and prosperity was crowned by a painless death.*

---

* We shall subjoin in a note the estimates of Lord Mansfield formed by not incompetent authorities. Smollett, the historian, refers to his "keen intuitive spirit of apprehension, that seemed to seize every object at first glance ; an innate sagacity, that saved the trouble of intense application ; and an irresistible stream of eloquence, that flowed pure and classical, strong and copious, reflecting in the most conspicuous point of view the subjects over which it rolled, and sweeping before it all the slime of formal hesitation and all the entangling weeds of chicanery." Bishop Newton says :—"Lord Mansfield's is a character above all praise ; the oracle of law, the standard of eloquence, and pattern of all virtue, both in public and private life. It was happy for the nation, as well as for himself, that at his age there appeared not the least symptom of decay in his bodily or in his mental faculties ; but he had all the quickness and vivacity

of youth, tempered with all the knowledge and experience of old age. He had almost an immediate intuition into the merits of every cause or question which came before him ; and, comprehending it clearly himself, could readily explain it to others : persuasion flowed from his lips, conviction was wrought in all unprejudiced minds when he concluded ; and, for many years, the House of Lords paid greater attention to his authority than to that of any man living." Bishop Hurd says :—" He was so extraordinary a person, and made so great a figure in the world, that his name must go down to posterity with distinguished honour in the public records of the nation ; for his shining talents displayed themselves in every department of the State, as well as in the Supreme Court of Justice, his peculiar province, which he filled with lustre of reputation not equalled perhaps, certainly not exceeded, by any of his predecessors. Of his conduct in the House of Lords I can speak with the more confidence, because I speak from my own observation. Too good to be the leader, and too able to be the dupe, of any party, he was believed to speak his own sense of public measures ; and the authority of his judgment was so high that, in regular times, the House was usually decided by it. He was no forward or frequent speaker, but reserved himself, as was fit, for occasions worthy of him. In debate he was eloquent as well as wise ; or rather, he became eloquent by his wisdom. His countenance and tone of voice imprinted the ideas of penetration, probity, and candour ; but what secured your attention and assent to all he said, was his constant good sense, flowing in apt terms and in the clearest method. He affected no sallies of the imagination or bursts of passion ; much less would he condescend to personal abuse, or to petulant altercation. All was clear, candid reason, letting itself so candidly into the minds of his hearers as to carry information and conviction with it. In a word, his public oratorical character very much resembled that of Messala, of whom Cicero says, addressing himself to Brutus : ' Do not imagine, Brutus, that for worth, honour, and a warm love of his country, any one is comparable to Messala.' So that his eloquence, in which he wonderfully excels, is almost eclipsed by those virtues, and even in his display of that faculty, his superior good sense shows itself most ; with so much care and skill has he formed himself to the truest manner of speaking ! His powers of genius and invention are confessedly of the first size ; yet he almost owes less to them than to the diligent and studious cultivation of judgment. In the commerce of private life, Lord Mansfield was easy, friendly, and very entertaining, extremely sensible of worth in other men, and ready on all occasions to countenance and patronise it." Of Lord Mansfield as a companion and conversationalist, Richard Cumberland, the dramatist, says:—"I cannot recollect the time when, sitting at the table with Lord Mansfield, I ever failed to remark that happy and engaging art which he possessed of putting the company present in good humour with themselves; I am convinced they naturally liked him the more for his seeming to like them so well: this has not been the general property of all the witty, great, and learned men whom I have looked up to in my course of life. He would lend his ear most condescendingly to his company, and cheer the least attempt at humour with the prompt payment of a species of laugh, which cost his muscles no exertion, but was merely a subscription that he readily threw in towards the general hilarity of the table. He would take his share in the small talk of the ladies with all imaginable affability; he was, in fact, like most men, not in the least degree displeased at being incensed by their flattery. He was no great starter of new topics, but easily led into anecdotes of past times: these he detailed with pleasure; but he told them correctly rather than amusingly. I am inclined to think that he did not covet that kind of conversation that gave him any pains to carry on: his professional labours were great, and it was natural that he should resort to society more for relaxation and rest of mind than for any thing that could put him upon fresh exertions. Even dulness, so long as it was accompanied with placidity, was no absolute disrecommendation of the companion of his private hours; it was a kind of cushion to his understanding." Lastly, of Lord Mansfield as a lawyer, the following portrait is drawn by Lord Campbell:—"He must, I think, be considered the most prominent legal character, and the brightest ornament to the profession of the law, that appeared in England during the last century. As an advocate he did not display the impassioned eloquence of Erskine, but he was for many years the first man at the bar among powerful competitors. Both before a jury in the Common Law Courts, and addressing a single judge in the Courts of Equity, by the calm exertion of reason, he won every cause in which *right* was with him, or which was doubtful. There was a common saying in those days: ' Mr. Murray's *statement* is of itself worth the argument of any other man.' Avoiding the vulgar fault of misrepresenting and exaggerating facts, he placed them in a point of view so perspicuous and so favourable to his client, that the verdict was secure before the narrative was closed.   The observations which followed seemed to suggest trains of thinking rather than to draw conclusions ; and so skilfully did he conceal his art, that the hearers thought they formed their opinion in consequence of the workings of their own minds, when in truth it was the effect of the most refined dialectics.   For parliamentary oratory he was more considerable than any lawyer our profession could boast of till the appearance of Henry Brougham,—having been for many years in both Houses in the very first rank of debaters. . . . Nothing remains to be said for the purpose of proving that he was the first of common law judges."

# Edmund Burke.

EDMUND BURKE was born in a house on Arran Quay, Dublin, January 1st, 1730 (O. S.) He was the younger son of a reputable Protestant attorney, Richard Burke or Bourke, and of his wife, a Miss Nagle. In his early years he suffered severely from the pains and penalties inflicted by a delicate constitution; so that when his brothers were pleasantly occupied in the athletic games and exercises of boyhood, he might be seen reclining on a sofa, diligently reading. His elder brother, Richard, himself a man of considerable parts, when found in later life deeply meditating after one of Edmund's magnificent orations in the House of Commons, excused himself by saying, " I have been wondering how Ned has contrived to monopolize all the talents of the family; but now I remember, when we were at play he was always at work." It is consolatory to some of us to reflect that delicate health in childhood is not always a bar to success in after-life. The law of compensation prevails in all things ; and a volume might be filled with the names of men whose ability to serve their country—or themselves—has closely been connected with the patient industry rendered compulsory or possible by early " invalidism."

That he might enjoy the benefit of country air, young

Burke, while still a child, was sent to his uncle's house at Castletown Roche, where he received the rudiments of education from the village schoolmaster, and learned, perhaps, that the neighbourhood was hallowed ground—hallowed by the memories of Spenser, Essex, and Raleigh. In 1741 he was sent to the "classical academy" at Ballitore. His untiring application, his keen apprehension, and his tenacious memory, soon lifted him above his school-fellows. In his leisure hours he applied himself with particular delight to the study of history and poetry; and we are pleased to conjecture that his eloquence owed some of its imaginative colouring to his frequent perusal of the old chivalrous romances, such as the " Palemerin of England " and " Don Belianis of Greece." It is not necessary for an orator to be a poet, or for a poet to be an orator ; but I am disposed to believe that every great poet must possess the oratorical instinct, as Homer, Milton, and Shakespeare possessed it, and that a great orator must have a certain measure of the poetic insight, as was the case with Demosthenes and Cicero, with Chatham and with Burke. The last-named, like most lads with a literary taste, made several attempts in verse during his school days—beginning a drama on the story of King Alfred, and translating the idyll of Theocritus on the death of Adonis.

The schoolmaster at Ballitore was a man of capacity and enlightenment ; and it seems to have been by him that Burke was early indoctrinated in the principle of tolerance, and from him that he imbibed his enthusiasm for civil and religious freedom. In one of his House of Commons speeches he remarked, that he had been educated as a Protestant of the Church of England, by a Dissenter who was an honour to his sect [the Society of

Friends], though that sect was one of the purest. Under his eye he had read the Bible, morning, noon, and night, and had ever since been the happier and the better for such reading. The lad afterwards turned his attention to the theological treatises of all shades of opinion that had been so ably written in the last and present century; but eventually discovering, that they confounded and bewildered instead of instructing and assisting him, he had thrown them aside, resolved to hold firmly the faith of the Church of England. But towards Protestant Nonconformists, as towards Romanists, he cherished the most equitable feelings, and protested against any restriction being placed upon the rights of conscience.

In April, 1743, Burke entered Trinity College, Dublin, as a pensioner.* He took his degree as Bachelor of Arts in 1748, and as Master of Arts in 1751. As a student his tastes disposed him to devote his time and energies to the classics, history, metaphysics, and general literature. He had the good sense to be partial to a well-written novel, and, as might have been expected of so judicious a critic, he preferred Fielding and Smollett to Richardson. He read Le Sage with pleasure, as well as Addison, and, of course, Shakespeare. In a letter written about this time he expresses his strong admiration of Plutarch. Among the Greek orators he preferred Demosthenes, and among the Greek dramatists Sophocles. He placed a higher value upon the Greek historians than upon the Latin. I suppose it was the picturesqueness and amplitude of Thucydides which pleased him more than the terse and thought-weighted sentences of Tacitus. To Lucretius, Virgil, and Horace he was exceedingly

---

* Oliver Goldsmith was one of his contemporaries.

partial. That he regarded the Æneid as superior to the Iliad, most scholars will consider a serious error of taste ; but he modified his judgment to some extent by admitting that the elder poet surpassed the younger in sublimity, strength, and invention. If it be true that a man is known by the company he keeps, it is still more true that the bent of his genius and the strain of his character may be ascertained from the books he reads ; and therefore Burke's literary partialities become a matter of interest to his biographer.

The reader will not object, perhaps, to a specimen of Burke's powers as a versifier and translator. While at Trinity College he rendered the latter portion of Virgil's second Georgic into English heroic couplets. That his version is equal to Dryden's we cannot allow, but it is very smooth and correct :—

> " Oh, happy swains ! did they know how to prize
> The many blessings rural life supplies ;
> When in safe huts from clattering arms afar,
> The pomp of cities and the din of war,
> Indulgent earth, to pay his labouring hand,
> Pours in his arms the blessings of the land.
> Calm through the valley flows along his life,
> He knows no danger, as he knows no strife.
> What ! though no marble portals, rooms of state,
> Vomit the cringing torrent from his gate ;
> Though no proud purple hang his stately halls,
> Nor lives the breathing brass along his walls,
> Though the sheep clothe him without colour's aid,
> Nor seeks he foreign luxury from trade ;
> Yet peace and honesty adorn his days _
> With rural riches and a life of ease."

Burke's earliest published effort, however, was, fitly enough, of a political character. In 1749, just before leaving Trinity College, he attacked the pretentious

productions of Henry Brooke, the author of a dull tragedy
on the subject of "Gustavus Vasa," which gained a temporary popularity by its application to Sir Robert Walpole.

Being designed for the legal profession, Burke repaired
to London, to keep his terms in the Middle Temple.
During the next two or three years he studied deeply, so
that he became fully conversant with the scientific principles of jurisprudence, and acquired a wide and accurate
knowledge of English law. This knowledge proved of
very considerable value to him in his after-career, and the
influence of it may be traced in many of his speeches and
writings. Thus, though he never practised as a barrister,
or as an advocate sought the suffrages of juries, he fairly
deserves to rank among the "learned in the law." One
cannot but wonder that English gentlemen do not more
generally include a study of the law in their educational
curriculum ; and especially would it seem to be a desirable, nay, an indispensable preliminary for all who aim
at playing a part in public life. The relations between
classes would assuredly be improved if our local authorities,
who have so much to do with the working of the social
machinery,—our guardians, justices of the peace, and
civil magistrates,—knew even the mere elements of
jurisprudence.

But Burke was all-embracing in his range of knowledge.
His studies, as Mr. Buckle remarks, not only covered the
whole field of political inquiry, but extended to an
immense variety of subjects, which, though apparently
unconnected with politics, do in reality bear upon them
as important adjuncts ; since, to a philosophic mind, every
branch of knowledge lights up even those that seem most
remote from it. "Thus it is, that while his insight into
the philosophy of jurisprudence had gained the applause

of lawyers, his acquaintance with the whole range and
theory of the fine arts has won the admiration of artists ;
a striking combination of two pursuits, often, though
erroneously, held to be incompatible with each other." *
" The excursions of his genius," as Robert Hall says,†
" were immense.   His imperial fancy laid all nature
under tribute, and collected riches from every source of
the creation and every walk of art."   Or to put it in the
language of Wilberforce :—" The field from which he drew
his illustrations was magnificent.   Like the fabled object
of the fairy's favours, whenever he opened his mouth
pearls and diamonds dropped from him."   Sir Joshua
Reynolds considered him ‡ the best judge of pictures he
ever knew ; and Winstanley, the Camden Professor of
Ancient History, remarks § that it would have been
difficult to have met with a person who knew more than
Burke did of the philosophy, the history, the filiation of
language, or of the principles of etymological deduction.
And, to close this accumulation of evidence which Burke's
own writings render superfluous, Charles James Fox
asserted ‖ that if he had put all the political information
he had gathered from books, all that he had gained from
science, and all which any knowledge of the world and its
affairs had taught him, into one scale, and the improvement which he had derived from Burke's instruction and
conversation were placed in the other, he should have
been at a loss to decide to which to give the preference.
   Burke would seem to have given up all thought of the

* Buckle, " History of Civilisation," i. 413-416.
† Mr. Robert Hall, " Works," p. 190.
‡ *Annual Register* for 1798, p. 329.
§ Prior, " Life of Burke," p. 427.
‖ " Parliamentary History," xxviii. 363.

law as a career, in 1753, when, it is said, he applied for
the professorship of logic at Glasgow, but was unsuccessful.  He had already made a reputation among London
men of letters and London actors, and we read of Garrick
and Macklin, and Murphy the playwright, as among his
associates.  It is believed that at this time he contributed
to various periodicals; but his first avowed work, the
"Vindication of Natural Society," was not published
until 1756.  Both in conception and execution it was
original, though the idea has since had numerous imitations.  The style is deliberately modelled upon Lord
Bolingbroke's; and the object of the book is to expose
the fallacy of Bolingbroke's atheistic theories by pushing
them to their extreme but natural consequences.  So
admirably was the parody accomplished as to deceive at
first both Chesterfield and Bishop Warburton; the imitation is carried not only into the structure of the language,
but into the train of thought and method of argument.
And it is a curious fact, that not a few of the speculations
which Burke satirically bases on the dazzling but unsound
hypotheses of Bolingbroke, were afterwards seriously
adopted by that school of pseudo-philosophers which
found its Bible in the *Encyclopédie*.

A few months later appeared the once famous " Philosophical Inquiry into the Origin of our Ideas of the
Sublime and Beautiful."  Its popularity was immediate;
it was read in every polite circle, and discussed by every
literary club.  Not to have read it would have branded a
man with ignorance as unmistakably as in our own time
an ignorance of the writings of George Eliot would do.
Men of mark sought the acquaintance of its author, who
on his list of friends was soon able to inscribe the names
of Hume, Lord Lyttelton, Soame Jenyns, the author of

the "Origin of Evil," Bishop Warburton, Sir Joshua Reynolds, and Dr. Johnson. The author of "Rasselas" seems to have loved Burke as he loved Topham Beauclerk. At one time he spoke of him as the only man whose common conversation corresponded with the general fame he had in the world. At another time he would assert that no man of sense could meet Mr. Burke by accident, under a gateway, without being convinced that he was the first man in England. He was one of the first to recognise the merits of the "Philosophical Inquiry," which he pronounced a model of true and refined criticism. Posterity, however, has not endorsed this high eulogium. On the contrary, it holds that many of the canons put forward are erroneous, and not a few of the illustrations inapposite. At the very threshold, we take exception to our author's definitions of Beauty and Sublimity, as neither very precise, nor, which is more important, very accurate. Again, his analysis of their effects upon the mind cannot be considered satisfactory; it lacks comprehension and insight. Further, the style is repellantly bare and frigid ; and the most attractive lines of thought are followed up with a coldness and lack of animation usually supposed to be peculiar to theological statements of dogmatic difficulties. It is, as Macaulay says, the most unadorned—and not, therefore, adorned the most— of all Burke's writings; and this, though it belongs to a period of life when authors are generally prone to luxuriance of imagery and pomp of language. In truth, the reader feels chilled and dissatisfied with the coldness, the want of emotion, the absence of sympathy, which Burke exhibits while discoursing upon the influence of mountains, forests, and shining waterfalls, on the glorious masterpieces of Art, and the face and bosom of Beauty.

But from every point of view a page of Ruskin's
"Modern Painters" is worth the whole of Burke's frigid
disquisition.

Prolonged ill-health compelled Burke, in 1756, to
place himself under the care of Dr. Nugent, of Bath, a
man of some distinction both as a physician and a
scholar. Under his roof Burke made the acquaintance
of his daughter, whose graces of mind and person he
quickly learned to appreciate. Their intimacy soon
developed into an affectionate attachment. Burke
offered his hand — was accepted — and his marriage
ensured his domestic felicity. For Mrs. Burke was in all
respects a perfect wife; and those who knew her agreed
that the fond portrait drawn by her husband's loving
admiration did not err from excess of colouring. She
was a refined and cultured woman, with moral strength
of character, and a boundless capacity of loving, equally
fitted to rule in the household or shine in the social
circle, and possessed of an ardent sympathy with everything beautiful, good, and true.*

---

* Here is Burke's portrait-in-words of this admirable and admired
lady :—

"She is handsome, but it is a beauty not arising from features,
from complexion, or from shape. She has all these in a high degree,
but it is not by these she touches the heart; it is all that sweetness
of temper, benevolence, innocence, and sensibility which a face can
express that forms her beauty. She has a face that just raises your
attention at first sight; it grows on you every moment, and you
wonder it did no more than raise your attention at first.

"Her eyes have a mild light, but they awe when she pleases; they
command, like a good man out of office, not by authority, but by
virtue.

"Her stature is not tall ; she is not made to be the admiration of
everybody, but the happiness of one.

Though Burke had gained the attention of the reading public and the respect of literary society, he could not maintain his position without an arduous struggle. He

---

"She has all the firmness that does not exclude delicacy; she has all the softness that does not imply weakness.

"Her voice is a soft low music, not formed to rule in public assemblies, but to charm those who can distinguish a company from a crowd; it has this advantage—you must be close to her to hear it.

"To describe her body describes her mind—one is the transcript of the other; her understanding is not shown in the variety of matters it exerts itself on, but in the goodness of the choice she makes.

"She does not display it so much in saying or doing striking things, as in avoiding such as she ought not to say or do. . . .

"Her politeness flows rather from a natural disposition to oblige than from any rules on that subject, and therefore never fails to strike those who understand good breeding and those who do not.

"She discovers the right and wrong of things not by reasoning but by sagacity. She never disgraces her good nature by severe reflections on anybody, so she never degrades her judgment by immoderate or ill-placed praises.

"She has a steady and firm mind, which takes no more from the beauty of the female character than the solidity of marble does from its polish and lustre. She has such virtues as make us value the truly great of our own sex. She has all the winning graces that make us love even the faults we see in the weaker and beautiful,—in hers."

Compare with this Tennyson's picture of a perfect wife in his "Isabel:"—

> "The intuitive decision of a bright
> And thorough-edgèd intellect to part
> Error from crime. . . .
> A love still burning upward, giving light
> To read those laws; an accent very low
> In blandishment, but a most silver flow
> Of subtle-pacèd counsel in distress,
> Right to the heart and brain, though undescried;
> A courage to endure and to obey;
> A hate of gossip, parlance, and of sway."

Q

exercised his pen with persistent industry, compiling for the bookseller, Dodsley, the "Annual Register," at a yearly salary of £100, in which it is difficult to decide whether his record of contemporary history or his dispassionate judgments upon public men evince the finer art. He also prepared an "Account of the European Settlements in America," and began an "Abridgment of English History," which shows strong traces of his study of Montesquieu. It is certain, however, that, as an historian, he would not have made any permanent record in English literature. His genius was essentially oratorical, and he felt that public life was the sphere for which his abilities fitted him and his studies had prepared him. He waited patiently for his opportunity. It came to Burke as it comes to every man who waits. In 1759 he was introduced by his friend, the Earl of Charlemont, to Gerard Hamilton, better known as "Single-speech Hamilton," in allusion to a remarkable oration with which he had astonished and delighted the House of Commons, afterwards becoming as silent as an extinct volcano.* Hamilton was fully competent to appreciate Burke's great powers, and, having been appointed Chief Secretary for Ireland, he invited him to go to Dublin, partly as his private secretary, and partly as his friend.

In both capacities his services proved so valuable, and at first were so highly esteemed, that in 1763 he was granted a pension of £300 on the Irish Establishment. Within a twelvemonth, however, this payment was made by Hamilton an excuse for claims which Burke would not acknowledge, and for conduct which he warmly resented. With characteristic independence, he imme-

---

* In the Irish Parliament, however, he made several speeches of great eloquence.

diately resigned his pension, and broke off all connection with his patron. "The occasion of our difference," he wrote to a friend, "was not any act whatsoever on my part; it was entirely on his, by a voluntarily but most insolent and intolerable demand, amounting to no less than a claim of servitude during the whole course of my life, without leaving me at any time a power either of getting forward with honour, or of retiring with tranquillity." He took leave of Hamilton in a dignified letter which, many years afterwards, Hamilton candidly confessed was one of the finest compositions he had ever read. The definite cause of this strange quarrel has never been ascertained, but certain it is that, to the last, Burke considered himself to have been unjustly and even insolently treated.

Returning to England in 1764, Burke renewed his friendly intercourse with wits and politicians. In May he founded, in conjunction with Sir Joshua Reynolds, the "Literary Club," in imitation of that famous gathering at "the Monument," which had witnessed the *symposia* of Shakespeare and Ben Jonson, and that other coterie at Will's coffee-house, where Pope knelt at the feet of Dryden. Among its members was Burke's old fellow-collegian, Oliver Goldsmith. In the following year our rising politician accepted the post of private secretary to the Marquis of Rockingham, when that right-minded but somewhat ordinary nobleman was placed at the head of the Government.

"Being in a very private station," he said some nine years later, "free enough from any line of business, and not having the honour of a seat in this House, it was my fortune, unknowing and unknown to the then ministry, by the intervention of a common friend, to become connected with a very noble person, then at the head of the Treasury Department. It was indeed in a situation of little rank and no consequence, suitable to the mediocrity of my talents and pretensions. But a situation near enough to make me to see, as well as others, what was going on; and I did see in that noble person such sound principles, such an enlargement of mind, such clear and sagacious sense, and such unshaken fortitude, as have bound me, as well as others much better than me, by an inviolable attachment to him from that time forward. "

When the appointment was made, the Duke of Newcastle, on hearing of it, shuffled off to Rockingham with a warning to be on his guard against the adventurer, who, he said, was a wild Irishman, a concealed Papist, a Jesuit, a Jacobite, and, worst of all, an O'Bourke! Rockingham smilingly put aside these ridiculous calumnies, and at his instance Burke was brought into Parliament as member for Wendover, in Buckinghamshire. The times were out of joint; for the ill-advised measures of the Grenville Administration, and the obstinacy of the king in wrong-doing, had brought the American colonies to the brink of rebellion. It was in a debate upon American affairs (January 14th, 1766), that Burke first addressed that House which he was afterwards so frequently to astonish and delight, and sometimes, be it said, to weary, by the copiousness of his splendid oratory. The fire, force, and freedom with which he spoke, attracted the attention and called forth the commendation of the elder Pitt, who, though shattered in health, wrapped up in flannels, and leaning on his crutch, delivered one of those noble orations that exercised such an influence over his contemporaries. "He had himself," he said, "intended to enter at length into the details, but he had been anticipated with so much ingenuity and elo-

quence that there was little left for him to say." Severa
times in the course of the session Burke joined in the
debates, and each time with such success as to convince
the Whig party of the value of their new recruit. Sir
John Hawkins, author of a "History of Music," now
chiefly remembered through Dr. Callcott's popular
" catch," took occasion, at the Literary Club, to express
his surprise at Burke's rapidly increasing reputation.
"Sir," said Dr. Johnson, "there is no wonder at all.
We who know Mr. Burke know that he will be one of
the first men in the country." And, writing to his
friend Langton, he said:—"We have less of Burke's
company since he has been engaged in public business,
in which he has gained more reputation than perhaps
any man at his first appearance ever gained before. He
made two speeches in the House for repealing the Stamp
Act, which were publicly commended by Mr. Pitt, and
have filled the town with wonder. . . . Burke is a great
man by nature, and is expected soon to attain civil
greatness."

Coldly supported, if indeed not secretly opposed, by the
sovereign, and baffled by the intrigues of the party which
arrogated to themselves the title of " the king's friends,"
the Rockingham ministry fell in July, 1766, and was
succeeded by a government, of which Pitt (with the
title of Earl of Chatham), was the virtual head. Burke
went on a visit to Ireland, and did not return to
England until the opening of Parliament in November.
Chatham then offered him a seat at the Board of Trade ;
but he appears to have felt himself bound to the ex-
Premier, and refused the great Minister's offer. Perhaps
he felt that he enjoyed more power and independence in
the House of Commons as the recognised leader of the

" Rockingham Whigs," than he could have done as a
subordinate official.  But I do not see that any justification can be alleged for the hostility with which he and
his party embarrassed the measures of Lord Chatham,
and played into the hands of the Opposition.

   In the new Parliament, which met in May, 1768,
Burke again took his seat as member for Wendover.  At
the same time he purchased, for a sum of £20,000, part
of which was advanced by the Marquis of Rockingham,
the agreeable residence and small estate of the Gregories,
near Beaconsfield, in Buckinghamshire.  After a painful
interregnum, caused by his bodily infirmities, which had
temporarily enfeebled his intellectual powers, Chatham
resigned office in October, 1768, and was succeeded by
the Duke of Grafton, with the support of the Duke of
Bedford's party.  The new Cabinet plunged Parliament
into a contest with the country on the question of
Wilkes's election for Middlesex.  Burke united with
George Grenville in resisting the illegal and unconstitutional votes by which Wilkes was expelled from the
House, and the electors of Middlesex deprived of their
legal rights.  On other points he was generally opposed
to Grenville, who was a reactionist of the sternest type,
and in a remarkable pamphlet he exposed the fallacies,
and replied to the attacks of Grenville's diatribe, " On
the Present State of the Nation."  Such was the
cogency of Burke's argument, and such the strength
and eloquence of his language, that many began to suspect him as the author of those celebrated " Letters of
Junius," which had just begun to make their appearance.
But neither the style of these " Letters," nor the spirit,
is the style or spirit of Burke.  They fall infinitely
below the standard of his genius and his public virtue.

He would never have stooped to their coarse personalities; he would never have condescended to their misrepresentations. He was no midnight murderer, to stab a reputation with a secret dagger. I am not called upon to discuss in these pages the vexed question of the authorship of the "Letters," but it has sometimes occurred to us that, in all probability, and in spite of some vapouring expressions in his private correspondence with his printer, the writer may have been some less distinguished person than is supposed. Certainly the evidence adduced to connect them with Sir Philip Francis is not without a flaw. At all events, their renown is wholly out of proportion to their real merits. They are conspicuously deficient in political sagacity and knowledge; their strength lies in their deliberate and envenomed attacks upon individuals, and much of their former influence and present reputation is due to the mystery with which they were artfully surrounded.

Having to some extent recovered his physical and mental faculties, Chatham reappeared on the political stage in 1770. He found the Dukes of Grafton and Bedford in office, with Lord North as Chancellor of the Exchequer. He found the country convulsed with anger at the persecution of Wilkes, pushed on by the Court and the House of Commons. He found the American colonies in stern revolt against the measures of taxation projected by the Government. Wherever he looked, he saw the horizon black with clouds. His first care was to attempt the reconciliation of the two sections of the Opposition, the Grenville and the Rockingham, which had so long been at open feud, in order that a combined attack might be made upon the Government. He declared that a new ministry must be formed upon

Whig principles, with the Rockinghams, and Cavendishes, and other old Whig families to be represented in its combination. Earl Temple adopted the same opinion, and, in an interview which he had with Burke, urged that the past should be forgotten. "We have done each other," he said, "a thousand acts of unkindness; let us make amends by a thousand acts of friendship." Rockingham and Burke did not at first show any great willingness to accept these overtures; but the two parties in the House of Commons adopted to some extent a common plan of action, and were rapidly beginning to understand and draw nearer each other, when the death of Chatham convulsed the political world. A new order of things dated from that calamity; new combinations sprang into existence; old traditions were broken up by new prejudices and animosities; and for the next twelve years the political history of England was a history of disaster and intrigue, selfishness, incapacity, and ignorance.

But we are proceeding too rapidly.

In the session of 1770, Burke spoke frequently. On the 1st of May he introduced eight resolutions in condemnation of the folly and indecency with which Ministers had mismanaged the contention between the mother-country and the colonies. A few days later he supported George Grenville's bill for the regulation of controverted elections. It was about this time that he published his famous pamphlet, "On the Cause of the Present Discontents," which has been justly described as unequalled for the variety and depth of its political knowledge, and the ornate yet vigorous beauty of its style. It has, not inaptly, been characterised as "a text-book of Whig principles." A philosophical moderation permeates every page, and while a severe invective is delivered against Court influences and intrigues, not less severe is the censure bestowed on the revolutionary schemes of democratic agitators. A felicitous defence of party ties, as essential to the security of a constitutional system, is counterbalanced by an ingenious, though certainly not a successful, argument against Parliamentary reform. Burke once said that he pitched his Whiggism low, that he might not be tempted to deviate from it; and in this celebrated essay, unquestionably it never rises very high. It is the Whiggism of the practical statesman rather than of a philosophical theorist; of a statesman who recognised the disorders of the time, and was prepared to apply the necessary remedies, but felt no inclination to deal with hypothetical maladies. He had not as yet adopted those strong unmonarchical opinions, which in some of his later writings are so disagreeably prominent, colouring the whole of his political system. Nor had he yet fallen into the vice of his later style, that extravagance of imagery and luxuriance of verbiage which embarrass and oppress it. Thoughts luminous and deep are embodied in language refined and elevated, are impressed upon the reader by terse and apposite illustration. We venture to quote a few isolated sentences, marked by a *curiosa felicitas* of expression :—

" We have not relegated Religion to obscure municipalities or rustic villages. No! we will have her to exalt her mitred front in Courts and Parliaments."

" A great deal of the furniture of ancient tyranny is worn to rags ; the rest is entirely out of fashion."

" No lines can be laid down for civil or political wisdom. They are a matter incapable of exact definition."

" The king is the representative of the people ; so are the lords ; so are the judges ; they are all trustees for the people, as well as the commons, because no power is given for the sole sake of the holder ; and although government is certainly an institution of divine authority, yet its forms, and the persons who administer it, all originate from the people."

" It is no inconsiderable part of wisdom to know how much of an evil ought to be tolerated ; lest by attempting a degree of purity impracticable in degenerate times and manners, instead of cutting off the subsisting ill practices, new conceptions might be produced for the concealment and security of the old."

Burke's pamphlet was answered from the Tory standpoint by Dr. Johnson, and from the Republican by Mrs. Macaulay ; but while their compositions are forgotten, Burke's is still read and admired. As Lord Brougham says :—" It is the best weighed and most deliberately pronounced, the calmest of all his productions, and the most fully considered."

In the session of 1770-71, Burke delivered one of his finest speeches in denunciation of the power then possessed by the Attorney-General of filing *ex-officio* informations ; a power which had been employed against Almon, the bookseller, for publishing the " Letters of Junius to the King." In this speech runs a fine reference to *Junius*, which seems to us a fair example of Burke's earlier and chaster style :—

" How comes this Junius to have broke through the cobwebs of the law, and to range uncontrolled, unpunished, through the land ? The myrmidons of the court have been long, and are still pursuing him in vain. They will not spend their time upon me or upon you, when the mighty boar of the forest that has broke through all their toils is before them. But what will all their efforts avail ? No sooner has he wounded one, than he strikes down another dead at his feet. For my own part, when I saw his attack upon the king, I own my blood ran cold. I thought he had ventured too far, and that there was an end to his triumphs ; not that he had not asserted many bold truths. Yes, sir, there are in that composition many bold truths by which a wise prince might profit. It was the rancour and venom with which I was struck. But while I expected from this daring flight his final ruin and fall, behold him rising still higher, and coming down *souse* upon both Houses of Parliament. Yes, he made you his quarry ; and you still bleed from the effects of his talons. You crouched, and still crouch beneath his rage. Nor has he dreaded the terror of your brow, sir,* for he has attacked even you ; and I believe you have no reason to triumph in the encounter. Not content with carrying our royal eagle away in his pounces, and dashing him against a rock, he has laid you prostrate, and king, lords, and commons thus become but the sport of his fury. Were he a member of this House, what might not be expected from his knowledge, his firmness, and his integrity ? He would be easily known by his contempt of all danger, by his penetration, and by his vigour. Nothing would escape his vigilance and activity. But ministers could conceal nothing from his sagacity, nor could promises nor threats induce him to conceal anything from the public."

At this time Burke was the acknowledged leader of his party. He had not yet exhausted the attention of the House by his excursive prolixity and endless " refining ;" and in all the political questions which came before Parliament, he displayed the vast scope of his intellectual powers, the breadth of his sympathies, and the soundness of his judgment. As yet the French Revolution had not thrown him off his balance ; he was fully master of himself and his resources, *totus in se.* The State of New

---

* An allusion to the heavy black eyebrows of the Speaker, Sir Fletcher Norton.

York recognised the generosity and vigour of his defence of colonial liberties by appointing him its agent (1771). He was on the side of freedom as against privilege when the House of Commons unwisely attempted to prohibit the publication of reports of its proceedings, and summoned to its bar the printers of the principal London newspapers.* In this warfare Colonel Onslow was foremost ; he had been ridiculed as " little Cockney George," and his *amour propre* grievously wounded. To his motion for summoning the printers, a member moved an amendment to the effect that they should bring with them their " compositors, pressmen, correctors, blackers, and devils ; " and Burke supported it, remarking, " It would be as irregular for the printer to come to your bar without them, as it would be for you, sir, to come to the House without your mace, or a Marshal of the King's Bench without his tipstaff, or a First Lord of the Treasury without his majority." When Colonel Onslow boasted of the part he had played as specially befitting one who was descended from three Speakers, Burke retorted :— " I have not the advantage of a parliamentary genealogy. I was not born, like the honourable gentleman, with ' Order ' running through my veins. But as that gentleman boasts of his father, his son will never boast of *him*. The parliamentary line is cut off." It is needless to say that the House was beaten in the struggle, and did not retire from it without some loss of dignity.

We again find Burke on the side of moderation and enlightenment when, in 1772, a proposal was submitted for the relief of Dissenting ministers from the necessity of subscribing the Thirty-Nine Articles. This he fervidly

---

* The three papers attacked were the *Gazetteer*, the *Middlesex Chronicle*, and the *London Evening Post*.

supported, while at the same time opposing the concession of a similar relief to clergymen of the Established Church, because their subscription was the condition under which they held their benefices.   In 1773, when advocating a further measure of relief, he defined in beautiful language what he conceived to be the true position and duty of the Church of England.

" At the same time," he said, " that I would cut up the very roots of Atheism, I would respect all conscience—all conscience that is really such, and which perhaps its very tenderness proves to be sincere.   I wish to see the Established Church of England great and powerful ; I wish to see her foundations laid low and deep, that she may crush the giant powers of rebellious darkness ; I would have her head raised up to that heaven to which she conducts me.   I would have her open wide her hospitable gates by a noble and liberal comprehension, but I would have no breaches in her wall ; I would have her cherish all those who are within, and pity all those who are without ; I would have her a common blessing to the world, an example, if not an instructor, to those who have not the happiness to belong to her ; I would have her give a lesson of peace to mankind, that a vexed and wandering generation might be taught to seek for repose and toleration in the maternal bosom of Christian charity, and not in the harlot lap of infidelity and indifference.   Nothing has driven people more into that house of seduction than the mutual hatred of Christian congregations.   Long may we enjoy our Church under a learned and edifying Episcopacy."

In the debates upon the affairs of British India, which occupied the House in the Session of 1773, Burke gave astonishing proof of the variety and extent of his information, and the statesman-like breadth and solidity of his views.   During the recess he paid a visit to Paris, and saw the young queen, Marie Antoinette, in all the grace

and radiance of her young beauty. He was appalled by
the social disorganisation which had overtaken the
country, and especially by the absolute contempt into
which religion had fallen; and in the following session of
Parliament he took occasion to point out this "conspiracy of Atheism" to the vigilance of Government. Though
it was contrary to his political principles to call in the aid
of the secular arm to suppress doctrines and opinions, yet,
if ever it were raised, he said, it should be against those
enemies of their kind, who would take from man the
noblest prerogative of his nature—that of being a religious animal. "Already, under the systematic attacks of
these men, I see many of the props of good government
beginning to fail. I see propagated principles which
will not leave to religion even a toleration, and make
virtue herself less than a name."

The dispute between England and her American
colonies was daily assuming a graver character, and the
Whig statesmen perceived that an amicable settlement
of it was essential to the honour and security of the
mother-country. The rift, at first so inconsiderable, was
rapidly broadening, and threatened to open into a chasm
which it would be impossible to close up or bridge over.
In December 1773, when the English tea-ships arrived
at Boston, the townsmen boarded them at night, and
threw their cargoes into the sea. The news of this decisive act reached England in January. The Government
unhappily determined at once on a policy of repression,
while the Opposition urged the adoption of a policy of
conciliation. Burke in vain poured forth his most vehement
eloquence in support of moderate measures. It had been
said that the tax upon tea imposed by the English Government, which was the *fons et origo mali,* not in itself,

but in the principle underlying it—the principle of taxation *without* representation—was trifling :—

"Could anything," said Burke, "be a subject of more just
alarm to America than to see you go out of the plain highroad
of finance, and give up your most certain revenues and your
dearest interest, merely for the sake of insulting your colonies?
No man ever doubted that the commodity of tea would bear an
imposition of threepence. But no commodity will bear threepence, or will bear a penny, when the general feelings of men
are irritated, and two millions of people are resolved not to pay.
The feelings of the colonies were probably the feelings of Great
Britain. Theirs were formerly the feelings of Mr. Hampden,
when called upon for the payment of twenty shillings. Would
twenty shillings have ruined Mr. Hampden's fortune? No!
but the payment of half twenty shillings, on the principle it was
demanded, would have made him a slave."

Referring to a speech made by Lord Carmarthen—
his maiden speech—Burke continued :—

"A noble lord, who spoke some time ago, is full of the fire
of ingenuous youth; and when he has modelled the ideas of a
lively imagination by further experience, he will be an ornament to his country in either House. He has said that the
Americans are our children, and how can they revolt against
their parent? He says that if they are not free in their present
state, England is not free; because Manchester and other considerable places are not represented. So then, because some
towns in England are not represented, America is to have no
representative at all. They are 'our children,' but when children ask for bread, we are not to give a stone. Is it because the
natural resistance of things, and the various mutations of time,
hinder our Government, or any scheme of government, from being
any more than a sort of approximation to the right—is it therefore
that the colonies are to recede from it infinitely? When this child
of ours wishes to assimilate to its parent, and to reflect with a true

filial resemblance the beauteous countenance of British liberty,
are we to turn to them the shameful parts of our constitution?
Are we to give them our weakness for their strength, our opprobrium for their glory, and the slough of slavery, which we are
not able to work off, to serve them for their freedom?"

In the session of 1775 Burke introduced a series of
thirteen resolutions, founded on a bill drawn by Chatham,*
and embodying a proposal for a pacific settlement of the
points in dispute between England and America. The
House rejected them by a majority of 270 against 78
(March 22, 1775). Burke's speech in explanation and
support was one of his finest bursts of argumentative
eloquence, and I do not know that in any other of his
orations the great qualities of his genius are more
abundantly shown :—

"My proposition," he said, "is peace. Not peace through
the medium of war; not peace to be hunted through the laby-
rinth of intricate and endless negotiations; not peace to arise
out of universal discord, fomented on principle in all parts of
the empire. Not peace to depend on the judicial determination
of perplexing questions, or the precise marking of the shadowy
boundaries of a complex government. It is simple peace,
sought in its natural course, and in its ordinary haunts. It is
peace, sought in the spirit of peace."

Again:

"I look on force not only as an odious but as a feeble instrument for preserving a people so numerous, so active, so growing,
so spirited as this, in a profitable and subordinate connection
with us. First, the use of force alone is but temporary. It may
subdue for a moment, but it does not remove the necessity of

---

* "A provisional Bill for settling the troubles in America," introduced into the House of Lords, February 1.

subduing again. A nation is not governed, which is perpetually to be governed."

He added :—

"Three thousand miles of ocean lie between you and the colonies. No contrivance can weaken the effect of this distance in weakening government. Seas roll and months pass between the order and the execution ; and the want of a speedy explanation on a single point is enough to defeat a whole system. You have, indeed, winged ministers of vengeance who carry your bolts in their talons to the uttermost verge of the sea. But then a power steps in, which limits the arrogance of raging passions and furious elements, and says, 'So far shalt thou go, and no farther!' Who are you that should fret and rage, and bite the chains of nature? Nothing more happens to you than does to all nations who have extensive empire. From all these causes a fierce spirit of liberty has grown up. The question is, not whether the spirit deserves praise or blame, but what, in the name of God, shall we do with it? You have before you the object, such as it is, with all its glories, all its imperfections on its head. We are strongly urged to determine something concerning it."

In a splendid passage he adverted to the remarkable growth of the American colonies, in an allusion to the aged Earl Bathurst,* father of the then Lord Chancellor :—

"We stand where we have an immense view of what is, and what is past. Clouds, indeed, and darkness rest upon the future. Let us, however, before we descend from this noble eminence, reflect that this growth of our national prosperity has happened within the short period of the life of man. It has happened within sixty-eight years. There are those alive whose memory

---

* This was the Allen, Lord Bathurst, to whom Pope addressed his "Epistle on the Use of Riches."

might touch the two extremities. For instance, my Lord
Bathurst might remember all the stages of the progress. He
was, in 1704, of an age at least to be made to comprehend such
things. He was then old enough *acta parentum jam legere, et
quæ sit cognoscere virtus.* Suppose, sir, that the angel of this
auspicious youth, foreseeing the many virtues which made him
one of the most fortunate men of his age, had opened to him in
a vision that, when, in the fourth generation, the third prince of·
the House of Brunswick had sat twelve years on the throne of
that nation which (by the happy issue of moderate and healing
counsels) was to be made Great Britain, he should see his son,
Lord Chancellor of England, turn back the current of hereditary
dignity to its fountain, and raise him to a higher rank of peerage, whilst he enriched the family with a new one. If amidst
these bright and happy scenes of honour and prosperity, that
angel should have drawn up the curtain, and unfolded the rising
glories of his country, and whilst he was gazing with admiration on the then commercial grandeur of England, the genius
should point out to him a little speck, scarce visible in the mass
of the national interest, a small seminal principle rather than a
formed body, and should tell him, ' Young man, there is America,
which at this day serves for little more than to amuse you with
stories of savage men and uncouth manners ; yet shall, before you
taste of death, show itself equal to the whole of that commerce
which now attracts the envy of the world. Whatever England
has been growing to by a progressive increase of improvement
brought in by varieties of people, by succession of civilising
conquests and civilising settlements, in a series of seventeen
hundred years, you shall see as much added to her by America
in the course of a single life !' If the state of his country had
thus been foretold to him, would it not require all the sanguine
credulity of youth, and all the fervid glow of enthusiasm, to
make him believe it ? "

In another speech on American affairs, discussing the
alleged right of taxation, which the Ministerial orators

described as inherent in the mother-country, Burke said :—

"I do not examine whether the giving away a man's money be a power excepted and reserved out of the general trust of Government, and how far all forms of policy are entitled to an exercise of that right by the charter of nature. Or whether, on the contrary, the right of taxation is necessarily involved in the general principle of legislation, and inseparable from the ordinary supreme power. These are deep questions when great names militate against each other ; when reason is perplexed ; and an appeal to authorities only thickens the confusion. For high and reverend authorities lift up their heads on both sides, and there is no sure footing in the middle. This point is

> 'The great Serbonian bog,
> 'Twixt Dalmiata and Mount Casius old,
> Where armies whole have sunk.'

I do not intend to be overwhelmed in that bog, though in such respectable company. The question with me is not whether you have a right to render your people miserable, but whether it is not your interest to make them happy. It is not what a lawyer tells me I *may* do, but what humanity, reason, and justice tell me I *ought* to do. Is a politic art the worse for being a generous one ? Is no concession proper but that which is made from your want of right to keep what you grant ? Or does it lessen the grace and dignity of relaxing in the exercise of an odious claim, because you have your evidence-room full of titles, and your magazines stuffed with arms to enforce them ?

"What signify all these titles and all these arms : Of what avail are they when the reason of the thing tells me that the assertion of my title is the loss of my suit ; and that I could do nothing but wound myself by the use of my own weapons ? Such is steadfastly my opinion of the absolute necessity of keeping up the concord of this empire by a union of spirit, though in a diversity of operations, that if I were sure the colonists had,

at their leaving this country, sealed a regular compact of servitude; that they had solemnly abjured all the rights of citizens; that they had made a vow to renounce all ideas of liberty
for them and their posterity to all generations, yet I should hold
myself obliged to conform to the temper I found universally
prevalent in my own day, and to govern two millions of men
impatient of servitude on the principles of freedom.  I am not
determining a point of law; I am restoring tranquillity; and the
general character and situation of a people must determine what
sort of government is fitted for them."

In spite of the eloquence and arguments of Burke and
Chatham, Lord North's disastrous government persevered
in its efforts to subdue the rebellion of the colonists, until
France and Spain leagued with the United States to crush
and humiliate their great adversary and rival.  History
records with what courage, with how much hopeless
persistency England faced this formidable coalition ; and
how, while the incapacity of her commanders and the
blind policy of her Ministers overwhelmed her with
disgrace in the West, the honour of her arms was retrieved,
and the valour of her sons vindicated, by her triumphs in
the East, where the bold, audacious, yet wary genius of
Warren Hastings laid firm and sure the foundations of her
Indian Empire.  The surrender of Lord Cornwallis's army
at York Town to the American forces under Washington
(October 19, 1772), was " the beginning of the end."
England was exhausted and over-weighted; and only the
naval victories of Rodney saved her from a shameful
peace.  As it was, bleeding at every pore, she found
herself compelled, in November, 1772, to sign the Treaties
of Paris and Versailles, by which she recognised the
Independence of America.

The result, I imagine, was as painful to Burke as to

any of his political opponents. Like Chatham, he had never advocated the separation of the colonies, but their conciliation ; and it was only when he saw, as he thought, the liberties of his own country in danger that he came to look upon their independence as a necessity. As Mr. Morley puts it*:—

"All his reflections upon the subject of America, notwithstanding his conviction that her independence was the necessary price of the maintenance of free government in England, must have been tinged with bitterness. Great as America might become, and as he honestly wished her to become, her greatness would bring no renown or laud to the mother-country or its incomparable constitution. Though above the narrow vices incident to patriotism in weaker and less loftily moral souls, it could not have been more grievous to him to look back upon the circumstances under which England and her sons parted company, than it was mortifying to look forward to a glory for America, which, if statesmen had been prescient and nations just, might have been added to the abundant glories of England. Burke, we may be sure, had none of that speculative fortitude which enabled Adam Smith to anticipate with compo- sure the possible removal of the seat of empire to that part of the empire which in a century [from 1776] would probably contribute most to the general defence. He was intellectually capable of foreseeing much which he was not morally capable of allowing himself fully to realise, and certainly not of con- straining himself to dwell upon."

The intellectual activity of Burke was almost as wonderful as is that of our greatest living statesman. He seemed to make every subject his own, and to have something to say upon it better than any specialist could

---

* John Morley, "Edmund Burke : a Historical Study," pp. 162-163.

say. His mind was ever open to new impressions, and
of each rising movement he became, as if by some natural
and unconscious act, the brain and heart. In 1780, he
surprised the House by the breadth and solidity of his
views upon commercial reform, of which he may be said
to have been the Parliamentary pioneer. He declared
his object to be " the reduction of that corrupt influence
which is itself the perennial spring of all prodigality and
all disorder; which loads us more than millions of debt;
which takes away vigour from our arms, wisdom from our
councils, and every shadow of authority and credit from
the most venerable parts of our constitution." It is
sometimes unwise, or at least dangerous, for a man to be
in advance of his contemporaries. Burke had been
returned for Bristol in 1774, but when his constituents
found him protesting against the corruption on which so
many of them fattened, advocating toleration for Roman
Catholics, and denouncing the restrictions which English
jealousy had unfairly imposed upon Irish commerce, they
would have no more of him; his enlightened and liberal
policy offended them; and he was glad to take shelter in
his former seat for the little borough of Malton, which,
during the remainder of his political career, he continued
to represent.

When, in the spring of 1782, it became evident that
the American war could no longer be prosecuted, Lord
North resigned (March 20); and the king was reluctantly compelled to recall to his councils the Marquis of
Rockingham. Through Thurlow, the Lord Chancellor,
he endeavoured at first to make such conditions as would
preserve unimpaired his personal power; but Rockingham insisted upon a change of measures as well as of
men; and that the measures, of which he would require

the king's acceptance, should be those he had advocated while in Opposition. The king, he said, must agree to the recognition of the Independence of the American colonies. Peace and Retrenchment, he said, would form the cardinal principles of his policy; and among the bills which the Cabinet would introduce and press forward would be one for the exclusion of contractors from the House of Commons; another, disqualifying revenue officers from voting at elections; and a third, Burke's great scheme for the better security of the independence of Parliament, and the economical reformation of the civil and other establishments. After some vapouring talk about abdication, the king sent for the Earl of Shelbourne, the leader of the Chatham Whigs, and afterwards for Earl Gower, the leader of the Bedford section; but finding each to be pledged to the union of the party, he was forced to accept Rockingham on his own terms. Charles James Fox took the seals of Secretary of State and the leadership of the Commons. Dunning, an admirable debater, received the Chancellorship of the Duchy of Lancaster, and was created Baron Ashburton. The Chancellorship of the Exchequer devolved upon Lord John Cavendish. Shelbourne was made Secretary of State for Home, Irish, and Colonial affairs. To Burke was given the Paymastership of the Forces, but without a seat in the Cabinet.

There is no doubt that Burke resented this exclusion, and felt indignant at the aristocratic superciliousness of the Whig nobles, who " almost avowedly regarded power as an heirloom in certain houses." But Rockingham probably felt that in the Cabinet he would be dangerous to its amenity; he was impetuous, apt to be dominated too completely by a pre-conceived opinion, hasty in his conclusions, and too easily influenced by a warm and luxuriant imagination. But while these were grave faults, which would certainly have unfitted him for such a post as that of Prime Minister or Foreign Secretary—to neither of which, however, did he aspire—they were just the faults which the responsibility of a Cabinet office would have corrected. And his claims to such promotion were indisputable. Inferior to Charles James Fox in parliamentary tact, in persuasiveness, in the debating faculty, he was his superior in the higher qualities of the highest eloquence. As a philosophic statesman he towered head and shoulders above his contemporaries. He was emphatically a man of ideas, and those ideas were always broad, enlightened, progressive, and exalted. The question of religious freedom, the question of freedom of commerce, the question of the rights of the citizen—these he had made his own, and so completely that most of us now-a-days, like his fellow-candidate at Bristol, do but say " ditto to Mr. Burke." Then, again, he had untiringly advocated the introduction of greater purity and a more rigid economy into every department of the administration. Moreover, not only by his voice and his pen had he zealously and ably served his party, but for years he had been the friend and trusted adviser of its leader; so that we cannot but marvel that that leader, when he assumed the reins of government, could find for such a man no seat in his Cabinet.

At no time, however, was Burke's influence in the House or with the country—except, perhaps, during the paroxysm of terror caused by the outbreak of the French Revolution—commensurate either with his genius or his services. He never attracted towards himself any of that personal popularity which attended Pitt and Fox, as in our own day it has attended Palmerston and Gladstone. His name fell coldly on the public ear; to his eloquence the heart of the people made no response. He was respected by many, admired by not a few, and his great speeches frequently drew a large and approving audience. His legislative proposals were adopted by the Government; and yet his name was never on the lips of the people. I suppose the explanation of this apparent phenomenon is to be found in the character of his oratory, which appealed to the limited circle of the cultured rather than to the uneducated masses. Gradually his style became cumbrous with ornament, and obscure through excessive redundancy. What is more surprising is, that it was sometimes coarse. Lord Brougham, noticing Burke's want of success in his later Parliamentary career, endeavours to explain it on the score of Burke's deficiency in judgment:—

" He regarded not," he says "the degree of interest felt by his audience in the topics which deeply occupied himself; and seldom knew when he had said enough on those which affected them as well as him. . . . He was essentially didactic, except when the violence of his invective carried him away, and then he offended the correct taste of the House of Commons. His declamation was addressed to the head, as from the head it proceeded—learned, fanciful, ingenious, but not impassioned. Of him, as a combatant, we may say what Aristotle said of the old philosophers, when he compared them to unskilful boxers, who hit round about, and not straight forward, and fought with little effect, though they may by chance sometimes deal a hard blow."

His redundance of statement and elaboration of argument justified Goldsmith's good-humoured satire in the " Retaliation : "—

"Who, too deep for his hearers, still went on refining,
And thought of convincing, while they thought of dining." *

Of his too frequent coarseness I shall give only two
specimens :—

" The vital powers, wasted in an unequal struggle, are pushed
back upon themselves, and fester to gangrene—to death; and
instead of what was but just now the delight of the creations,
there will be cast out in the face of the sun a bloated, putrid,
noisome carcass, full of stench and poison, an offence, a horror,
a lesson to the world."

" With six great chopping bastards, each as lusty as an infant
Hercules, this delicate creature blushes at the sight of her own
bridegroom, assumes a virgin delicacy; or, to use a more fit as
well as a more poetical comparison, the person so squeamish, so
timid, so trembling lest the winds of heaven should visit too
roughly, is expanded to broad sunshine, exposed like the sow
of imperial augury, lying in the mud with all the prodigies of
her fertility about her, as evidence of her delicate amour."

To such a depth as this, Chatham, we may be sure,
would never have descended.

---

* The whole passage must be quoted :—
" Here lies our good Edmund, whose genius was such,
We scarcely can praise it, or blame it too much;
Who, born for the universe, narrowed his mind,
And to party gave up what was meant for mankind.
Though fraught with all learning, yet straining his throat
To persuade Tommy Townshend to lend him a vote:
Who, too deep for his hearers, still went on refining,
And thought of convincing, while they thought of dining;
Though equal to all things, for all things unfit,
Too nice for a statesman, too proud for a wit;
For a patriot too cool, for a drudge disobedient
And too fond of the *right* to pursue the *expedient*.
In short, 'twas his fate, unemployed or in place, sir,
To eat mutton cold, and cut blocks with a razor."

His entire disinterestedness and disregard of pecuniary considerations was shown by his reform of the practice of his office. The Paymastership of the Forces had always been coveted on account of the splendid perquisites attached to it; but these, scanty as were his private means, he absolutely refused to touch; and he introduced into Parliament a bill for the future regulation of the office, which provided that no balances should in future accumulate in the Paymaster's hands. Previously he had been allowed to appropriate the interest of those amounts, sometimes not less than a million sterling, while the Chancellor of the Exchequer was imposing new taxes to meet the public expenditure. His measure of economical reform was taken up by the Cabinet, but sadly reduced from its original proportions. As submitted to the House, it did not touch the mode of supplying the royal household, or the two ancient but useless posts of treasurer and cofferer, or the cumbrous and extravagant staffs of the Principality of Wales, and the Duchies of Lancaster and Cornwall; but nevertheless it effected a very considerable improvement. It abolished numerous useless sinecures, usually held by members of Parliament, which succeeding administrations had found a ready means of corruption, and it brought the pension list within moderate limits. At all events, it deserves to be remembered as the first serious attempt to introduce the principles of economy and retrenchment into the administration of the national revenue.

But if in favour of economical reform, Burke was steadfastly opposed to Parliamentary reform, apparently unable to see that the former could never be effectively undertaken until the latter had been accomplished. When William Pitt moved, on the 7th of May, for a committee

" to inquire into the present state of the representation of the Commons of Great Britain," it was with difficulty Fox persuaded Burke to leave the House, and not to record a hostile vote. Again, when it was proposed to limit the duration of Parliaments, he attacked Pitt in "a scream of passion," and protested that Parliament was, and always had been, precisely what it ought to be, and that all people who thought of reforming it wanted to overturn the constitution. It has been put forward, as an apology for Burke's want of political prescience, that, in his intimate knowledge of the composition of parties, he might believe that an agitation for reform would then be dangerous, because it would be useless ; and Mr. Buckle contends " that he recognised in all its bearings that great doctrine which, even in our own day, is too often forgotten, that the aim of the legislator should be, not truth, but expediency." Is truth, then, ever other than expedient ? But it was on no question of " expediency " that Burke opposed Parliamentary reform ; it was on the question of " principles." He could not be brought to admit that it was, or had been, or ever could be necessary. The British Constitution was a sacred ark which no hand profane might touch. It was a palladium dropped from heaven, to be fenced round with all the precautions of a blind, unreasoning idolatry.

Thus a gradual divergence of policy and sentiment arose between Fox, who had been his political pupil and favourite, and himself, the former sympathising with the spirit of progress and movement which was astir in the nation, while the latter stood steadfast on the platform of the old orthodox Whiggism, if, indeed, he did not fall back to some extent from his earlier position. The elements which composed the Rockingham Ministry were

so discordant that it was impossible they should long
have existed in combination; but on the death of the
Premier, 1st May, 1782, they at once started asunder.
The king appointed Lord Shelbourne to the vacant office,
whereupon Fox and Cavendish at once resigned, and
Burke and Sheridan followed their example. This resignation was a political blunder; but it is not my business
to discuss it in these pages. It was followed by a greater
political error, the coalition between Fox and Lord
North—a coalition not less preposterous than would be
one between Mr. Gladstone and Lord Salisbury !—which
overthrew the Shelbourne Ministry on the 21st of February, 1783. The Duke of Portland then became First
Lord of the Treasury, and Fox and North were appointed
Secretaries of State. Burke returned to his former
office.

The condition of India had for some years engaged
Burke's most serious attention. It is easy to understand
that for a man of his peculiar genius it would necessarily have a very strong attraction. In the pomp and
splendour of Oriental life there was much to affect his
imagination; in the rapid extension of British supremacy
over the empire of the Great Mogul, and the territories
of powerful rajahs and nawaubs, over millions upon
millions of dusky Hindoos, over a country abounding in
gorgeous scenery, over a land with the associations of a
venerable antiquity, there was much to interest and
stimulate his intellect. Then, again, the wrongs inflicted upon the native population appealed very powerfully to his generous sympathies, and he entered upon
an investigation of those wrongs with an eager desire
to redress them. Of the committees of investigation
appointed by the House of Commons in 1780 and 1781

he had been a most industrious member; and probably
no one had so completely succeeded in unravelling the
intricate woof of Anglo-Indian policy.  It was natural,
therefore, that Fox, when, in 1783, he determined on
attempting the reform of the Government of India,
should call in Burke to assist in the preparation of the
necessary measures.  It was a work of great difficulty;
for though the Ministry had a large majority in the
House of Commons, they were unpopular with the
country, and heartily disliked by the king; and the
danger was lest any false action should move the royal
prejudices into open and active hostility, and so array
the Crown and the people in opposition to the Lower
Chamber.

The India Bill was introduced by Fox on the 18th of
November.  It proposed to transfer the authority of the
East India Company to a board of seven commissioners,
to be named by Parliament, and not removeable at the
pleasure of the Crown, under whose control the whole
government of India should be placed.  Eight assistants,
under the supervision of the board, were to take charge
of the commercial interests of the company.  The board
was to hold its sittings in England; it was to be
established on trial for four years; and if experience
demonstrated its success, the future nomination of its
members was to rest with the Crown.

A torrent of hostile criticism was directed against Fox
and Burke's measure, though, as Mr. Massey says :—

"It was no peddling temporising evasion of a great difficulty,
but a bold, a comprehensive, and a vigorous project.  Its
opponents objected, however, that as regarded the seven Commissioners, no link existed between them and the Ministers of the
Crown, and that, therefore, Parliament could exercise no real

control over them. Mr. Jenkinson described the proposed Commission as the setting up within the realm of a species of executive government independent of the Crown. The Common Council of London petitioned the House against the Bill, declaring that, as a measure which dictated a seizure and confiscation of powers, privileges, and property, granted by charter, and secured and confirmed by various Acts of Parliament, it had exceedingly alarmed the petitioners, and raised their fears and apprehensions.

The Bill was defended with great vigour by Fox and Burke. The speech of the latter was one of his grandest and most complete efforts. The driest details were rendered attractive by the graces of his eloquence. His fierce imagination seemed to have steeped itself in the Indian atmosphere, and the warmth and light thus derived was communicated to every part of the subject, which, vast as it was, proved not too vast for the great orator's consummate intellectual grasp. The Bill passed the Commons by large majorities ; in the Lords, owing to an unscrupulous use of the influence of the Crown, it was rejected by a majority of ninety-five to seventy-six. Within twenty-four hours of this hostile vote (December 7, 1783), the king sent a message to Mr. Fox and Lord North, requiring them to give up their seals of office by their under-secretaries, as a personal interview would be disagreeable to his Majesty. Next day, William Pitt was appointed First Lord of the Treasury and Chancellor of the Exchequer.

Thus terminated, for the time, the prolonged struggle between the Crown and the great Whig families, who, as custodians of constitutional right, had steadily resisted the encroachments of "privilege" and the extension of the personal influence of the Throne. The real contest in those days, remarks Sir George Lewis,* was not between aristocracy and democracy, but between aristocracy and monarchy. The Tories were, at least, as much aristocrats as the Whigs, but they submitted to the dominion of the Crown. The Whigs sought to maintain a Parliamentary party, independent of the king's personal influence, and to establish its supremacy over the royal will. The great Whig houses may have been an oligarchy, but they fought the battle of the people against the Crown, though the people withheld their support, and positively rejoiced at their downfall.

In opposition the Whigs had ample leisure to compose their internal dissensions, to mature their principles, and to educate the people politically, before they were carried back to office by that great movement of constitutional progress which culminated in the Reform Act of 1832.

William Pitt, when he assumed the Premiership, was only twenty-four years of age. It seemed at the outset impossible that he should prevail against the mixed ranks of the Opposition, led, as they were, by such veteran politicians as Fox, Burke, Sheridan, and Lord North. To his private friends he owned that he was doubtful of the result, while determined not to abandon the situation he had undertaken, but to make the best stand in his power. The Opposition were flushed with confidence, and sanguine that at any moment they could overthrow him. He enjoyed, however, the eager support of the Crown, and it was soon seen that he carried with him the suffrages of the nation. On the 14th of January, 1784, he brought in his India Bill; and on the 23rd it was rejected. Contrary to usage, he did not

---

* Sir G. Cornewall Lewis, "British Administration," p. 95.

resign, and the Opposition then moved an address to the king, praying for his dismissal. It was carried by a majority of twenty-one; but the king refused his consent. He was desirous that public affairs should be conducted by a firm and extended administration; but he did not conceive that object would be promoted by the dismissal of those at present in his service. Another address to the king, moved by Fox, and carried on the 1st of March, by a majority of twelve, received the same answer. Meanwhile, out-of-door demonstrations, and addresses from every quarter, proved his popularity with the people; and on the 8th of March, an elaborate Remonstrance, drawn up by Burke, and moved by Fox, was carried only by a majority of one. The battle was over, and Pitt was the victor. On the 25th Parliament was dissolved. A new Parliament assembled on the 1st of May, and in it the Whigs were represented by a scanty minority. One hundred and sixty members had lost their seats, and, but for the nomination boroughs owned by the great Whig families, the party must have been wholly unrepresented.

We now come to one of the most interesting episodes in Burke's career, his share in the prosecution of Warren Hastings. The "great proconsul," as Lord Macaulay terms him, had returned from India in 1785, at the close of a splendid administration, during which the bounds of English supremacy had been largely extended. He had accomplished more than Clive; he had made British India the most flourishing of all the Indian States. In his own proud language, he was entitled to say:—"It was I who made them so. The valour of others acquired—I enlarged and gave consistency to—the dominion which we hold there. I preserved it." His rule had been

s

characterised by a wonderful combination of boldness and
prudence; it had been marked by sagacity, courage,
and personal moderation ; and it had been crowned with
success.   To a successful statesman we forgive much ;
to an unsuccessful statesman, nothing.   To carry out his
subtle and audacious projects he had needed money, and
on money he had laid his hands whenever and wherever
he could.   One large sum had been obtained by binding
the services of British troops to coerce the Rohillas ;
another considerable amount had been extorted from the
Begums or Princesses of Oudh ; and a third from the
Rajah of Benares.   To consolidate and perpetuate his
power, he had resorted to expedients which might well
shock the conscience of a sensitive English statesman ;
but they had had no malignant influence on the mind, and
ample evidence exists that he was absolutely beloved
by the Hindu population.   " He enjoyed among the
natives a popularity," says Macaulay, " such as other
governors have, perhaps, better merited, but such as no
other governor has been able to attain."

Early in the session of 1786, Burke moved for the
production of papers relating to Indian affairs ; and after
these had been examined, he announced that he should
feel justified in proposing the impeachment of the ex-
Governor-General.   He had an uphill task before him ;
for the Government were not inclined to support such
a proceeding, and Warren Hastings had on his side the
King and Queen, Lord Mansfield, Lord Thurlow, Lord
Lansdowne, and many other men of influence.   Popular
feeling was with him ; for though he had been guilty of
grave errors, the nation remembered that he had rendered
magnificent services.   But Burke was not to be discouraged, beguiled, or defied.   He knew the purity of

his motives; he was inspired by a genuine hatred of the cruelties practised upon the unfortunate natives. The errors and political failures of his later years were many; but at least he was always consistent in his opposition to the outrages of power upon the weak. His blood was fired by the wrong and oppression which stained the relations between the English rulers and their Indian subjects. In a strong race like the English there is always a natural tendency to exalt and glorify the strong man, though he may have used his strength with an arbitrary disregard of the principles of justice and mercy; and this tendency, as it showed itself in the adulation heaped upon Hastings, Burke set himself to resist and combat. If in doing this he sometimes overstepped the borders of a frigid moderation, let it be remembered that the provocation was extreme. The acts of oppression which he denounced were not those of a victorious general, flushed with the heat of victorious warfare. They had been committed from policy, and not from passion or panic. They had been dictated, as Mr. Morley says, not by strategical necessity, but by a colossal stupidity. They had involved the sufferings of millions. And what so profoundly stirred Burke's sympathies was not " the woes of a sovereign despoiled of gold and silver, of silks and jewels," but the merciless hand that " tore the cloth from the loom, or wrested the scanty portion of rice and salt from the peasant of Bengal, or wrung from him the very opium in which he forgot his oppressions and his oppressors!"

In April Burke brought forward his charges. They were twenty-four in number, covering the entire range and field of the policy and government of Hastings. It is not necessary here to enumerate them. The first, relating to the employment of British troops in the Rohilla war, came on for debate in June; but as it failed to receive the support of the Government, it was rejected by forty-nine votes against sixty-seven. A few days later, Fox introduced the second, accusing Hastings of extorting money from Cheyte Sing, the Rajah of Benares. By this time Pitt had made up his mind to throw Hastings over, or he had really convinced himself that his conduct could not be defended. He declared his intention of supporting Mr. Fox, and the motion was accordingly carried by 119 to 79. It was not until the following year that the inquiry was resumed. The charge relating to the spoliation of the Begums of Oudh was introduced by Sheridan in a speech of extraordinary brilliancy, which still remains one of the most precious *souvenirs* of the House of Commons. Burke pronounced it — " The most astonishing effort of eloquence, argument, and wit united of which there was any record or tradition ;" and Pitt, who cannot be suspected of any party bias, affirmed that " it surpassed all the eloquence of ancient and modern times, and possessed everything that genius or art could furnish to agitate and control the human mind." The debate was adjourned, that members might not vote under the orator's immediate influence. When the vote was taken, it showed a majority against Hastings of 107. Eventually, after an almost interminable series of debates, the House agreed upon twenty articles of accusation, and directed Burke to go before the Lords, and impeach Warren Hastings of high crimes and misdemeanours.

A committee for managing the impeachment having been appointed, and the preliminaries completed, the great trial began on the 13th of February, 1788. It may be doubted whether that of Strafford, or even that of the " grey discrownèd " Charles, made a profounder impression on the public mind. All the circumstances with which it was surrounded were of a nature to arouse and fascinate the imagination. There was in it so much of romantic interest, that the most common-place person could not but be struck by the strange contrast it presented to the ordinary dulness of English public life. The scene was worthy of the occasion :—

" That great hall of William Rufus, the hall which had resounded with acclamations at the inauguration of thirty kings ; the hall which had witnessed the just sentence of Baum, and the just absolution of Somers ; the hall where the clergyman of Strafford had for a moment awed and united a victorious party inflamed with just resentment ; the hall where Charles had confronted the High Court of Justice with the placid courage which has half redeemed his fame."*

The prisoner was a man who might well engage the sympathies of all who looked upon him. For fifteen years he had maintained the power and renown of Britain in the remote East ; had annexed a vast territory to his sovereign's dominions ; had disposed of the destinies of alien races and subject populations ; had sent forth armies to execute his behests ; had raised and deposed princes. His judges were the peers, civil and spiritual, of England, nearly one hundred and seventy in number, and including the brothers and sons of the king, and the heir-apparent to England's ancient throne. And who were his accusers ? The Commons of England, repre-

---

* "Lord Macaulay, " Essay on Warren Hastings." The description of the opening of the trial is one of the brilliant historian's most brilliant passages, and no lesser pen can hope to rival it.

sented by five of their greatest orators—by Burke and
Fox, Sheridan, Windham, and Charles Grey.　And what
an audience !　The Queen and the three eldest Princesses were present.　The ambassadors' box held the
representatives of the European Powers.　Female loveliness softened the austerer features of the spectacle ;
and officers of the naval and military services crowded to
look upon the man who had done so much for England.
Nor did art and literature fail to grace the occasion ;
and many an eye turned from the prisoner and his
judges and accusers to gaze upon Gibbon, the most
learned historian, Sir Joshua Reynolds, the most successful painter, and Dr. Parr, the greatest scholar of his
time.

　　The first charge was opened by Burke in a speech
protracted over four days—an oration of unquestionable
splendour, but containing much that was irrelevant, and
a good deal that was superfluous.　He reviewed the
history of British India down to the period of the
administration of Hastings, and then plunged into an
animated discourse upon arbitrary power, of which,
he somewhat strangely asserted, on the authority of
the Koran, Tamerlane's Institutes, the Gentoo law,
and other formularies, the Eastern races had had no
experience until it was inflicted upon them by an English governor.　On the third day he took up numerous
vague charges of bribery and peculation, and dwelt upon
certain gross atrocities committed by Cheyte Sing, a
native lieutenant of Hastings, though he did not prove
that Hastings had either authorised or condoned them.
After reviewing the principal heads of his formidable
indictment, he concluded with the following noble
peroration :—

"Do we want a tribunal? My lords, no example of antiquity, nothing in the modern world, nothing in the range of human imagination, can supply us with a tribunal like this. Here we see virtually, in the mind's eye, that sacred majesty of the Crown under whose authority you sit, and whose power you exercise. We see in this invisible authority, what we all feel in reality and life, the beneficent powers and protecting justice of majesty. We have here the heir-apparent to the Crown, such as the fond wishes of the people of England wish an heir-apparent to the Crown to be. We have here all the branches of the royal family in a situation between majesty and subjection, between the sovereign and the subject, offering a pledge in that situation for the support of the rights of the Crown and the liberties of the people, both whose extremities they touch. My Lords, we have a great hereditary peerage here, those who have their own honour, the honour of their ancestors, and of their posterity to guard, and who will justify, as they have always justified, that provision in the Constitution by which justice is made a hereditary office. My Lords, we have a new nobility, who have risen, exalted by various merits, by great military services, which have extended the fame of this country from the rising to the setting sun. We have those who, by various civil merits and talents, have been exalted to a situation which they well deserve, and in which they will justify the favour of their sovereign.

"My lords, you have here also the lights of our religion—you have the bishops of England; you have that true image of the primitive Church in its ancient form, in its ancient ordinances, purified from the superstitions and the vices which a long succession of ages will bring upon the best institutions. . . . My lords, these are the securities which we have in all the constituent parts of the body of the House. We know them, we reckon upon them, we rest upon them, and commit safely the interests of India and humanity into your hands. Therefore, it is with confidence that, ordered by the Commons,

"I impeach Warren Hastings, esquire, of high crimes and misdemeanours.

"I impeach him in the name of the Commons of Great Britain, in Parliament assembled, whose Parliamentary trust he has betrayed.

"I impeach him in the name of all the Commons of Great Britain, whose national character he has dishonoured.

"I impeach him in the name of the people of India, whose laws, rights, and liberties he has subverted, whose properties he has destroyed, whose country he has laid waste and desolate.

"I impeach him in the name and by virtue of those eternal laws of justice which he has violated. I impeach him in the name of human virtue itself, which he has cruelly outraged, injured, and oppressed in both sexes, in every age, rank, situation, and condition.

Owing to the delays caused by George III.'s attack of insanity, and other political events, Burke did not speak again until April, 1789, when he introduced the sixth charge, that of bribery and corruption. Repeated postponements followed, and eventually the public grew thoroughly weary of the trial, which they came to regard as a gigantic sham. And, indeed, Burke was the only person who was in earnest. His earnestness, however, availed but little. He had lost his old Parliamentary influence, and his popularity out of doors had been greatly impaired by the violence and bad taste of his speeches on the Regency Bill. He persevered, nevertheless, in his difficult task, and courageously held his ground against the many powerful interests which Hastings had combined in his support. In June, 1794, the nine years' trial—it lasted almost as long as the Homeric siege of Troy—was brought to a conclusion by the general summing up of the charges of the different managers—Burke's reply, extending over nine days, forming an appropriate finale. Then came the rejoinder from Law, the prisoner's counsel (afterwards Lord Ellenborough). Eventually, the Peers acquitted Hastings by a large majority, whose verdict did but confirm the opinion of the nation.

As to the chief prosecutor, the highest tribute to the force and splendour of his eloquence was paid by Hastings himself, who, in reference to his opening speech, exclaimed, "For the first half hour I looked up to the orator in a reverie of wonder, and during that time I felt myself the most culpable man on earth; but then I recurred to my own bosom, and there found a consciousness that consoled me under all I heard and all I suffered."

England has long ago decided that this great trial ended exactly as it was desirable that it should end. It was right and fitting that a man who had rendered such vast services to his country, in a remote sphere, and under novel conditions, without example or precedent to guide him—should escape the punishment of the law, even though he had been guilty of some grievous errors. But it is felt that the object of the impeachment was, after all, secured; that it conveyed a very significant warning to future "proconsuls." It taught the great lesson, "that Asiatics have rights, and that companies have obligations; and that the authority of the English Legislature is not more entirely a trust for the benefit of this country, than the dominion of the English in India is a trust for the benefit of the inhabitants of India."

In a well-known passage of his brilliant essay on "Warren Hastings," Macaulay comments on the striking changes which had occurred in the long interval between the opening and the close of the great trial. Of all these, the most momentous, as it was the most melancholy, was that which had passed over the relations between Burke and his former colleagues. Their friendship, their close confidence, was at an end. It had been dissolved publicly and violently, with tears and reproaches, and outbursts of wrath and indignation. They no longer stood together on the same platform contending for the same object. Fox had gone in one direction, followed by Sheridan and Charles Grey; Burke in another, accompanied by William Windham. The causes of this separation, which so greatly influenced the political history of our country for a quarter of a century, I shall now proceed to trace with as much brevity as the importance of the subject will admit.*

## II.

It was in July, 1789, that the Bastille of Paris, which history seems to have accepted as the symbol of uncontrolled power and despotic cruelty, was attacked and captured by an infuriated multitude. Its downfall, by most lovers of freedom, was hailed with delight, as foreshadowing the advent in France of an era of law and order and constitutional government; and it might well be imagined that in England, at all events, the adherents to the principles of the "glorious Revolution of 1688" would rejoice at so direct a blow to the cause of tyranny. Yet were there many who either regarded it with timid feelings, or looked on with surprise and hesitation, not

---

* W. Massey, "History of England During the Reign of George the Third;" J. Prior, "Life of Edmund Burke;" John Morley, "Edmund Burke: a Biographical Study," etc.

knowing (as Burke remarked) whether to blame or
approve. "For whenever a separation," he wrote, "is made
between liberty and justice, neither is safe." As the great
revolt in France against the privileged classes took shape,
as it daily assumed larger and more formidable proportions, the generous heart of Fox glowed with enthusiasm;
while Burke, with his Conservative sympathies and
orthodox reverence for prudence and tradition, grew
more and more alarmed. He lost his intellectual balance; his imagination prevailed over his judgment; and
the night of the fourth of August, when all class interests
were ruthlessly swept away, and the gaunt figure of the
Revolution seemed to menace the supremacy of the law
and the preservation of social order, he denounced, in
strains of the most fiery invective. His apprehensions,
sharpened by his intellectual repugnance to all uncontrolled power, whether that of the one or the many,
seemed to detect the drift of the revolutionary current, and he declared that it was hurrying the people
unawares to a sea of blood. While even the calm and
sagacious Pitt was praising the new constitution which
the French deputies had constructed, Burke was crying
aloud that they had shown themselves the ablest archi-
tects of ruin who had ever existed in the world. In a
short space of time, he exclaimed with exaggerated
passion, they had pulled to the ground their army, their
navy, their commerce, their arts, and their manufactures;
in a word, wherever he looked he saw—chaos!

At first Burke stood almost alone in his fear and
his wrath. The Tories followed Pitt, who had not yet
thrown off his early Liberalism, and was cordial in his
relations with the new French Government. The Whigs,
who acknowledged the leadership of Fox, naturally hailed

with satisfaction the apparent adoption by the French of
the constitutional principles they had so steadfastly advocated.   The course of events strengthened the general
confidence, so that Burke, like another Cassandra, shouted
his prophecies to the winds.   When, in its jealous anger
at the foundation of an English settlement at Nootka
Sound, Spain sought the assistance of France, the Revolutionary party warmly opposed, and eventually prevented,
the war in which the ministers of Louis XVI. were anxious
to engage.   Pitt was led to enunciate a maxim of policy,
unhappily not accepted as a fundamental principle until
our own times—that changes of government in France
afforded no reason for distrust or interference on the part
of Great Britain.   This was a maxim which, a few years
before, Burke would eagerly have endorsed and confirmed
by the abundant illustration he had always at his command; but now he chose to put it aside as a fallacy, in
the distempered view he had conceived of the Revolution
as the enemy of all he loved and valued; the enemy of
the landmarks of the past; the enemy of a well-ordered
fabric of social organisation, with " respectability " as its
corner-stone ; the enemy of the traditional graduation of
ranks and nicety of class distinctions; the enemy of the
Church and the old nobility.   He refused to keep any
terms with a people who had overthrown the associations
and conventionalities of the past.

We have seen in our own generation what may be
accomplished by the genius and enthusiasm of one man
when he has, as he believes, a noble and righteous cause
to advocate.   But the work which at this time Burke
undertook was infinitely greater and more laborious than
Mr. Gladstone's, because he had no personal following,
had lost the ear of the House, and had never had

any strong hold upon the nation. It is strange how completely his influence in Parliament had perished. His speeches were too redundant, too protracted; his arguments too subtle and complex; and while his earnestness wearied an audience of broad-acred squires and wealthy merchants, his want of discretion and his extravagance of language disgusted them. Yet even this is scarcely sufficient to explain the fact that, at his rising the crowded benches would thin rapidly, and that his splendid perorations were generally wasted on an almost empty House. The impeachment of Hastings had been the occasion of some noble orations which, for a while, had retrieved his reputation; but as the trial drew its slow length along, he sank again into the sere and yellow leaf of a statesman's decay. But the French Revolution came, like the sound of a trumpet, to awaken all his best energies. A new fervour inspired him; a new, if mistaken, spirit of enthusiasm. With all his old vigour he rose in defence of the things he most loved and revered; of the old order against the new, of conservatism and orthodoxy against speculative boldness in politics and religion.

On the 9th of February, 1790, Burke went down to the House prepared to deliver a solemn protest against the sympathy which Fox, the leader of his party, had avowed with what seemed to him an outrageous defiance of law and authority. The speech was in his best manner; absolutely free from the exaggeration and vulgar rant which had disfigured his latter orations; noble, pathetic, eloquent, replete with vigorous thought. It embodied a dignified and not unmerited rebuke of Fox's hasty panegyric on the French generals who had proved false to their colours and their allegiance. It contained a declaration against every form of despotism; against the despotism of an absolute monarch, and against the worse despotism of a plundering, furious, tyrannical democracy, democracy without a single virtue of republicanism to redeem its crimes. Pitt, in following Burke, expressed his warm admiration of the speech the House had just heard. "Former differences," he said, "could not preclude him from expressing his strongest feelings of gratitude and reverence for the speaker of such sentiments; sentiments which would be received with the greatest esteem by his country, and would hand down his name to posterity with respect and honour." Fox in his turn hastened to retract his ill-advised language; and it was evident he felt doubtful of the wisdom of the unbounded admiration he had lavished on the French ideas of liberty, fraternity, and equality. Nor was it less evident that he shrank from a rupture with his former friend and colleague, by whom, he used to say, he had been instructed more than by all other men and books together; by whom he had been taught to love the constitution; from whom he had acquired nearly all his political knowledge. But Sheridan quietly fanned into a destructive flame the mouldering embers of doubt and distrust. Prompted in part by his jealousy of Burke, and in part by his ready sympathy with extreme opinions, he broke forth into a rhapsodical eulogium upon the French Revolution and of its leaders; and concluded by inveighing against Burke as a deserter from the camp, as an assailant of the very principles of freedom, as the defender and apologist of an odious tyranny, and the obtrusive libeller of liberty abroad. Burke then rose, and in accents of lofty anger remonstrated against language which ought to have been spared, were it only as a sacrifice to the ghost of departed friendship. It was true that the language was not novel, and might be heard nightly at the reforming clubs and societies with which Sheridan was connected; clubs for whose plaudits he had chosen to sacrifice his friends, though he might in time discover that the value of such plaudits was not equal to the price at which they were purchased. Henceforward they were separated in politics for ever.

It was essential to the interests of the Whig party that a reconciliation should be effected; and a meeting for this purpose was held at the house of the Duke of Portland. Unfortunately, the difference of feeling and sentiment proved to be too great for any compromise to bridge it over. Fox adhered to the opinions he had deliberately expressed; Windham sided with Burke; and the result was a schism which almost annihilated Whig influence in Parliament and the country for many years.

As an anti-revolutionist, Burke did not limit his exertions to the Parliamentary arena. With the view of awakening the country to a true sense of the danger of the crisis, he had recourse to his pen, and by the month of October, his genius and industry had produced his " Reflections on the French Revolution ; " a book of surprising eloquence, impetuous in appeal, luxuriant in imagery, often very noble and beautiful in thought, but marked almost throughout by a curious narrowness of view. It is still remembered for the beauty of some of its passages. As, for instance :—

"The age of chivalry is gone ; that of sophisters, economists, and calculators has succeeded ; and the glory of Europe is extinguished for ever."

And the allusion to Queen Marie Antoinette :—

"And surely never lighted on this orb, which she hardly seemed to touch, a more delightful vision. I saw her just above the horizon, decorating and cheering the elevated sphere she just began to move in—glittering like the morning star, full of life and splendour and joy. Oh! what a revolution! and what a heart must I have to contemplate without emotion that elevation and that fall! Little did I dream, when she added titles of veneration to that enthusiastic, distant, respectful love, that she should ever be obliged to carry the sharp antidote against disgrace concealed in that bosom; little did I dream that I should have lived to see such disasters fallen upon her in a nation of gallant men, a nation of men of honour and of cavaliers. I thought ten thousand swords must have leaped from their scabbards to avenge even a look that threatened her with insult."

I venture to believe that, throughout all the writings and speeches of Burke on the French Revolution, thickly sown as they are with the maxims of political wisdom, you can trace the influence of a morbid imagination. He had thrown himself into the new crusade with so much ardour that all prudence and sobriety deserted him. He was blinded by the glow and glare of his passions to the impressions made on his very senses. As Lord Brougham put it, "he saw not what other men beheld, but what he wished to see, or what his prejudices and fancies suggested; and having once laid down a dogma, his mind refused to acknowledge the most astounding contradiction that events could offer."

Early in 1790, when France had already sent large armies into the field, Burke pronounced her external power at an end. Even in 1793, when the second European invasion had ignominiously failed, except in provoking her people to threaten the security of Europe, he could see nothing in her situation but " complete

ruin, without the chance of resurrection;" and was still
sanguine enough to believe, when she recovered, as he
supposed, a nominal existence by the restoration of her
monarchy, that it would be necessary for her neighbours
to keep her on her basis by their combined guarantee.
That a man of his political sagacity should be involved
in so wild a delusion is curious and instructive. Not
less extraordinary was the way in which he confounded
under one general torrent of reproach, calumny, and
indignation, men and things of the most diverse and
opposite character. "We are much astonished," says
Lord Brougham, "at finding him repeatedly class the
humane and chivalrous Lafayette with the monster
Robespierre; but when we find him pressing his theory,
that all atheists are Jacobins, so far as to charge Hume
with being a heathen, and pressing the converse of the
proposition so far as to insinuate that Priestley was an
atheist, we pause incredulous over the sad devastation
which a disordered fancy can make in the finest understanding."

Mr. Buckle has brought together a number of examples of the violent language which Burke was wont to
employ towards France and the French.* France was
" Cannibal Castle," " a hell," " the republic of assassins."
Its Government consisted of " the dirtiest, lowest, most
fraudulent, most knavish of chicaners." Its people were
" a gang of robbers," " a desperate gang of plunderers,
murderers, tyrants, and atheists," " the prostitute out-
casts of mankind," " a nation of murderers." He was
not ashamed to speak of the amiable Lafayette as " a
horrid ruffian," and of the philosophical Condorcet as " a

* Buckle, " History of Civilisation," i. 428, 429.

fanatic, atheist, and furious democratic republican, capable
of the lowest as well as the highest and most determined
villainies." To enter into negotiations with France was
" exposing our lazar sores at the door of every proud
servitor of the French Republic, where the court-dogs will
not deign to lick them." So foul was the atmosphere of
Paris, that our ambassadors could not but be corrupted
by it. " They may easily return as good courtiers as
they went; but can they ever return from that degrading residence loyal and faithful subjects, or with any
true affection to their master, or true attachment to the
constitution, religion, or laws of their country? There
is great danger that they who enter smiling into this
Typhonian cave will come out of it sad and serious
conspirators, and such will continue as long as they live."
To learn the French language or to travel in France was
a crime, so complete was the insularism of Burke's mind
under the domination of its anti-revolutionary frenzy.
" No young man," he cries aloud, " can go to any part
of Europe without taking this place of pestilential contagion in his way; and, whilst the less active part of the
community will be debauched by their travel, whilst
children are poisoned at their schools, our trade will put
the finishing touch to our ruin. No factory will be
settled in France that will not become a club of complete French Jacobins. The minds of young men of
that description will receive a taint in their religion,
their morals, and their politics which they will in a
short time communicate to the whole kingdom." Burke
was incessantly crying out for war—a general war
against Jacobins and Jacobinism; a war of conquest;
" a war not confined to the vain attempt of raising a
barrier to the lawless and savage power of France, but

directed to the only rational end it could pursue, namely, the utter destruction of the desperate horde which gave it birth."* "A long war," he wrote emphatically;† "a religious war,"‡ as in the colossal madness of his passionate egotism he dared to term it.

The wider intellect of Pitt rose superior at first to Burke's terrible apprehensions, and he assured the French Government that England would scrupulously persevere in the neutrality she had hitherto observed with respect to the internal dissensions of France, and would not depart from it unless compelled to do so in self-defence. With a wisdom shared by few of his own followers, he boldly gave his support at this critical time to Fox's Libel Act, which accomplished the liberty of the press by transferring the decision in libel cases from the judge to the jury; whilst he initiated the wise policy of colonial self-government by granting a representative constitution to the two Canadas. It is needless to say that the anti-revolutionist theories found no favour with the Whigs. It was the 4th of May, 1793, which witnessed the final disruption of the party, and its division into Foxites and Burkeites, into Old Whigs and New. In the course of a debate on the Government bill for the better government of the Canadas, Burke rose to speak, and, according to his customary practice, plunged into a torrent of invective against the French Revolution and its leaders. He made a violent attack upon the doctrine set forth in Thomas Paine's "Rights of Man," and then glided away into a highly-coloured description of the

---

* Parliamentary History, xxxi. 427.
† "Letters on a Regicide Peace." Burke's Works, ii. 291.
‡ "Remarks on the Policy of the Allies." Works, i. 600.

insults offered by the Parisian rabble to Louis XVI. and
the royal family of France.  He was called to order,
and a scene of intense excitement took place.  Fox,
starting to his feet, reprimanded him for the irrelevancy
of his remarks.  " This, however," he said, " was a day
of license, on which any gentleman might get up and
abuse any Government he pleased.  True it was that
the French Revolution had no more to do with the
question before the House than the Government of
Turkey or the laws of Confucius ; but what of that ? "

Burke retorted with vehemence, comparing his position to that of Caylus, the great French orator, and
Conservative leader of the French National Assembly,
whose speeches were always interrupted by the clamour
of the so-called friends of liberty.  The cries of
" Order ! " grew louder, and Fox, Charles Grey, Pitt,
and others became involved in an angry conversation.
At length Lord Sheffield moved, and Fox seconded, a
motion, " that dissertations on the French Constitution,
and to read a narrative of the transactions in France, are
not regular or orderly on the question ; and that the
clauses of the Quebec Bill be read a second time."  But
in seconding this amendment, Fox fell into the very
breach of order for which he had censured Burke.  He
entered upon an animated defence of the principles of
the French Revolution ; and, contending that the rights
of man were and must be the foundation of every social
or political system, he observed that he had learned this
doctrine from the lips of Burke himself, whom, in
passionate words, he accused of betraying his cause and
party, and—quoting the language employed by Burke at
the time of the American war—of drawing an indictment against a whole people.

The House was hushed in profound silence, as, pale and agitated, Burke rose to reply. Speaking at first in a low tone, and struggling to subdue his evident excitement, he complained of the bitter personal attack that had been made upon him by one of his oldest friends, and then proceeded to review the political relations which for a quarter of a century had existed between Fox and himself, indicating the few questions on which they had differed, and rejoicing that those differences had not sundered the bonds of their private friendship. It was indiscreet, he said, at his time of life, to provoke enemies or lose friends; but if his steadfast adherence to the British Constitution placed him in such a dilemma, he would risk all, and, as public duty and public prudence taught him, with his last breath exclaim, "Fly from the French Constitution!" In faltering tones, Fox exclaimed, "There is no loss of friendship!" "I regret to say there *is*," rejoined Burke. "I know the value of my line of conduct. I have indeed made a great sacrifice. I have done my duty, though I have lost my friends. There is something in the detested French Constitution that envenoms everything it touches." And he concluded with a fervid apostrophe to the two great political leaders, beseeching them, whatever their other differences, to unite in guarding the British Constitution against innovations and new theories.

Fox was so powerfully moved that, on rising to reply, he could hardly speak at first for tears. In broken tones, while the House listened in sympathetic silence, he made a pathetic appeal to his old and revered friend, reminding him of their ancient friendship, of their reciprocal affection, as dear and almost as binding as the ties of nature between father and son. Burke remained unshaken. On the altar of public duty he had sacrificed his private feelings; and with great earnestness he declared that he could not maintain a friendly inter-course with a man who upheld anarchy and revolution in their most hideous aspects.

Thus was the long-tried and close connection of five-and-twenty years " trampled "—to use the words of Wilberforce —" trampled to pieces in the conflict of a single night."

So far as popular opinion was concerned, the evidence soon became unmistakeable that it sided with Burke rather than with the Opposition. Of his " Reflections on the Revolution in France," no fewer than 30,000 copies were sold in a few weeks. It may be doubted whether any literary production—except, perhaps, in our own time, Mr. Gladstone's pamphlet on " Bulgarian Horrors "—ever exercised so powerful and immediate an influence on the public mind. I believe it created the prejudice and hostility in England which eventually plunged Europe into a long and sanguinary war, and that the responsibility of that war rests on the shoulders of its author. It has been well said that—

" The reputation of the author as the greatest political philo-sopher of his age ; his predilections for freedom, displayed through the whole course of the American Revolution ; his hatred of despotic power, as manifested in his unceasing denunciations of atrocities in India ; his consistent adherence to Whig prin-ciples, as established by the Bill of Rights ; this acquaintance with the character and sentiments of Burke first raised an unbounded curiosity to trace the arguments against the struggle for liberty in another country, coming from a man who had so long contended for what was deemed the popular cause at home. The perusal of this remarkable book converted the inquirer into an enthusiast. In proportion as the liberal institutions of our own country were held up to admiration, so were the attempts of France to build up a new system of government upon the ruins of the old system described as the acts of men ' devoted to every description of tyranny and cruelty employed to bring about and to uphold this revolution.' "

The great change that came over the caricatures, so popular in those days, as an expression of public opinion, must here be noted. Previously Burke had always been represented in the dress of a Jesuit. Now he was shown as confounding by his oratorical successes, the defenders and apologists of the French Revolution, while Fox appeared in every kind of degrading and offensive attitude and position. To do honour to Burke seemed the leading thought of all sorts and conditions of men. From the University of Dublin he received the degree of Doctor of Laws ; the Oxford graduates presented him, through Mr. Windham, with a congratulatory address ; the Bishop of Aix, and the expatriated French clergy, poured out their emotions of gratitude and admiration in the most enthusiastic language. His Parliamentary influence had so completely revived that the Irish Roman Catholics requested him to advocate their claims in the House ; nor did his exertions prove wholly unsuccessful. The activity of his mind, under the pressure of its new excitement, was surprising ; and the interest he took in the great questions of the day appears very strikingly in his pamphlet, entitled " Heads for Consideration on the Present State of Affairs."

Burke, however, in spite of all this popular adulation, felt the shame and bitterness of separation from the political party with which he had been so long identified ; and he resolved on retiring from parliamentary life so soon as the protracted trial of Hastings came to a conclusion. Arrangements were made for his son, whom he loved with a passionate love, and who promised to be worthy of it, to succeed him in the representation of Malton. His last appearance in the House of Commons was on the 25th of June, 1794, when, with the other managers of the impeachment of Hastings, he received the formal thanks of the House. Almost immediately afterwards he accepted the Chiltern Hundreds.

His son was duly elected for Malton, and was on the point of starting for Ireland, as secretary to the new Viceroy, Lord Fitz-William, when he was seized with a mortal illness, and died on the 2nd of August. The blow fell with a crushing effect upon the unhappy father. His friend, Dr. Laurence, writes :—

"During the past day he was at times truly terrible in his grief. He occasionally worked himself up to an agony of affliction, and then, bursting away from all control, would rush to the room where his son lay, and throw himself headlong on the bed or on the floor. Yet at intervals he attended, and gave directions relative to any little arrangement, pleasing himself most with thinking what would be most consonant to the living wishes of his son."

He afterwards told Dr. Laurence that he lamented having seen his son after death, as the dead countenance had made such an impression on his imagination, that he could not retrace in his memory the features and air of his living Richard.

From the day that he lost the heir of his genius, and hopes, and ambition, the great statesman may be said to have rapidly drawn nearer to the grave. He never afterwards entered Beaconsfield Church ; could not bear even to turn his eyes towards it. Thenceforth he walked with head bowed down like one oppressed by the burden of his sorrow, and all who saw him felt, in the old historic and expressive phrase, that " a waft of death came from him." He was desolate and solitary. " I am alone," he wrote; "I have none to meet my enemies in the gate; stripped of my boast, my hope, my consolation, my helper, my counsellor, and my pride."

He was roused from this despondent and dejected condition by the violent attack made upon him by the Duke of Bedford. From the Government he had received, at the king's suggestion, a pension of £3700, though on what ground it was granted, it is not easy to determine. In the House of Lords " the job" was strongly denounced by the Duke of Bedford, as well as by the Earl of Lauderdale. Burke was stung to the quick, and replied in his celebrated " Letters to a Noble Lord ; " a masterpiece of satirical eloquence and rhetorical invective, which, however, carefully avoids any definite line of argument, and depends for much of its force upon its *tu quoques*.

I quote a few specimen passages :—

" The grants to the House of Russell (by Henry VIII.) were so enormous, as not only to outrage economy, but even to stagger credibility. The Duke of Bedford is the leviathan among all the creatures of the Crown. He tumbles about his unwieldy bulk ; he plays and frolics in the ocean of the royal bounty. Huge as he is, and whilst 'he is floating many a rood,' he is still a creature. His ribs, his fins, his whalebone, his blubber, the very spiracles through which he spouts a torrent of brine against his origin, and covers one all over with the spray—everything of him, and about him, is from the Crown.

" The first peer of the name, the first purchaser of the grants, was a Mr. Russell, a person of an ancient gentleman's family, raised by being a minion of Henry VIII. As there generally is some resemblance of character to create these relations, the favourite was in all likelihood much such another as his master. The first of these immoderate grants was not taken from the ancient demesne of the Crown, but from the vast recent confiscation of the ancient nobility of the land. The lion having sucked the blood of his prey, threw the offal carcase to the jackal in waiting. Having tasted once the food of confiscation, the favourites became fierce and ravenous. This worthy favourite's first grant was from the lay nobility. The second, infinitely improving upon the amenity of the first, was from the plunder of the Church. In truth, his Grace is somewhat excusable for his dislike to a grant like mine, not only in its quantity, but in its kind so different from his own.

"Mine was from a mild and benevolent sovereign; his from Henry VIII.

"The merit of the grantee whom he derives from, was that of being a prompt and greedy instrument of a *levelling* tyrant, who oppressed all descriptions of his people, but who fell with particular fury on anything that was *great and noble.*

"Mine has been, in endeavouring to screen every man, in every class, from oppression, and particularly in defending the high and eminent, who, in the bad times of confiscating princes, confiscating chief governors, or confiscating demagogues, were the most exposed to jealousy, avarice, and envy.

"The merit of the original grantee of his Grace's pensions was in giving his heart to this work, and partaking the spoil with a prince who plundered a part of the national church of his time and country.

"Mine was in defending the whole of the national church of my own time and my own country, and the whole of the national churches of all countries, from the principles and the examples which lead to ecclesiastical pillage, thence to a contempt of *all* prescriptive titles, thence to the pillage of *all* property, and thence to universal desolation.

"The merit of the origin of his Grace's fortune was in being a favourite and chief adviser to a prince who left no liberty to their native country.

"My endeavour was to obtain liberty for the municipal country in which I was born, and for all descriptions and denominations in it. Mine was to support with unrelaxing vigilance every right, every privilege, every franchise, in this my adopted, my dearer, and more comprehensive country; and not only to preserve these rights in this chief seat of empire, but in every nation, every land, in every climate, language, and religion, in the vast domain that is still under the protection, and the larger that was once under the protection, of the British Crown."

It is worth observing that, though the "Letter" is the defence of a man who, to use a popular phrase, was "self-made," it is thoroughly aristocratic in tone. I find in it no trace of popular sympathies; and the Duke is assailed as an individual, and not as the representative of a faction.

In a pathetic passage he alludes to the heavy domestic calamity that had overshadowed his later years :—

"Had it pleased God," he says, "to continue to me the hopes of succession, I should have been, according to my mediocrity and the mediocrity of the age I live in, a sort of founder of a family. I should have left a son, who, in all the points in which personal merit can be viewed—in science, in erudition, in honour, in genius, in humanity, in every liberal sentiment and every liberal accomplishment, would not have shown himself inferior to the Duke of Bedford, or to any of those whom he terms in his line. His Grace very soon would have wanted all plausibility in his attack upon this provision, which belonged more to mine than to me. He soon would have supplied every deficiency, and symmetrised every disproportion. It would not have been for that successor to resort to any stagnant, wasting reservoir of merit in me, or in any of my ancestry. He had in him-

self a salient, living spring of generous and manly action.   Every
day he lived he would have repurchased the bounty of the
Crown, and ten times more.   He was made a public creature,
had no enjoyment whatever but in the performance of some
duty.   At this exigent moment, the loss of a finished man is
not so easily supplied.

" But a Disposer, whose power we are little able to resist, and
whose wisdom it behoves us not at all to dispute, has ordained it
in another manner, and (whatever my querulous weakness might
suggest) a far better.   The storm has gone over me, and I lie,
like one of those old oaks, which the late hurricane has scattered
about me.   I am stripped of all my honours ; I am torn up by
the roots, and lie prostrate on the earth.   There, and prostrate
there, I must unfeignedly recognise the Divine justice.      But
while I humble myself before God, I do not know that it is
forbidden to repel the attacks of unjust and inconsiderate man.
The patience of Job is proverbial ; after some of the convulsive
struggles of our irritable nature, he submitted himself, and
repented in dust and ashes; but even so, I do not find him
blamed for reprehending those ill-natured neighbours of his, who
visited his dung-hill to read moral, political, and economical
lectures on his misery."

To the last, Burke's intellectual powers burned brightly,
and were actively employed.   The stores of learning and
reflection which he had accumulated were too vast to
fear exhaustion.   He was physically feeble and broken-
down, but his hand had lost none of its cunning, nor his
spirit of its fire.   The anti-revolutionary fever still
excited his blood, and disturbed him with a panic fear
lest English society should be exposed to the evils by
which French society had been degraded and demoralised.
When the numerous great victories of the French soldiers,
and the not less numerous disasters of the Allied troops,
had suggested to the Ministry the desirability of opening up

negotiations with the French Government, his passionate
excitement could scarcely be controlled. The Cassandra
vein was once more opened, and in his " Letters on a
Regicide Peace," published in the summer of 1796, he
gave free course to his powers of prophecy and denunciation. Amid much exaggeration and much morbidity of
sentiment, these " Letters " contain passages of the keenest philosophical insight ; and no one will pretend that
they present any indications of intellectual decay.

We shall quote two or three admirable reflections :—

" The nature of courage is to be conversant with danger ; but
in the palpable night of their terrors, even under consternation,
suppose, not that it is the danger which calls out the courage
to resist it, but that it is the courage which produces the
danger. They, therefore, seek for a refuge from their fears in
the fears themselves, and consider a temporising meanness as
the only source of safety."

" None can aspire to act greatly but those who are of force
greatly to suffer. They who make their arrangements in the
first run of misadventures, and in a temper of mind the common guest of disappointment and dismay, set a seal on their
calamities. So far as their power goes, they take a security
against any favours which they might hope from the usual
inconstancy of fortune."

" Never can a vehement and sustained spirit of fortitude be
kindled in a people by a war of calculation. It has nothing
that can keep the mind erect under the gusts of adversity. Even
when men are willing, as sometimes they are, to barter their
blood for lucre, to hazard their safety for the gratification of
their avarice, the passion which animates them to that sort of
conflict, like all other short-sighted passions, must see its objects
distinct and at hand. Speculative plunder, contingent spoil ;
future, long-adjourned, contingent booty ; pillage which must
enrich a late posterity, and which possibly may not reach

posterity at all: these for any length of time will not support a mercenary war. The people are in the right. The calculation of profit in all such wars is false. On balancing the account of such wars, ten thousand hogsheads of sugar are purchased at ten thousand times their price. The blood of man should never be shed but to redeem the blood of man. It is well shed for our family, for our friends, for our God, for our country, for our kind. The rest is vanity, the rest is crime."

Meantime, the physical strength of Burke was rapidly declining, and he grew too feeble to enjoy his ordinary amount of daily exercise. Early in February, 1797, he repaired to Bath, to try the effect of the waters; but they could not counteract the decay incident upon a prolonged exertion of the intellect, and the pressure of an irreparable loss. He was confined to his bed or his couch almost the whole time he lingered at Bath. "Since I came hither," he wrote to a friend, "my sufferings have been greatly aggravated, and my little strength still further reduced, so that, though I am told the symptoms of my disorder begin to carry a more favourable aspect, I pass the far longer part of the twenty-four hours—indeed, almost the whole—either in my bed or lying upon the couch, from which I dictate this." He was fully aware of his imminent danger, and looked forward to the end with great courage and composure. On the 24th of May, at his own earnest request, he was carried back to Beaconsfield; and throughout he made careful preparation for the death that hovered near. Touching messages of remembrance were sent to his old friends, and kindly words of forgiveness to his old foes. Only to Fox would he not consent on being reconciled, though Fox anxiously desired that they might part in peace.

On the last day of his life (9th July, 1797) he occupied himself in giving directions for his funeral, and in listening to one of Addison's beautiful essays " On the Immortality of the Soul." When the reading was finished he complained of faintness, and asked to be conveyed to his bed. But his attendants and his kinsman, Mr. Nagle, had scarcely taken him in their arms before his breathing became difficult, and in a few minutes, low murmuring an inarticulate blessing, he expired. " His end," says Dr. Laurence, " was suited to the simple greatness of mind which he displayed through life—every way unaffected, without levity, without ostentation, full of natural grace and dignity." He was in his sixty-eighth year."

On the 15th he was buried in Beaconsfield Church, by the side of his well-beloved son and his brother Richard.

The private life and character of Burke were without spot or stain. He was deeply religious ; not, perhaps, in the sense in which religion is understood by the bigots of the Calvinistic school or the Pharisees of any sect, but in the true spirit of the Church of England, with moderation and sobriety—a firm faith, a sincere practice, and a cheerful, vivid, and unpretending piety. Churchman as he was, towards both Romanists and Protestant Dissenters he displayed a sagacious charity and enlightened tolerance. No shadow of doubt or suspicion has rested upon his integrity ; his moral character is as unsullied as the shield of Bayard. For his cultivated taste and elevated nature the dice and the bottle, which misled so many of his contemporaries, had no attractions. But in truth he had no leisure for self-indulgence, no time to be idle. The hours not devoted to public affairs or social intercourse were occupied by literary labour, and in the country by agricultural pursuits. He had a liberal hand and a warm heart. No worthy applicant ever told him a tale of distress and want unrelieved. The kindly, generous patronage he bestowed on James Barry, the artist—who was scarcely less beholden to his sagacious advice than to his active benevolence—will always be remembered to his honour.

Burke excelled as a conversationalist. Being always full of information, fluent in speech, prompt in reply, ingenious in the development of an argument, with considerable resources of humour and vivacity, he was one of the first of Talkers in an age of Great Talkers. "Burke," said Dr. Johnson, "is never what we call hum-drum; never in a hurry to begin conversation, at a loss to carry it on, or eager to leave off." He was entirely free from a vice often found in great conversationalists: he never showed a desire to monopolise the talk. He was able to listen, and delighted in drawing out the best powers and gifts of his friends. It is much to be wished that he had had a Boswell to perpetuate his sayings, for that they were wise and witty we have the testimony of his contemporaries. Hearing a "Life of Dr. Young," the author of the "Night Thoughts," described as a good imitation of Johnson, he exclaimed, "No, no; it is not a good imitation of Dr. Johnson. It has all his pomp without his force; it has all the nodosi-ties of the oak without its strength; it has all the contortions of the Sibyl without the inspiration." In reference to Godwin's curious definition of gratitude in his "Political Justice" he remarked, "I should take care to spare him the commission of that vice, by never conferring upon him a favour." His severe judgment upon Gay's "Beggar's Opera" was expressed in an epigram : " There is nothing exhibited in it which a correct man would wish to see, and nothing taught in it which any man would wish to learn."

We have commented, in the earlier part of this essay, on Burke's versatility of genius and acquirements, a versatility which would surely have delighted Milton! It is not enough to say of him that he was a great scholar, and an eminent politician, and a potent party leader; you must add that he was a successful conversationalist, a philosophic inquirer, a judicious critic, and an accomplished scholar. That his imagination sometimes overpowered his judgment is unfortunately true. In all that related to the French Revolution he was so fevered and overwrought that his usual clearness of discrimination and moderation of view utterly disappeared; yet he possessed a rare gift of political foresight. Whatever Burke did, he did thoroughly; he was never superficial; he poured upon every subject he took up a flood of fresh light; and the profusion of his ideas was not less remarkable than the copiousness of his eloquence.

It may have been this very prodigality and exuberance of thought and suggestion that made him, as a practical statesman, inferior to Pitt and Fox. He forgot what was expedient while dwelling upon the ideal. In the full sweep and rush of his imagination, he advanced far beyond the goal at which intellects more prudent, and more attentive to the immediate necessities of present action, were content to halt their forces. This was the secret both of his success and failure in regard to the French Revolution. He never paused to contemplate its beneficial side—the good it had effected, and was designed to effect, in the release of Europe from its bondage to ancient prejudices and its dread of mediæval

U

spectres, and in the abolition of the iron traditions and
practices of feudalism.   All he could see, in his too
rapid survey, was the vehemence of a movement which
seemed to shake the foundations of society, and threatened to involve the civilised world, with all its law, and
order, and religion, in a chaos of broken faiths and
wrecked institutions.   In the fever of his soul, he saw
everything through a blood-red atmosphere.   The truth
is that, with all his professed Whiggism, Burke at heart
was a Conservative.   He clung with a strange affection
to the altar of the past.   He looked back with a tear
in his eye to the picturesque aspect of "the age of
chivalry."   The associations of antiquity he invested with
an imaginary sacredness ; and whatever was established
he sought to place above the reach of the innovating
or irreverent hand.

In person Burke was neither commanding nor graceful.
He measured five feet ten inches in height, was erect and
well made, but not robust.   In early life he was partial
to rural sports, and down to the date of his last illness
he delighted in active exercise.   His features were good
and sufficiently regular ; but the chief expression of his
countenance was one of benevolence.   His manners were
attractive, combining dignity with frankness, and simplicity with ease.   Finally, it may interest the reader
to know—since one of Burke's biographers thinks it
worthy of record—that his customary dress was a light
brown coat, so made that it seemed to cramp and con-
strain his movements, and a little bob-wig, with curls.

Such was Edmund Burke.

# Sir William Jones.

1746–1794.

———◆◇◆———

**M**Y acquaintance with Sir William Jones began in my boyhood with my perusal of that charming book which has been a help and an inspiration to so many young minds, "The Pursuit of Knowledge under Difficulties." There, if I remember rightly, he is put forward as a remarkable example of what may be accomplished by patience and perseverance. In my later life, having had occasion to look into his career and character, I have been led to the conclusion that he furnishes one of the best illustrations to be found in all biography of the truth of Gibbon's saying, that "Every person has two educations—one which he receives from others, and one, more important, which he gives to himself." This saying we should take with Sir Walter Scott's corollary, "The best part of every man's education is that which he gives to himself." Sir William Jones was all his life —unhappily it was not a long one—*educating himself*, and doing so with a wonderful tenacity and thoroughness. His vast stores of knowledge were accumulated by his own industry—an industry guided by intelligence, and sustained by an unwavering firmness of purpose. His intellectual activity was ceaseless; his brain was never at rest; and he seems to have been consumed by a fever of acquisition. Like Alexander, he was always sighing for new worlds to conquer. He was, I think, only twenty-seven years old when he mapped out a field of study of such wide area that most minds would look at it aghast. With lofty resolution, he noted down that he would learn no more "rudiments," but perfect himself in twelve languages—not as a mere linguistic triumph, but for the purpose of acquiring an accurate knowledge of

I.—History.
(a.) Man.   (b.) Nature.

II. Arts.
(a.) Rhetoric.  (b.) Poetry.  (c.) Painting.  (d.) Music.

III. Sciences.
(a.) Law.  (b.) Mathematics.  (c.) Dialectics.

The twelve languages which he proposed to acquire were—Greek, Latin, Italian, French, Spanish, Portuguese, Hebrew, Arabic, Persian, Turkish, German, English.

An accomplished critic, Lord Jeffrey, makes some admirable remarks upon the career of this indomitable seeker after knowledge, which may be accepted as a just statement of the lesson that career teaches:—

"From the very commencement," he says, "he appears to have taxed himself very highly; and having in early youth set before his eyes the standard of a noble and accomplished character in every department of excellence, he seems never to have lost sight of this object of emulation, and never to have remitted his exertions to elevate and conform himself to it in every particular. Though born in a condition very remote from affluence, he soon determined to give himself the education of a finished gentleman, and not only to cultivate all the elegance and refinement implied in that appellation, but to carry into the practice of an honourable profession all the lights and ornaments of philosophy and learning, and, extending his ambition beyond the attainment of mere literary or professional eminence, to qualify himself for the management of public affairs, and to look forward to the higher rewards of patriotism, virtue, and political skill.

"The perseverance and exemplary industry with which he laboured to carry out his magnificent plan, and the distinguished success attending the accomplishment of all that part of it which the shortness of his life permitted him to execute, afford an instructive lesson to all who may be inclined by equal diligence to deserve an equal reward. The more we learn, indeed, of the early history of those who have bequeathed a great name, the more shall we be persuaded that no substantial or permanent excellence can ever be attained without much pains, labour, and preparation, and that extraordinary talents are less necessary to the most brilliant success than perseverance and application."

William Jones was born in London in 1746. His father, who was the friend of Newton, and a man of considerable scientific acquirements, died when his son was only three years old. Under the care of his mother, however, the boy throve rapidly, developing an active spirit of inquiry, and a love and an appreciation of knowledge such as is seldom met with in young minds. His mother was an accomplished woman, with a natural genius for teaching; and it was from her his intellect received its earliest impulse. Our teachers can do so much with us when the first thing they teach us is to love them! In his fifth year the boy's imagination was attracted by the fine figure of the angel in the 10th chapter of the Apocalypse. The impression produced

was never forgotten.  It is evident, therefore, that his
mother had good material to work upon.

In 1753 he was sent to Harrow School, then under
the charge of Dr. Thackeray.  For the first two years, it
is said, he was remarked for his great diligence rather
than the superiority of his talents, which, as the boy
was barely nine, is scarcely a matter of surprise.  Having
the misfortune to break his thigh-bone, he was laid up at
home for more than a twelvemonth, and exchanged the
curriculum of Harrow for a course of home-reading,
which, as it included some of the best English writers,
was certainly more profitable for him.  On returning to
school, he was promoted at once to the class in which he
would have stood had his studies been uninterrupted—a
judicious promotion, as it inspired him with confidence
in himself, and a resolve to keep the position he had
gained.  His great powers of apprehension and recep-
tivity were now disclosed, and he strode so far ahead of
his compeers that, in his twelfth year, he was removed
into the Upper School.  While performing his appointed
exercises with the greatest care and credit, he lost no
opportunity of adding to his store of general information.
He gained an acquaintance with Arabic characters, and
mastered Hebrew so far as to be able to read the Psalms.
His leisure hours, instead of appropriating to the usual
recreation, he devoted to study, and he even encroached
upon the hours of sleep, drinking tea and coffee to keep
him awake.  His eyesight becoming affected, he was
compelled to desist from this dangerous practice.

Among his intimate associates at this time were two
lads, who, like himself, rose to future eminence—Dr.
Parr; Burnett, Bishop of Cloyne.  The latter afterwards
said of him :—" I knew him from the age of eight or

nine years, and he was always an uncommon boy. Great abilities, great particularity of thinking, fondness for writing verses and plays of various kinds, and a degree of integrity and manly courage, of which I remember instances, distinguished him even at that period. I loved him and revered him; and, though one or two years older than he was, was always instructed by him from my earliest age." Dr. Thackeray formed a high estimate of the talents and character of the young student. " So active was the mind of Jones," he said, "that if he were left, naked and friendless, on Salisbury Plain, he would, nevertheless, find the road to fame and riches."

In 1764, he was entered of University College, Oxford. That was not a time when the University did much for her children; if they asked for bread, she gave them a stone; and Jones, disgusted by the barrenness of the prescribed course of study, drew back upon his own resources. He worked with ardour and persistency, reading the best classic writers, and indulging his early inclination for the Oriental languages. A native of Aleppo whom he had found out in London, he engaged to assist him in Arabic and Persian. In his celebrated " Treatise on Education," Milton, when sketching out a complete educational system, is careful to include certain " exercises and recreations." And

" The exercise which I commend first," he says, " is the exact use of their weapon, to guard, and to strike safely with edge or point ; this will keep them healthy, nimble, strong, and well in health ; is also the likeliest means to make them grow large and tall, and to inspire them with a gallant and fearless courage, which being tempered with seasonable lectures and precepts to them of their fortitude and patience, will turn into a native and heroic valour, and make them hate the cowardice of doing wrong."

Jones acted upon this principle, and during his vacations, which he spent in London, he took lessons of Angelo, the famous fencing-master. At the same time, he read, by way of entertainment, the chief authors in the Spanish, Portuguese, and Italian languages.

In his nineteenth year, he was induced, through the narrowness of his means, to accept an offer from Earl Spencer, to act as private tutor to his son, Lord Althorpe, then only nine years of age. Soon afterwards, he was elected to a fellowship, and the income he derived from the two posts enabled him to pursue his studies without any fear of pecuniary embarrassment, a fear which has so often tied down the wings of genius.

We may gain some idea of the amplitude of our young student's acquirements by noting that he was not twenty-one when he began his "Commentaries on Asiatic Poetry,"—which presupposes an intimate acquaintance with Persian and Arabic. We know that he was also an accomplished Greek and Latin scholar; that he was conversant with all the best English literature; that he could read five European languages; and that he had made himself master of Hebrew. It must be averred that, for a young man of twenty, he was not badly equipped! Obviously his natural capacity must have been large, but how persistent must have been his industry! How resolute his perseverance! What admirable and methodical use must he have made of his time! No wonder that his name figures so conspicuously in our manuals of self-culture; in all books designed to awaken the emulation of the young, and stimulate them to contend bravely against ignorance and physical indulgence. Of the love of knowledge, in its highest, truest development, where shall we find a nobler example than William Jones? To him knowledge was its own exceeding great reward.

In 1767 he accompanied Earl Spencer's family on a Continental tour, and it is a characteristic illustration of his versatility, that while at Spa he took lessons in dancing. For several years he continued to reside with his pupils at Harrow, and in Lord Spencer's family at Althorpe. When the King of Denmark visited England in 1768, he brought with him a Persian MS., containing the life of Nadir Shah, which he wished to have translated into French. Jones was immediately introduced to him as the only Oriental scholar in England capable of performing the work. He undertook the commission, and discharged it with elegance and accuracy.

In 1770, at the instigation of his friends, or from a desire to be independent, he resigned his tutorship, and entering himself a student of the Temple, applied himself with ardour to the study of the law. His first bias in this direction seems to have been given him some years before by a chance perusal of Sir John Fortescue's treatise, *De Laudibus Legum Angliæ*. Writing to his friend, Count Reviczki, he says :—

"On my late return to England" [he had paid a second visit to the Continent in the preceding year] "I found myself entangled, as it were, in a variety of important considerations. My friends, companions, relatives, all attacked me with urgent solicitations to banish poetry and Oriental literature for a time, and apply myself to oratory and the study of the law; in other words, to become a barrister, and pursue the track of ambition. Their advice, in truth, was conformable to my own inclinations; for the only road to the highest stations in this

country is that of the law, and I need not add how ambitious
and laborious I am."

In what spirit he addressed himself to his new course
of life, we may learn from his letter to his friend, Mr.
Wilmot, son of Lord Chief-Justice Wilmot :—*

"I have just begun," he says, "to contemplate the stately
edifice of the laws of England—

"The gathered wisdom of a thousand years,"

if you will allow me to parody a line of Pope. I do not see
why the study of the law is called dry and unpleasant ; and I
very much suspect that it seems so to those only who would
think any study unpleasant which required a great application
of the mind and exertion of the memory. I have just read
most attentively the two first volumes of Blackstone's ' Commentaries,' and the two others will require much less attention. I
am much pleased with the care he takes to quote his authorities
in the margin, which not only give a sanction to what he asserts,
but point out the sources to which the student may refer for
more diffusive knowledge.

"I have opened two common-place books—the one of the
law, the other of oratory, which is surely too much neglected by
our modern speakers. I do not mean the popular eloquence
which cannot be tolerated at the bar ; but that correctness of
style and elegance of method which at once pleases and per-
suades the hearer. But I must lay aside my studies for about
six weeks, while I am printing my Grammar, from which a
good deal is expected, and which I must endeavour to make as
perfect as a human work can be. When that is finished, I
shall attend the Court of King's Bench very constantly."

From a letter to another friend I take a not less illus-
trative extract :—

* Lord Teignmouth, "Life of Sir William Jones."

"I have learned so much, seen so much, written so much, said so much, and thought so much, since I conversed with you that, were I to attempt to tell half what I have learned, seen, writ, said, and thought, my letter would have no end. I spend the whole winter in attending the public speeches of our greatest lawyers and senators, and in studying our own admirable laws, which exhibit the most noble example of human wisdom that the mind of man can contemplate. I give up my leisure hours to a political treatise on the Turks, from which I expect some reputation; and I have several objects of ambition which I cannot trust to a letter, but will impart to you when we meet. If I am in England, I shall print my *De Poesi Asiatica* next summer, though I shall be at least two hundred pounds out of pocket by it. In short, if you wish to know my occupations, read the beginning of Middleton's 'Cicero,' pp. 13-18, and you will see my model, for I would willingly lose my head at the age of sixty, if I could pass a life at all analogous to that which Middleton describes."

But the generation to which Jones belonged was, in many respects, intensely conservative and bigoted. It was an axiom of general belief that a good lawyer could be nothing else than a lawyer; that in proportion as he cultivated his mind by the study of letters, did he deteriorate in the application of " precedents" and "cases." A lawyer who was known to write poetry and read foreign languages was shunned by the public with honest aversion and mistrust. No clients came to his door; no fees jingled in his pockets. "It would hurt me as a student at the bar," writes Jones, in reference to this extraordinary superstition, " to have it thought that I continue to apply myself to poetry." So that, after he was called to the bar in 1774, he abandoned his literary pursuits, and devoted himself wholly to legal studies. " As the law is a jealous science," he writes, " and will not have any partnership with the Eastern Muses, I must absolutely renounce their acquaintance for ten or twelve years to come."

Sir William Jones was not a poet; he had the poetic taste, but not the vision and the faculty divine, not the creative gift, or the soaring sweep of the poet's imagination. But an accomplished student of polite letters, he wrote with ease and elegance, and his translations are admirably executed.　From a volume which he published in 1772 I quote a few stanzas, " A Persian Song of Hafiz," the smoothness of which not unfairly represents the liquid fluency of the original :—

> " Sweet maid, if thou wouldst charm my sight,
> And bid these arms thy neck enfold ;
> That rosy cheek, that lily hand,
> Would give thy poet more delight
> Than all Bokhara's haunted gold,
> Than all the gems of Samarcand.　.　.
>
> " Speak not of Fate ; ah, change the theme,
> And talk of odours, talk of wine,
> Talk of the flowers that round us bloom ;
> 'Tis all a cloud ; 'tis all a dream ;
> To love and joy thy thoughts confine,
> Nor hope to pierce the sacred gloom.
>
> " Beauty has such resistless power
> That even the chaste Egyptian dame
> Sighed for the blooming Hebrew boy ;
> For her how fatal was the hour
> When to the banks of Nilus came
> A youth so lovely and so coy !
>
> " But, ah, sweet maid ! my counsel hear—
> Youth should attend when those advise
> Whom long experience renders sage.
> While music charms the ravished ear,
> While sparkling cups delight our eyes,
> Be gay, and scorn the frowns of age.

" Go boldly forth, my simple lay,
Whose accents flow with artless ease,
Like orient pearls at random strung : *
Thy notes are sweet, the damsels say ;
But, oh ! far sweeter if they please
The nymph for whom these notes are sung !"

This is very graceful, though it is a paraphrase rather than a translation. As an original writer, little of Jones's poetry is now read or remembered; but in one of his lyrics he strikes an unusually elevated note, and exhibits a considerable power of condensed thought. I refer to the " Ode, in imitation of Alcæus : "—

" What constitutes a State ?
Not high-raised battlement or laboured mound,
Thick wall or moated gate ;
Not cities proud, with spires and turrets crowned ;
Not bays and broad armed ports,
Where, laughing at the storm, rich navies ride ;
Not starred and spangled courts,
Where low-browed baseness wafts perfume to pride.
No ; men, high-minded men,
With powers as far above dull brutes endued
In forest, brake, or den,
As beasts excel cold rocks and brambles rude ;
Men who their duties know,
But know their rights, and, knowing, dare maintain,
Prevent the long-aimed blow,
And crush the tyrant while they rend the chain.
These constitute a State ;
And sovereign law, that State's collected will,
O'er thrones and globes elate
Sits empress, crowning good, repressing ill ;
Smit by her sacred frown,
The fiend Dissension like a vapour sinks,
And even the all-dazzling crown
Hides his faint rays, and at her bidding shrinks.

---

* A happy line, which has become familiar as household words.

" Such was this heaven-loved isle,
Than Lesbos fairer, and the Cretan shore !
No more shall Freedom smile ?
Shall Britons languish and be men no more ?
Since all must life resign,
Those meet rewards which decorate the brave
'Tis folly to decline,
And steal inglorious to the silent grave."

For a few months after he was called to the bar Mr.
Jones did not seek to practise, from an idea, it is supposed,
that he had not sufficiently mastered the principles
of jurisprudence.   For he took as comprehensive a view
of the study of law as he had taken of his other and
lighter studies ; and, regarding it as a science, proceeded
to investigate it with scientific method, comparing the
legal systems of ancient times with those of modern
Europe, all of which he carefully examined and compared.    In a wider and deeper sense than usually
attaches to the words, he was "learned in the law" when
he began his regular attendance at Westminster Hall in
1775.    His remarkable acquirements and high character
secured him a very easy promotion; for in the following year,
Lord Chancellor Bathurst, unsolicited by Jones himself,
and uninfluenced by any friend, presented him to a com-
missionership of bankruptcy, he dedicating to his patron
his translation of " Isæus " (1778).   Jones says :—

" I cannot let slip this opportunity of informing the public—
who have hitherto indulgently approved and encouraged my
labours—that although I have received many signal marks of
friendship from a number of illustrious persons, to whose favours
I can never proportion my thanks, yet your Lordship has been
my greatest, my only benefactor ; that, without any solicitation,
or even request, on my part, you gave me a substantial and
permanent token of regard, which you rendered still more valu-

able by your obliging manner of giving it, and which has been literally the sole fruit that I have gathered from an incessant course of very painful toil."

His noble Alcaic Ode shows that he was animated by a wise and genuine spirit of patriotism; and though he did not interfere actively in political life, his sympathies were all with the cause of enlightenment and progress. He was strongly opposed to the American war, and lifted his voice in favour of the abolition of the slave trade. He appears to have contemplated for himself in the future a parliamentary career, under such circumstances, however, as should secure his independence. His ambition was as high-toned as his character; and it was not personal advancement he sought, but the means and opportunity of contributing to the public welfare. Writing to his old pupil, Lord Althorpe, in 1778, he says :— " I wish to have twenty thousand pounds in my pocket before I am eight-and-thirty years old, and then I might contribute in some degree towards the service of my country in Parliament, as well as at the bar, without selling my liberty to a patron, as too many of my profession are not ashamed of doing; and I might be a speaker in the House of Commons in the full vigour and maturity of my age." *  It happened, however, that a different channel was opened up to him for the suitable employment of his abilities. His acquirements as an Oriental linguist and a lawyer pointed him out as a man eminently fitted to adorn the Indian judicature; and in 1783, during the Administration of the Earl of Shelbourne, he was appointed a judge of the Supreme Court

---

* It was about this time that he published his " Essay on the Law of Bailments," of which lawyers still speak highly.  He also issued a pamphlet in favour of Parliamentary reform.

at Fort William (Calcutta), in Bengal. This appointment enabled him to offer his hand to a lady who had long enjoyed his esteem and affection, Miss Shipley, the eldest daughter of his friend the Bishop of St. Asaph.

Accompanied by his wife, Sir William Jones—he had received the honour of knighthood as the necessary appanage of the judicial office—embarked for India in April, 1773. On the voyage he addressed a letter to Lord Ashburton, to whose influence he owed his promotion :—

" As to you, my dear Lord," he said, " we consider you as the spring and fountain of our happiness, as the author and parent (a Roman would have added—what the coldness of our northern language will hardly admit—the god) of our fortunes. It is possible, indeed, that, by incessant labour and irksome attendance at the bar, I might in due time have attained all that my limited ambition could aspire to ; but in no other station than that which I owe to your friendship would I have gratified at once my boundless curiosity concerning the people of the East, continued the exercise of my profession, in which I sincerely delight, and enjoyed at the same time the comforts of domestic life.

" The grand jury of the county of Denbigh have proved, I understand, the bill against the Dean of St. Asaph for publishing my Dialogue ;* but as an indictment for a theoretical essay on government was,'I believe, never before known, I have no apprehension for the consequences. As to the doctrines of the tract, though I shall certainly not preach them to the Indians, who must and will be governed by absolute power, yet I shall go through life with a persuasion that they are just and

---

* He had written a tract entitled " A Dialogue between a Farmer and a Country Gentleman on the Principles of Government," of which the Dean of St. Asaph published a Welsh edition.

rational; that substantial freedom is both the daughter and parent of virtue; and that virtue is the only source of public and private felicity."

In December, 1783, Sir William Jones took his seat on the bench, and delivered his first charge to the grand jury. Lord Teignmouth tells us that the public—that is, the English community—had formed a high estimate of his oratorical powers, and that they were not disappointed. His address, we are told, was concise, graceful, and appropriate. He expounded his principles and sentiments with manly candour, but in a conciliatory manner; and from the known sincerity of his character, it was felt that his promises would not fail in the act of performance. Alluding with tact and good taste to the dissensions that at no remote period had unhappily prevailed between the executive and the judicial bench in Bengal, he showed that they ought to have been and might be avoided; that the functions of both were distinct, and could be exercised without risk of collision in promoting what should be the common object—the public good.

In the following year, his health becoming affected by the climate and his excessive application to his many duties, Sir William went on a tour through various parts of India, in the course of which he wrote "The Enchanted Fruit, or the Hindu Wife," a tale in verse, and a "Treatise on the Gods of Greece, Italy, and India." On his return he resumed his official duties with characteristic earnestness; but he seems always to have been a valetudinarian. Nothing, however, was allowed to interfere with his indefatigable pursuit of knowledge, or his eager desire to benefit the teeming millions of India. He planned a grand "Digest of Hindu and Mohammedan

x

Laws," on the model of Justinian's celebrated code ; and the plan having been approved by the Governor-General, he superintended its execution by native lawyers, devoting nearly the whole of his leisure to its advancement. To develop among the Anglo-Indian public a love of oriental literature, he founded the Asiatic Society, of which he was the first president. In order that he might investigate the principles of the Hindu law, without a servile dependence on the statements of the Pandects, he applied himself to the study of Sanskrit. To the *Asiatic Miscellany*, a periodical published at Calcutta, he contributed several translations, essays, and original poems. His energy was inexhaustible, and his activity ceaseless. It was impossible for him to desist from doing while there was anything to be done. Writing to a friend, he says :—" My private life is similar to that which you remember. Seven hours a-day, on an average, are occupied by my duties as a magistrate, and one hour is given to the new Indian Digest. For an hour in the evening I read aloud to Lady Jones." We are reminded of the division of time he suggests in the couplet which he improved from Sir Edward Coke. Coke wrote :—

> " Six hours in sleep, in law's grave study six,
> Four spend in prayer, the rest on nature fix."

Sir William Jones laid down a wiser rule :—

> " Seven hours to law, to soothing slumber seven,
> Ten to the world allot, and all to heaven."

In 1789 he translated the famous Indian drama of " Sakontala, or⋅ the Fatal Ring," which supplies us with some interesting pictures of Hindu characteristics and manners. This translation of Kâlidâsa's great dramatic poem has been to some extent superseded by Professor Monier Williams's; but it deserves to be ever held in respectful remembrance as the starting-point of Sanskrit philology in Europe. To Sir William Jones belongs the credit which is always ascribed to the pioneer who opens up a new path to man's intellectual enterprise.

Three years later, in pursuance of his great object of adapting the European administration of justice in India to the forms and principles of the old Indian laws, he published a translation of the "Ordinances of Menu." This great work is something more than a system of jurisprudence; it is also a system of cosmogony, an exposition of the art of government, and a treatise upon metaphysics. It is divided into twelve books, which treat respectively of—1. Creation; 2. Education, and the duties of a pupil, or the first order; 3. Marriage, and the duties of a householder, or the second order; 4. Means of subsistence, and the morals of the individual; 5. Diet, purification, and the duties of women; 6. Duties of an anchorite and an ascetic, or the third and fourth orders; 7. Government, and the duties of a king and the military caste; 8. Judicature and law, private and criminal; 9. Duties of the commercial and servile castes; 10. Mixed castes, and the duties of the castes in time of distress; 11. Penance and expiation; and 12. Transmigration and final beatitude.

In December, 1793, Lady Jones, by the impaired condition of her health, was compelled to return to England, leaving her husband to complete the "Digest," and then to join her in the happy rural retreat which his imagination, weary of its old ambitions, had pictured to him as the home of his later years. But this was not to be. One evening, in April, 1794, after remaining imprudently in the open air till a late hour, he called upon his friend, Sir John Shore (afterwards Lord Teignmouth), and complained of aguish symptoms. These, unfortunately, were found to indicate the existence of inflammation of the liver, when, two or three days afterwards, medical advice was obtained. His enfeebled constitution could not resist the disease ; it ran its course with increased swiftness ; and on the 27th of April proved fatal. On the morning of that day, his attendants, alarmed at the signs of approaching dissolution, hastened to summon Lord Teignmouth to the bedside of his friend. He found him lying on his bed in a posture of meditation, and the sole indication of lingering life was a small degree of action in the heart: this, after a few seconds, ceased, and he expired without a pang or groan. From the complacency of his features, and the ease of his position, it was evident that he had suffered little ; and no doubt he had found consolation from those sources where he had always been accustomed to seek it, —where alone, as we pass through the valley of the shadow, we can hope to find it successfully.

Sir William Jones, at the time of his death, was only forty-eight years old. But of his short life he had made admirable use. He had devoted himself to the acquisition of knowledge from no selfish motives. He had made it a means of advancing the cause of civilisation and human progress. His sympathies were always with right and justice and freedom ; his mind was as pure and as lofty as his life. Those last lines of Berkeley's " Siris," of which he was so fond—" He that would make a real progress in knowledge must dedicate his age as well as youth, the latter growth as well as the first-fruits, at the altar of Truth " *—seem to me the exact epitome, as it were of his career; or rather, I should say, perhaps, they gave its keynote. Truth was his guiding-star, his inspiration. In every relation of life, and in every capacity, he commanded esteem by his rectitude of conduct and loftiness of purpose. As a judge, his inflexible integrity was long remembered in Calcutta, both by Europeans and natives.

"So cautious was he," says Lord Teignmouth, "to guard the independence of his character from any possibility of violation or imputation, that no solicitation could prevail upon him to use his personal influence with the members of administration in India to advance the private interests of friends whom he esteemed, and which he would have been happy to promote. He knew the dignity and felt the importance of his office, and, convinced that none could afford him more ample scope for exerting his talents for the benefit of mankind, his ambition never extended beyond it."

As a linguist, Sir William Jones has been surpassed by few. He acquired a complete critical knowledge of eight languages :—English, Latin, French, Italian, Greek, Arabic, Persian, and Sanskrit. Eight more he knew less perfectly, but could read with some small assistance from a dictionary — Spanish, Portuguese, German, Runic, Hebrew, Bengali, Hindu, and Turkish. And with twelve others he had a varying degree of acquaintance—Tibetan, Pati, Phalari, Deri, Russian, Syrian, Ethiopic, Coptic,

---

* This sentence is the germ of the following lines by Sir William Jones :—

"Before thy mystic altar, heavenly Truth,
I kneel in manhood as I knelt in youth ;
Thus let me kneel till this dull form decay,
And life's last shade be brightened by thy ray ;
Then shall my soul, now lost in clouds below,
Soar without bound, without consuming grow."

Welsh, Swedish, Dutch, and Chinese. But, as we have seen, his acquirements in this direction did not prevent him from pursuing with energy and success the other branches of knowledge ; and he nourished his mind, fed his imagination, and guided his life by " the doctrines of philosophy, the records of history, and the teachings of science." *

---

* Our chief authority for the foregoing sketch is, of course, Lord Teignmouth's " Life of Sir William Jones."

# Sir Samuel Romilly.

1757-1818.

———◆◇◆———

SAMUEL ROMILLY was born on the 1st of March, 1757, in Frith Street, Soho, London. Like some other illustrious Englishmen, he sprang from a Huguenot family, who at one time held land at Mont-pelier, in the south of France. His grandfather, after the revocation of the Edict of Nantes—the great act of toleration which France owed to the wisdom of Henri Quatre—withdrew from his native country for conscience' sake, and settled in England. The patrimonial estates having passed away from him, he struggled as best he might against the pressure of poverty, but at a compara-tively early age fell in the unequal fight. His eldest son, Peter, born in 1712, was brought up to the trade of a jeweller. He married a lady of the name of Gamaule, who, like himself, was of French extraction, and by her had several children, of whom only three, Thomas, Catherine, and the subject of this sketch, escaped the perils of childhood.

Few particulars of the early life of Samuel Romily have come down to us, but it is known that he showed much sensibility of temperament, an amiable disposition, and exceptional activity of intellect. When very young he and his brother were sent to a neighbouring day-school, where they contrived to acquire, through their own exertions rather than any effort on the part of their master, some knowledge of writing, arithmetic, and the rules of the French grammar. At the age of fourteen Samuel Romilly left school, and for a couple of years gave assistance to his father in keeping his accounts, and occasionally taking the orders of his customers. This occupation left him a good deal of leisure, which he occupied in reading—reading all such books as he could possibly procure, while preferring those in ancient history, criticism, and English poetry. I suppose that most young men with a taste for letters dabble in rhyme, and think themselves poets. Romilly did not escape the delusion, and scrawled an infinite number of eclogues, songs, and satires, translated Boileau, and imitated Spenser. There is one advantage in this form of composition—the practice of it chastens the taste, trains the ear, and accustoms the writer to the choice of words.

A young man who writes verses can soon persuade himself that he is a genius. This was the case with Romilly, but he had good sense enough to perceive that even genius needs culture. He applied himself, therefore, to the study of Latin, and in the course of three or four years mastered the principal Latin authors in poetry and prose, and attained to some degree of facility in Latin composition. In Greek he was unable to make much progress, but he read the Greek writers in Latin and English versions. Meanwhile, by his process of desultory reading, he had gained some knowledge of a good many sciences, and an inherited taste had led him to study the works of the great painters,—so that, at eighteen, young

Romilly would have been justified in considering himself tolerably well educated, and certainly knew a great deal more than most young men of his age with far greater educational advantages.

His home-life was of a sort well calculated to encourage and develop in him a love of culture. He drew a picture of it which I cannot but contemplate with pleasure, and I sometimes think it may have suggested an idea to the author of "Daniel Deronda" for her admirable description of the household of the Meyricks. Here it is :—

" I love," he says, " to transport myself in idea into our little parlour, with its green paper, and the beautiful prints of Vivares, Bartolozzi, and Strange, from the pictures of Claude, Caracci, Raphael, and Correggio, with which its walls were elegantly adorned ; and to call again to mind the familiar and affectionate society of young and old intermixed, which was gathered round the fire ; and even the Italian greyhound, the cat, and the spaniel, which lay in perfect harmony looking before it." Here might be found " a lively, youthful, and accomplished society, blest with every enjoyment that an endearing home can afford, —a society united by a similarity of tastes, dispositions, and affections, as well as by the strongest ties of blood. They would have admired our lively, varied, and innocent pleasures ; our summer rides and walks in the cheerful country, which was close to us ; our winter evening occupations of drawing, while one of us read aloud some interesting book, or the eldest of my cousins played and sung to us with exquisite taste and expression ; the little banquets with which we celebrated the anniversary of my father's wedding, and of the birth of every member of our happy society ; and the dances with which, in spite of the smallness of our rooms, we were frequently indulged."

From such an atmosphere as this Romilly imbibed that refinement of taste and feeling which distinguished

him throughout his later life, and he also derived from
it, perhaps, that keen susceptibility which became both
his pleasure and his pain.

By the time that he was eighteen Romilly had ceased
to think himself a genius, but he had formed a strong
dislike to his father's business, and an earnest desire for
a more intellectual employment. It was determined,
therefore, that he should enter into some department of
the law; and the office of the Six Clerks in Chancery
being selected, he was duly articled to a Mr. Lally. He
still continued to reside at home, and in his leisure,
which was ample, to pursue his favourite studies and
amusements. His scheme of life he had duly settled;
he was to follow up his profession for a subsistence, and
to aspire to fame by his literary pursuits. That he was
no poet he had convinced himself, and, having given up
versifying, he sought to exercise himself in prose composition; and judging translations to be exceedingly
useful in forming a style, he rendered into English the
finest passages in the Latin literature; almost all the
speeches in Livy, very copious extracts from Tacitus, the
whole of Sallust, and much of the best of Cicero. For
the same purpose of improving his style, he read and
studied the best English writers, Addison, Swift, Bolingbroke, Robertson, Hume, carefully noting down every
*curiosa felicitas* of expression. No doubt these exercises
were exceedingly useful in guiding his judgment and
enlarging his vocabulary; but, after all, a man's style is
as much a part of himself as his thoughts or feelings are,
and if he have anything to say, he will find a way of his
own in which to say it.

It was a fortunate circumstance for the young student
that he made, while he was thus engaged, the acquaint-

ance of the Rev. John Royet, a native of Geneva, who had left that city of the mountains, and been appointed minister of the French chapel attended by the Romilly family. He was an eloquent preacher, but he was something more—he was a man of original mind, richly cultivated, and his hints and suggestions proved of great value to Romilly. I know not indeed of any circumstance of greater profit to a young man than that he should obtain the guidance of a trained and thoughtful intellect in his studies, to save him from wasting time by a fatal but enticing desultoriness of pursuit, to cheer him in his seasons of despondency, to control him in his moods of extravagant self-esteem and self-assertion, and to set before him an elevated ideal as that to which all his hopes and aspirations must be directed.

It was partly the influence of this valued friend which led Romilly into his true career.* In the Six Clerks' office there was no room for the development of his higher capabilities; and that fame and fortune which sometimes coloured his dreams, could be obtained only in a more important branch of the profession. He resolved, therefore, to study for the bar; and in May, 1778, became a member of Gray's Inn. Under the supervision of a Mr. Spranger, he pushed forward his legal reading with all the warmth of his nature. Writing to his friend, Royet, he thus details his daily order of work :—

"At six or sooner I rise, go into the cold bath, walk to

---

* In his autobiography Romilly says that he was influenced also by his perusal of Thomas's "Eloge of Daguesseau;" the career of glory which he represents that illustrious magistrate to have run, had greatly excited his ardour and ambition, and opened to his imagination new paths of glory.

Islington to drink a chalybeate water (from which I have found great benefit); return and write or read to ten ; then go to Mr. Spranger's, where I study till three ; dine in Frith Street, and afterwards return to Mr. Spranger's. This is the history of every day, with little other variation than that of my frequently attending the courts of justice in the morning, instead of going to Mr. Spranger's, and of often passing my afternoons at one of the Houses of Parliament."

We shall see that Romilly became a great lawyer, but he was also much more than a lawyer, and this was owing to his incessant and extensive reading. He was always athirst for general knowledge. He read a great deal of history; he continued to improve himself in the classics ; he translated, composed, and sedulously aimed at the formation of a correct and elegant style; the best passages of the best authors he assiduously rendered into English ; he wrote political essays, which he sent anonymously to the newspapers, being not a little elated at their constant appearance in print; and he strove to obtain a great facility of elocution. Adopting a device, suggested by Quinctilian, he expressed to himself, in the best language he could, whatever he had been reading, using the arguments employed by Tacitus or Livy, and building them, mentally, into speeches of his own. Occasionally, too, he attended the two Houses of Parliament, and would recite in thought, or answer, the speeches he heard there. And for the better economy of his time, he reserved these exercises for the hour devoted to walking or riding ; and before long, had so grown into the habit, that he would think these compositions as he was passing through the most crowded streets.

It is no marvel that intellectual labour so continuous,

and at such high pressure, eventually injured his health. He was naturally of a very nervous and sensitive temperament, which he ought to have managed with great care, and strengthened by adequate rest and open-air exercise; but throughout his life he put too great a strain upon it, with a result which should be a warning to all persons similarly constituted. In the spring of 1780 he spent six weeks at Bath, but without feeling any definite improvement. Then came the "No Popery" riots, headed by Lord George Gordon; and the consequent excitement still further disturbed his nervous system. Fortunately for him, a pressing occasion—the ill-health of Royet, who had married his sister, and sought a residence in Lausanne—called him away from England ; and a journey through Switzerland, followed by a visit to Paris, recruited both his physical and mental energies. While at Geneva, he formed the acquaintance of Dumont, afterwards the friend and editor of Bentham; and at Paris he was introduced to the philosophers of the *Encyclopædia*, D'Alembert and Diderot.* On a second visit to Paris, two years later, he had the satisfaction of conversing with Dr. Franklin, whose venerable patriarchal appearance, the simplicity of his manner and language, and the novelty of his observations, impressed Romilly with a conviction that he was "one of the most extraordinary men that ever existed."

On the 2nd of June, 1783, he was called to the bar. In a letter written a few weeks before to his friend,

---

* His letters at this time are marked by many interesting descriptions of the men and places he saw, and contain some curious sketches of a social order which was then unconsciously trembling on the brink of revolution.

Royet, he describes in elevated language the feelings with which he contemplated the career before him :—

"It would seem," he says, "that you thought I had affected doubt of succeeding in the way of life on which I am to enter, only to draw from you such praises as might encourage me in my pursuit. That object, had it been mine, must have been fully gratified by your silence, which, introduced as it is, is a greater encouragement to me, and is more offensive to modesty even than a panegyric upon talents which your indulgence might have supposed me to possess. However, I assure you I had no such wish, and that what I wrote to you was but a faithful transcript of what I felt. Could I but realise the partial hopes and expectations of my friends, there could be no doubt of my success, almost beyond my wishes ; but in myself I have a much less indulgent censor, and in this, perhaps alone, I cannot suffer their judgment to have equal weight with my own. I have taught myself, however, a very useful lesson of practical philosophy, in order to make myself easy in my situation, which is, not to suffer my happiness to depend upon my success. Should my wishes be gratified, *I promise myself to employ all the talents and all the authority I may acquire for the public good.* Should I fail in my pursuit, I console myself with thinking that the humblest situation of life has its duties, which one must feel a satisfaction in discharging ; that, at least, my conscience will have ever the pleasing testimony of having intended well ; and that, after all, true happiness is much less likely to be found in the high walks of ambition than in the *secretum iter et fallentis semita vitæ.* Were it not for these consolations, and did I consider my success at the bar as decisive of my future happiness, my apprehension would be such that I might truly say, ' *cum illius dici mihi venit in mentem, quo mihi dicendum sit, non solum commoveor animo, sed etiam toto corpore perhorresco.*' " *

* Cicero, in Q. Cæcil. Div. 13. "Memoirs of Sir Samuel Romilly," i. 257, 258.

To the high key-note pitched in these remarks, Romilly's whole life responded. I often think that men's failure in life is due to the low standard which they set up for themselves at the start; we make more misses by aiming too low than too high. But, after all, "success" and "failure" are relative terms; and what the world calls "success," God and angels may regard as "failure."

Again in May, 1783, he writes:—

"I am soon to enter on a career which possibly (though I grant not very probably) may place me in important and critical situations, which will certainly give one practical and selfish interests incompatible with the good of others, and which will throw me amidst mankind, and condemn me to hear the profession of dishonourable sentiments without opposing them, and to be a mere spectator of selfish and degrading conduct without discovering any detestation of it. It will in part depend on you to save me from the contagion of such examples; for though my heart still recoils from them with an antipathy that seems quite insurmountable, I have I know not what kind of terror, which I cannot overcome, of the force of habit, of perpetual temptations, of being familiarised with a contempt for virtue, and, above all, of our habitual attachment to the miserable gold which one earns."

For the first four or five years, Romilly's professional progress was very slow. His sensitive and nervous temperament was a grave obstacle, as it prevented him in public from doing justice to his really great powers. But if it were a source of weakness, it was also a source of strength. It refined and elevated his genius; quickened his sympathies; and promoted that human and compassionate disposition which animated his efforts for the amelioration of our universal law. Meanwhile, he continued to persevere in the performance of his professional duties, labouring patiently and assiduously, and preparing himself for the fit discharge of any responsibility that might devolve upon him. He attended the courts of law at Westminster, and went on the Midland circuit with exemplary regularity. He contrived in some measure to overcome his diffidence, and to acquire a greater degree of self-possession. By degrees it began to be known that his knowledge of law was sound and extensive, his judgment accurate, his perception rapid and exact; solicitors saw in him a man to be trusted; and in 1791 his practice as junior counsel was very considerable. In society he had established a reputation for grace of manner and charm of conversation which made him a welcome guest in the most distinguished circles, and the Marquis of Lansdowne, no mean judge of character, delighted in his company.

In 1797 he began to be employed as a leader, and in several important cases his success confirmed and extended his reputation. In 1800 he was appointed one of His Majesty's counsel, and thenceforth took a prominent position in the Court of Chancery. Having secured a moderate independence, he felt himself at liberty to seek a wider and nobler field of exercise than his profession in itself could offer, and waited only for an opening to enter upon that public life to which his hopes and aspirations had always pointed. His political views were those of the Whig party, but he was incapable of becoming a vehement or narrow partisan; his intellect was too philosophical, his judgment too impartial, his views of public duty too broad and lofty. Hence he desired to enter Parliament unshackled by promises. In 1805—the same year in which the Bishop of Durham appointed him his

Chancellor—he was offered a seat in the House of Commons by the Prince of Wales, but he respectfully declined. In the following year, in Mr. Fox's ministry, he was appointed Solicitor-General, and was immediately returned to Parliament as member for Queenborough. He was sworn in on the 12th of March, and, according to custom, knighted. Thus favourably, at the age of forty, did he enter upon his public career.

A few days after taking his seat in the House, Sir Samuel was appointed one of the managers in the impeachment of Lord Melville for peculation and jobbery during his tenure of office as First Lord of the Admiralty; and a duty which was not less disagreeable than onerous he discharged with great ability and scrupulous impartiality. On the 10th of May he summed up the case for the prosecution in a luminous and effective speech which lasted three hours and twenty minutes.

The philanthropical bias of his mind was shown in the warmth and eloquence with which he attacked the slave trade, in support of Mr. Fox's motion for its abolition. He tells us that he did not attempt to argue the question, whether the slave trade should be abolished; *this* he took as long ago decided; his object was to impress on the House a sense of the "reproachful situation" in which England stood with respect to this subject. Fifteen years before it had had the courage to inquire minutely into the subject, and had ascertained, by a mass of evidence which had been carefully sifted and recorded, that the trade was carried on by "robbery, rapine, and murder." And yet, with the full knowledge of this fact, it had persisted in the inhuman traffic, and dragged from the coasts of Africa no fewer than 360,000 human beings.

Y

At the time of Romilly's entering upon public life, the
English law was an Augean stable, offering ample work
to any reforming Hercules who would undertake its
cleansing. Romilly was anxious to do something in this
direction ; but, aware of the small result that is ever to
be obtained from a *general* attack, he wisely resolved to
bring his efforts to bear upon some particular abuse. The
bias of his mind and the natural benevolence of his
disposition led him to select, as the field in which he
might hope to employ his energies most advantageously,
the amelioration of our criminal code. To this his
attention had early been directed, and he was painfully
aware of the urgent necessity for prompt and efficient
action. The criminal code, as it then existed, was more
than Draconian in its severity ; it was written in blood ;
almost every clause ended in " death." Crimes and
offences, ranging from the nadir to the zenith of enormity,
met with the same penalty ; a man was hung for murder,
and he might be hung for stealing five shillings. Such
rigour was as impolitic as it was inhuman, not alone
from its ill effect upon the criminal classes, whom it
only hardened and exasperated, but from its influence
upon juries, whom it not unnaturally deterred from
pronouncing verdicts which carried with them the possibility of so awful a penalty.

Mr. Roscoe remarks that it has been sometimes
objected to Romilly that he did not apply himself to the
correction of the abuses which then discredited the
administration of justice in his own court, the Court of
Chancery ; and he adds that it ought surely never to be
regretted that he preferred the noble labour of reforming
a code, the excessive severity of which had for centuries
disgraced the institutions of our country. The former,

at the worst, struck only at men's property; the latter, at men's lives.

"That portion of the community which is affected by our civil polity are never without the means of making their complaints heard; but the poor, the destitute, the uninformed, and the misled, the objects upon whom our criminal jurisprudence operates, have no voice to protest against the severities which the Legislature may please to denounce. To watch over the interests of this wretched and degraded portion of society; to become the friend of those against whom every other hand was raised, and the protector of those who were abandoned, even by themselves, seemed to Sir Samuel Romilly a duty which claimed a decided pre-eminence."

It was a duty undertaken and carried out in the true spirit of that religion of humanity which was consecrated on Calvary by the blood of our Lord.

Romilly opened his protracted warfare on the 18th of May, 1808. In the previous year he had retired from office, on the fall of the Whig administration; and it was as a private member that he invited Parliament to repeal the Act of Queen Elizabeth which inflicted the punishment of death for privately stealing from the person to the extent of five shillings—in other words, for picking pockets! Even so obviously humane a measure met with vehement opposition. Romilly relates that a young man, the brother of a peer of the realm, came up to him at the bar of the House of Commons, and, breathing in his face "the nauseous fumes of his undigested debauch," stammered out, "I am against your bill; I am for hanging all." Romilly stood confounded; but, with his usual generosity, endeavouring to find some excuse for the brutal speech, observed that he supposed his interlocutor meant that the certainty of punishment affording the only prospect of suppressing crimes, the laws, whatever they were, ought to be executed. Over this golden bridge the young man had no wish to retreat; and he replied : "No, no ; it is not that. There is no good done by mercy; they only get worse. I would hang them all up at once."

Eventually the bill was passed; but Romilly was forced to strike out the declaration of principle embodied in the preamble : "Whereas, the extreme severity of penal law hath not been found effectual for the prevention of crimes, but, on the contrary, by increasing the difficulty of convicting offenders, in some cases affords them impunity, and in most cases renders their punishment extremely uncertain."

His next legislation was in amendment of the Bankruptcy Law; and then, in 1810, he resumed his attack upon the penal code, introducing three bills to repeal the statutes of William III., Queen Anne, and George II., by which the capital penalty might be inflicted for privately stealing in a shop goods to the value of five shillings, or in a dwelling-house, or on board a vessel in a navigable river. It is difficult now to believe that these measures would be bitterly opposed by such men as Windham, an orator of genius, a scholar, and a gentleman; and by Percival, the Prime Minister. Yet such was the fact ; and almost every member of the Government followed on the same side. Romilly had the satisfaction, however, of being supported by the eloquence of Canning and the authority of Wilberforce. Notwithstanding their valuable assistance, notwithstanding the strength of his arguments and the accumulated testimony of his facts, he was defeated. His first bill passed the Commons, but was rejected by the Lords; his second, the Commons rejected; the third was postponed, and afterwards withdrawn.

The opposition in the Lords was led by the Lord Chancellor, Eldon, and the Chief Justice, Lord Ellenborough, both great lawyers, but men bred in a narrow school, and fettered by tradition and precedent. The strange argument was put forward that the punishment must not be abolished, because the crime against which it was directed had increased; which would justify a physician in continuing to administer a powerful remedy because his patient grew worse!

"I trust," said Lord Ellenborough solemnly, "your Lordships will pause before you assent to a measure pregnant with danger to the security of property, and before you repeal a statute which has been so long held necessary for public security, and which I am not conscious has produced the smallest injury to the merciful administration of justice. After all that has been stated in favour of this speculative humanity, it must be admitted that the law as it stands is but seldom carried into execution; and yet it ceases not to hold out that terror which alone will be sufficient to prevent the frequent commission of the offence. It has been urged, by persons speculating in modern legislation, that a certainty of punishment is preferable to severity—that it should invariably be proportioned to the magnitude of the crime, thereby forming a known rate of punishment commensurate with the degree of the offence. Whatever may be my opinion of the theory of this doctrine, I am convinced of its absurdity in practice.

"Retaining the terror, and leaving the execution uncertain and dependent on circumstances which may aggravate or mitigate the enormity of the crime, does not prove the severity of any criminal law; whereas, to remove that salutary dread of punishment would produce injury to the criminal, and break down the barrier which prevents the frequent commission of crime. The learned judges are *unanimously agreed* that the expediency of justice and public security require there should not be a remission of capital punishment in this part of the criminal law. My lords, if we suffer this bill to pass, we shall not know where to stand; we shall not know whether we are on our heads or on our feet. If you repeal the Act which inflicts the penalty of death for stealing to the value of five shillings in a shop, you will be called upon next year to repeal a law which prescribes the penalty of death for stealing five shillings in a dwelling-house, there being no person therein—a law, your lordships must know, on the security of which, and the application of it, stands the security of every poor cottager who goes out to his daily labour (!). He, my lords, can leave no one behind to watch his little dwelling, and preserve it from the attacks of lawless plunderers. Confident in the protection of the laws of the land—[that is, their supposed readiness to hang a man for stealing a rush-bottomed chair !]—he cheerfully pursues his daily labours, trusting that on his return he shall find all his property safe and unmolested."

One stands lost in amazement at the absolute futility of the arguments thus elaborately put forth by a Lord Chief-Justice of England. Let the *laudatores temporis acti* reflect upon them, and the cause they were intended to support, and admit that in some things we have improved upon our forefathers. But it should be added, for the further enlightenment of the reader, that the sole legislative achievement of this truculent judge was an act (43 Geo. III. c. 58) which created ten new capital felonies, and greatly increased the already " revolting severity " of our criminal code.

With infinite patience pursuing his labours in the cause of humanity, Sir Samuel Romilly, in 1811, carried two bills which abolished the punishment of death for stealing from bleaching grounds; and in the following year, he persuaded Parliament to repeal the Act of Eliza-beth, by which soldiers and mariners wandering about the realm without a pass were doomed to death. A pamphlet on the " Criminal Law," which he had published, produced a great impression on the mind of the public, and helped to create a feeling in favour of further reform. The esteem in which he was held for his high character, scrupulous integrity, and great powers was agreeably manifested by an invitation from a number of respectable citizens of Bristol to become a candidate for the repre-sentation of their city. Two of his opponents, however, formed a strong coalition against him, and as he refused to sanction any lavish expenditure for corrupt purposes, he was defeated. Through the kindness of the Duke of Norfolk, he was afterwards elected for the borough of Arundel.

In the new Parliament our undaunted reformer once more proposed the abolition of capital punishment in cases of shop-lifting. The Commons passed the measure, but it was again rejected by the Lords. Sir Samuel then rested for a while from a crusade which seemed almost hopeless. But he was not idle. I have carefully examined the votes he gave in successive sessions on the various questions brought before Parliament, and I am prepared to say that he on no occasion flinched from his duty, and on no occasion gave a vote contrary to the principles of truth, justice, and freedom. Few of his contemporaries can show a record so unstained. He was a reformer before the day of reform, and on all subjects of foreign and domestic policy his views were in favour of enlightenment and progress. His efforts to promote the abolition of the slave trade never slackened, and Wilber-force had no more earnest or eloquent supporter. The persecutions to which the French Protestants were exposed, the disabilities imposed upon aliens, the iniquitous severities of the game laws : against these he strenuously protested, while he opposed the measures taken by Lord Liverpool's Government for restricting the liberty of the subject, such as the suspension of the Habeas Corpus Act, and the bill against so-called seditious meetings. The employment of spies and informers, who incriminated innocent men by their fictitious evidence ; the imprisonment for libels, urged on by a Government which was tyrannical because it was weak, he denounced with a just indignation. But what is noticeable is, that though thus opposing the policy of a powerful majority, he secured and preserved the esteem of his opponents no less than of his friends. There was a charm about that fine nature, in its simplicity, its unselfishness, its profound truthfulness, its purity, which everybody felt. It is impossible for some men not to make enemies ; it was impossible for Romilly not to make friends. His career is a proof of the instinctive deference which the world pays to *goodness*. For Romilly was not a man of genius, though gifted with considerable talents ; his intellect was not of that high order which compels instant and universal acknowledgement. His influence was the influence of character ; and it was *himself*, and not his gifts, which was loved and admired.

His efforts for the amelioration of the Criminal Code were resumed in 1816, when, after the downfall of Napoleon, he probably thought the country would have leisure for the consideration of legal reforms. On the 16th of February he obtained leave to bring in a bill repealing William III.'s shop-lifting statute. He justly described it as the severest and most sanguinary in our statute-book ; as inconsistent with the spirit of a later age ; and as repugnant to the law of nature, which could inflict no severer punishment upon the most atrocious of crimes. As recently as 1785, no fewer than ninety-five persons were executed in London for this offence alone; and on one occasion the hideous spectacle was exhibited of twenty hanging from the same gibbet. The result of such barbarity was, that, in order to evade the capital sentence, juries committed a pious fraud, and found the property of less value than the statute required. But if severe laws were never executed, the consequence was that crimes constantly increased, and more particularly the crimes of juvenile offenders.

On moving the third reading of the bill, on the 15th of March, Sir Samuel called attention to the great number of persons of tender age who had recently been sentenced to death for petty larceny. At that very moment, he said, a boy, not ten years of age, was lying in Newgate with this doom recorded against him ; and the Recorder of London was reported to have declared that it was intended to enforce the law strictly in future, to interpose some check, if possible, to the increase of youthful depravity. The bill passed the Commons, but was again thrown out by the Lords, though supported by the Dukes of Sussex and Gloucester. Nor was it until 1821 that the peers could be persuaded to assent to this humane measure. Other reforms initiated by Sir Samuel Romilly have long since been carried out. The system of raising money by State lotteries,—a singularly demoralising practice ; the use of spring guns for the protection of game ; the penalties inflicted on insolvent debtors, have all been abolished. A general and, on the whole, a thorough revision of our criminal law has been accomplished. The slave trade has for half-a-century ceased to be a reproach on the name and fame of England; and for even a longer period Catholics have ceased to suffer the disabilities imposed upon them by the tyranny of bigotry. These were objects which Sir Samuel had deeply at heart,—for which he laboured with admirable disinterestedness and splendid energy; and his efforts must not be the less cordially acknowledged because he did not live to share in the joy of victory.

A great tribute to his public services and high character was paid him in 1818, when, on the dissolution of Parliament, he was put in nomination as one of the candidates for Westminster. Though he took no personal part in the election, he was returned at the head of the poll with 5339 votes. Sir Francis Burdett, his colleague, polled 5328, against the 4808 of the Tory candidate, Sir Murray Maxwell, who was defeated. The spirit in which he accepted this honour will best be understood from the following passage in one of his private memoranda :*—

" The honour which has lately been conferred on me, that of being elected to represent the city of Westminster in Parliament, has in some respects added to my means of being useful. It has drawn upon me an additional portion of public attention; it has placed me, as it were, in a more conspicuous theatre; and has given some importance to my actions, and even to my speeches. It has, however, at the same time, brought with it some difficulties to which I was not before exposed. I seem to be not quite so much the master of my own conduct as I used to be. Chosen by popular election to represent the metropolis, which on all great questions of public interest has, of late years, taken the lead in supporting the claims and pretensions of the

---

* Memoirs, iii. 411-13.

people, it will be expected of me that I shall maintain such pretensions more strenuously than I have ever done before; that I should pay my court to the people, and be ever ready to attend the call of those who shall think proper, as they have been accustomed to do, to summon popular meetings on great public questions as they may occur.

"I feel, however, no inclination to act any such part. I am the servant of the people, but I am determined not to be their slave; and I should think the proud distinction which has been conferred on me had lost half its value if it had been obtained, or was to be preserved, by acting the part of a factious demagogue. I do not say that I will attend no popular meetings, but I will attend them only on extraordinary occasions, and when these occur I will endeavour to temper the violence and to remove the prejudices which I may find prevailing there. No conduct can, in my eyes, be more criminal than that of availing one's self of the prejudiced clamours of the ignorant or misinformed to accomplish any political purpose, however good or desirable in itself. If I use strong language, and take a bold part for the people, it shall be in the House of Commons, not in Palace Yard. If I cannot serve those of my fellow-citizens who are in the humblest situations of life, at least I will not injure them. I will be careful, not by inflaming their passions, and encouraging them to enter upon courses of which the danger would exclusively be theirs, to draw ruin upon their heads."

Sir Samuel Romilly was exceptionally happy in his domestic relations. His wife was a woman of many graces, with a refined taste and an accomplished mind; in every way a suitable helpmate, sympathising with her husband's objects, sharing his aspirations, and by her thoughtful partnership lightening the burden of his labours. He loved her with the devotedness of a passionate lover and the confidence of an attached husband. It is something of the irony of fate that she who made

all the light and joy of his life was to prove the immediate instrument of his death. The satisfaction he
naturally experienced at the honour conferred upon him
by the constituency of Westminster was not a little
clouded by the anxiety his wife's declining health began
to cause him. Towards the close of the summer he
repaired with her to East Cowes Castle, the seat of his
friend, Mr. Nash, in the Isle of Wight, in the hope that
the milder air would improve her condition. There,
as her disease fluctuated, his mind continued in a state
of alarming disquietude, pulsating from hope to despair,
and from despair to hope. On the 27th of September
he wrote to his friend Dumont :—

"Since I last wrote to you Anne has been worse, and was
certainly considered by both her medical attendants as being in
some danger. She is at present a little better ; but, for myself,
I still apprehend the worst. I take care to let neither her nor
the poor children see the anxiety I feel ; but it costs me a good
deal. With all this, do not suppose that I have not quite resolution enough to undergo everything, and to preserve my health
for my children's sake."

On the receipt of this letter, Mr. Dumont seems to
have started for Cowes, where he found Lady Romilly so
much improved as to be able to spend two or three hours
daily in the society of her family and friends. Unfortunately, this improvement was only temporary. A severe
relapse followed, and several days of acute suffering; during
which, we are told, her husband's anguish could be
equalled only by the pious fortitude and resolution with
which he strove to control his emotions. But the nervous strain was excessive. Night after night he passed
sleeplessly, or, if he slept, it was to be disturbed by such

terrible dreams that he awoke unrefreshed and profoundly shaken. At times he believed his faculties to be injured, and began to entertain fears of mental derangement, whilst still discharging with anxious regularity the duties he owed to his God, his country, his family. Struggling against the agony that threatened to overwhelm him, he devoted to his children and friends the time that remained to him from his attendance in the sick chamber of his wife. With Mr. Dumont he held the most intimate and unrestrained conversations, discussing his projects for the future, and his plans for the education and establishment of his children.

There is something sadly significant in the last few entries in his diary.* He was evidently unable to sit down and record the day's events with his usual calmness :—

"Sept. 3rd. Arrived at Cowes.
   12th. Anne went into the sea-bath.
   13th. Taken ill.
   14th. Sailed with Mr. Fazakerley to Southampton.
   16th. Consulted with Mr. Bloxam [a local medical practitioner].
   19th. [Dr.] Royet and William arrived, and Mr. Nash.
 Oct. 9th. Slept for the first time after many sleepless nights.
   10th. Relapse of Anne."

"Relapse of Anne !" These are the last few but most significant words. Having written them, he laid down his pen, as if he felt that his life's record was closed.

About the middle of October his sister, to whom he

---

* Memoirs, iii. 368.

was deeply attached, came to the Isle of Wight, with her daughter, at his own express desire. She was followed by his wife's two sisters; but he met them "without a tear or any visible emotion." On the night of the 29th Lady Romilly's gentle spirit passed away. The worst was made known to her husband on the following morning; he heard it with apparent resignation and in silent sorrow. But there was enough in his condition to impel his friends to remove him on the same day from the scene of his irreparable loss, and they journeyed by easy stages to London, arriving there on the 1st of November. During the journey he had frequently been much agitated, and the violence of his feelings increased as he approached the home that to him could be home no more. " On one of these occasions," says his biographer, "as he was shutting his eyes and wringing his hands, Mr. Dumont, who had accompanied him from the Isle of Wight, took the hand of his daughter, and placed it in his, upon which, opening his eyes, and casting on his friend a look expressive of gratitude and affection, he tenderly embraced his daughter."

Having reached his house in Russell Square, he made repeated but ineffectual efforts to control his feelings. Throwing himself on a sofa, he joined his hands together for some moments, as if seeking the Divine mercy and assistance. He then became calm; but with a calmness that alarmed his friends more than his previous agitation; it was that of a man bleeding inly from some mortal wound. Dr. Royet, his nephew, was unremitting in his attentions, and he was joined with friendly solicitude by Drs. Marcet and Babington; but who can minister to a mind diseased? The spring of his mind snapped beneath the presence of a protracted agony; his heart broke! and in a moment of frenzy, he put an end to his existence.

At the time of his death, Sir Samuel Romilly was sixty-one years of age; and he had attained the highest position, both in the Courts of Law and in Parliament, which character and intellect without office could confer. No man was more generally admired, respected, and beloved. His triumphant return for Westminster, without having solicited a single vote or spent a shilling, or even made an appearance on the hustings, was a signal testimony to his popularity, and also, it may be added, to the purity of conduct and the rectitude of purpose by which he had acquired it. Miss Martineau has justly observed that "the charm of his beautiful nature" won its way even where wide difference of political principles and sentiment might have been expected to create a strong hostility. No two men could be more unlike than he and Lord Eldon, yet it is known that the latter was deeply affected by Sir Samuel's death. As he took his seat next morning in the Court where Romilly had practised for so many years, he was struck by the sight of the vacant place. His eyes filled with tears. "I cannot stay here," he exclaimed, and, rising in great agitation, sat no more that day.

According to his biographer, Sir Samuel, in person, was tall and well-proportioned, with a regular and pleasing countenance, which was "sicklied o'er," however, "with the pale cast of thought," and readily reflected the strongest or tenderest emotions. His manners were perfect in their graceful simplicity, unaffected modesty, and kind and courteous consideration for the wishes and feelings of others. His habits were strictly temperate and studious, and he was never so happy as when engaged in domestic intercourse and family pleasures. He rose regularly at six o'clock, and during the greater part of the day, and frequently to a late hour at night, applied himself to the conscientious discharge of his professional and Parliamentary duties or to his literary studies. For he was much more than a lawyer; he was a cultivated man of letters. On this point, Lord Campbell quotes the evidence of a bishop, who said to him : " I remember travelling, many years ago, with Sir Samuel Romilly, one stage in his carriage, which was filled with the best books of the general literature of the day. To a remark from me that I rejoiced to see that he found time for such reading, he answered, ' As soon as I found that I was to be a busy lawyer for life, I strenuously resolved to keep up my habit of non-professional reading, for I had witnessed so much misery in the last years of many great lawyers whom I had known, from their loss of all taste for books, that I regarded their fate as my warning.' "

His household was liberally but not extravagantly maintained. He had a willing hand and a generous heart, and to a true tale of distress or sorrow never closed his ears. It was with a noble enthusiasm that he stood forward in defence of the oppressed, the destitute, the friendless, and exerted on their behalf all his professional knowledge and intellectual vigour. Every movement in favour of freedom and progress, every humane and philanthropic measure, found in him an earnest supporter. Nor was his disinterestedness less marked than his philanthropy; he never thought of himself or his reward, and was absolutely indifferent to the possession of place and power, unless they promised to be the means towards the attainment of some object designed for the benefit of others. His religion was simple, sincere, and practical ; a religion of everyday life, which showed itself in deeds rather than in words—in devout gratitude to God and charity to all mankind.

The mainspring of his conduct is very clearly shown in the following passage from one of his speeches :*—

"It was not from light motives, it was from no fanciful notions of benevolence, that I have ventured to suggest any alteration in the criminal law of England. It has originated in many years' reflection, and in the long-established belief that a mitigation of the severe penalties of our law will be one of the most effectual modes to preserve and advance the humanity and justice for which this country is so universally distinguished. Since the last session of Parliament, I have repeatedly reconsidered the subject. I am more and more firmly convinced of the strength of the foundation upon which I stand ; and even if I had doubted my own conclusions, I cannot forget the ability with which I was supported within these walls ; nor can I be insensible to the humane and enlightened philosophy by which, in contemplative life, this advancement of kindness has been recommended. I cannot, therefore, hastily abandon a duty which, from my success in life, I owe to my profession ; which, as a member of this house, I owe to you and to my country ; and which, as a man blessed with more than common prosperity, I owe to the misguided and unfortunate.

"Actuated by these motives," he continued, "it is not to be imagined that I shall be easily discouraged by any of the various obstacles so commonly, and perhaps with propriety, opposed to every attempt to alter an established law ; upon such a resistance I calculated, but [by it] am not to be deterred. I knew that my motives must occasionally be misunderstood by many, and might possibly be misrepresented by others. I was not blind to the road where prudence pointed to preferment ; but I am not to be misled from comforts which no external honours

---

* "Speeches of Sir S. Romilly," i. 317-319.

can bestow. I have long thought that it was the duty of every man, unmoved either by bad report or by good report, to use all the means which he possessed for the purpose of advancing the well-being of his fellow-creatures; and I know not any mode by which I can so effectually advance that well-being as by endeavouring to improve the criminal laws of our country."

We should weaken the force of these simple but earnest remarks by adding any comment. No one can rise from the study of Romilly's life without a conviction that he was animated by motives of the highest and purest benevolence; that he was absolutely free from all stain of selfishness; and that his sole ambition was that true and honourable one—to be of some service to the State, some good to his fellow-creatures, and to assist, loyally and energetically, in promoting the principles of justice, truth, and enlightenment.

---

[The foregoing sketch is founded upon the biography, by Mr. Paton, prefixed to Sir Samuel Romilly's "Speeches in the House of Commons," 2 vols. 8vo, 1820; and Sir Samuel Romilly's "Memoirs of His Own Life," edited by his sons, in 3 vols., 1840. We have referred also to Roscoe's "Eminent British Lawyers," Miss Martineau's "History of England for Thirty Years after the Peace," and other authorities.]

# Henry, Lord Brougham.

HAVE now to deal with one of the most disappointing and perplexing characters in the long gallery of English worthies,—a man who, with great capacity and great acquirements, never achieved anything permanently great; whose abundant and splendid promise never ripened into full performance,—Henry, Lord Brougham. Notwithstanding the brilliancy of his career, and the conspicuous figure he made among his contemporaries, I have ever ranked him in the melancholy category of " Men who have Failed; " and I feel that, however useful the preceding biographies may prove in the way of encouragement and example, the life of Lord Brougham cannot be less useful in the way of warning—as a warning, let us say, against wasting our powers or abusing our opportunities. Few men have had richer natural gifts. He was a clear and prompt thinker, a powerful orator, a fluent writer. There was scarcely anything he could not do and do well. It is not often that a great speaker attains so considerable a position as a man of letters, yet this good fortune was reserved for Brougham. A clever, rather than a profound lawyer, he gained the highest prize of his profession—the Lord Chancellorship of England. As a scientific investigator

339

he was rash and empirical, yet on some points his investigations were marked by ability and crowned with success. Still, on the whole, he was "a failure," and chiefly because he gave up to many pursuits the powers which should have been devoted to two or three. A man of brilliant talents, he was without the moderation, the calmness, the sweet repose, and the patience which belong to the higher genius. So he outlived his own fame, and made no lasting mark in literature, science, or politics. He expended his energy in such a vast number of channels, that it dribbled away into shallows and stagnant pools. Miss Martineau has happily said that, when we think of Lord Brougham, the oft-quoted apologue which the Duchess of Orleans applied to her son, the regent, involuntarily occurs to the mind. He was one on whom, in his cradle, the beneficent fairies had lavished every intellectual grace, but a single malignant spirit rendered them all unavailing by adding the fatal ingredient of waywardness. And she relates an anecdote of much significance. Lord Brougham, she says, was at his château at Cannes, when the daguerreotype process, the precursor of photography, was introduced there; and an accomplished neighbour proposed to take a view of the château, with a group of guests in the balcony. The artist explained the necessity of complete immobility, and asked his lordship and friends to keep still only for "five seconds." His lordship vehemently promised that he would not stir. Alas! he moved too soon, and the consequence was, where Lord Brougham should have been, *a blurr*. So stands the daguerreotype view to this hour. "There is something," remarks Miss Martineau, "very typical in this. In the picture of our century, as taken from the life by history, this very man should have been a central figure; but now, owing to his want of steadfastness, there will be for ever a blur where Brougham should have been." His restless ambition, his uneasy egotism, his want of consistency, and deliberateness, and moderation — these were the faults that marred the career of Henry, Lord Brougham.

Henry Brougham came of a respectable and ancient family in the north of England. At the time of his birth his father, who had married Miss Syme, the niece of Robertson the historian, was residing in St. Andrew Square, Edinburgh, where Henry Brougham was born on the 19th of September, 1778. His mother, a woman of rare accomplishments and fine character, was his first instructor; but at an early age he was sent to the High School of Edinburgh. His remarkable talents were precociously manifested; his thirst after knowledge seemed insatiable, and in classics, modern languages, and mathematics he attained a considerable proficiency. He became *dux* of his school when he was only thirteen, and in the following year left school with the reputation of a " prodigy." Entering the University of Edinburgh in 1792, he attended almost all the classes, exercising with great success his unconquerable energies and splendid abilities. He was only eighteen when, in 1795, he sent to the Royal Society of London a paper entitled, " Experiments and Observations on the Inflexion, Reflexion, and Colours of Light." Next year he communicated to the same body a paper entitled, " Further Experiments and Observations on the Affections and Properties of Light; " and, in 1798, a mathematical paper, " General Theorems, chiefly Prisms." The views in these were immature and imperfect, and expressed with too much confidence; but they were remarkable as coming from a young man

under twenty, and the two optical papers were considered by Professor Prevost, of Geneva, of sufficient
importance to merit an elaborate examination.

While engaged in these scientific exercises, he found
time to attend the debates of the "Speculative Society,"
where Francis Horner and Lord Henry Petty (afterwards
Marquis of Lansdowne) were among his contemporaries.
Here he cultivated his talents for public speaking, astonishing his hearers by his copiousness, pungency, and
readiness, and also devoted himself assiduously to the
practice of composition. Even these occupations failed
to exhaust his superabundant vivacity; and after an
evening spent in literary and philosophical investigation,
he would sally forth into the streets of Edinburgh to
ring bells and smash lamps, and twist off bell-pulls and
knockers.*

---

* "One autumn, by way of seeing what was in Scotland considered
'fashionable life,' he went to the meeting of the Caledonian Hunt,
which was held at Dumfries. According to the prevailing custom,
all orders and degrees dined at a *table d'hôte*, and after dinner all sorts
of bets were laid. Brougham offered a wager against the whole
company that none of them would write down in a sealed packet the
manner in which he meant to travel to the races, which were to take
place a few miles from Dumfries the next day. As many as chose to
accept his challenge wrote down their conjectures, which were sealed
up along with his actual purpose. When the packets were opened
it was found that he would go in a sedan-chair, which none of them
had thought of. Accordingly, he made his progress to the races
carried in that way, and accompanied by an immense crowd. After
dinner he renewed the bet against all who chose to take it, and when
the packets were opened he was equally successful. He had written
down that he would go in a post-chaise and pair, all the persons who
had accepted the bet having written down the strangest and most
absurd modes of conveyance they could devise."—Lord Campbell,
"Lives of Lord Lyndhurst and Brougham," pp. 230, 231.

Brougham completed his four years' curriculum in 1795. He then had to choose his profession; and the law seeming to offer him the best prospect of fame and fortune, he decided in its favour. For two years he attended the lectures on civil law at the University, passed his examinations, and on the 16th of June, 1800, was called to the Scottish bar. In the same year he went the southern circuit as a brother of mercy—that is, as advocate for the defence of prisoners too poor to fee counsel. He showed much ingenuity and more assiduity in the cases intrusted to him; but it is to be feared he was more successful in puzzling and perplexing the judge (Lord Eskgrove) than in exculpating his clients. The Faculty of Advocates seem to have held a favourable opinion of his legal qualifications, for they appointed him "Civil Law Examinator." But this was not enough to satisfy his insatiate energy. "Quiet to quick bosoms is a hell." As an intellectual diversion, and an effort to grasp the bubble reputation, he worked upon his elaborate "Inquiry into the Colonial Policy of the European Powers," a book of much interest and value, which may still be read with advantage, though many of its hypotheses would find little favour with modern politicians.

The "Inquiry" was not published until 1803. In the preceding year an event had occurred in the literary world which had stirred it to its stagnant depths. A few clever young Whigs, meeting in a room on the third flat of a house in Buccleuch Place, Edinburgh, conceived the idea of establishing a new Review, which should treat of political, literary, and social questions with freedom and facility. The principal projectors were Sydney Smith, Jeffrey, and Horner, to whom was afterwards added, though not without some dread of his indiscretion, Henry

Brougham. After a little hesitation, Brougham con-
sented to give his help; and, having done so, with
characteristic energy, contributed three (or, as he himself
says, seven) articles to the first number; five to the
second; eight to the third; and five to the fourth; in
only five of these being assisted by a collaborator. He
continued to be one of the most voluminous, and at times
the most valuable of contributors.

" It has been said that he once wrote a whole number, including
articles upon lithotomy and church music. It is more authentic
that he contributed six articles to one number at the very crisis
of his political career; and at the same period he boasts of
having written a fifth of the whole *Review* to that time. He
would sit down in a morning, and write off twenty pages at a
single effort."

A great deal of what he wrote bears evident marks of
this extemporaneousness of composition; and is certainly much inferior to the leader-writing in the great
newspapers of the present day. But at the time the
*Review* exercised a remarkable influence. It was plain-
spoken and pungent; its contributors were young men,
and wrote like young men, with no very great respect for
authority. They held what were then considered " advanced opinions," and expressed these opinions with a
novel amount of freedom.

Few of Brougham's articles have had a greater interest
for posterity than the one which (in 1808) dealt so
trenchantly with Byron's youthful effort, " Hours of
Idleness," and stimulated his genius into the production
of the satire of " English Bards and Scotch Reviewers."
As the poet had decidedly the better of the combat,
neither he nor his admirers had much reason to complain ;

and, in truth, the review, if flippantly written, was
by no means unjust. Few, if any, great poets have
ever put forth weaker stuff as their first-fruits than Byron
unwisely gave to the world in his "Hours of Idleness;"
and the keenest critic must have failed to detect in its
mawkish and mediocre pages a single indication of latent
or prospective power.   In Brougham's once famous
article it is not the severity which we notice, for that
was deserved ; nor the fun, for that was forced and
heavy ; but the slipshod composition, which makes us
wonder that the *Review* ever attained to so formidable
a position as a literary dictator.  I do not find in any of
Brougham's contributions that superiority, that surpassing
excellence which one naturally looks for when one re-
members the repute they once enjoyed.   I would venture
to say as much of most of the writing of his colleagues ;
and the secret of the undoubted success of the *Edinburgh Review* is to be found, I think, not in any special
merit of its own, but in the intolerable dulness and
feebleness of its contemporaries.*

As early as 1803 Brougham entered himself of
Lincoln's Inn, with the view of obtaining a wider field
for his immense energies and intense self-assurance than
the Scotch bar afforded ; but he did not finally remove to
London until two years later.   There he applied himself

---

* Mr. Leslie Stephen, after speaking of Brougham's portentous
activity, justly condemns his writings as poor in style and substance.
"His garden," he says, "offers a bushel of potatoes, instead of a
single peach.   Much of his work was up to the level necessary to
give effect to the manifesto of an active politician.   It was a forcible
exposition of the arguments common at the time, but it has nowhere
the stamp of originality in thought or brilliance in expression which
could confer upon it a permanent vitality."

with characteristic ardour to the study of the English law, while finding leisure for political discussion, literary criticism, and social intercourse. At the dinners of the Whig leaders he soon became a welcome guest, and in the brilliant coterie of Holland House he held his own by his conversational powers and ready sarcasm. He was speedily noted as a man sure to get on, and the Whigs were delighted at having gained so versatile and vigorous an adherent. To the metropolitan papers he furnished article after article, attacking the Tory Government with unfailing vivacity, and defending Whig principles with untiring ardour. Lord Holland bears witness to the extent and value of his services :—

" The management of our press," he says, " fell into the hands of Mr. Brougham. With that active and able man I had become acquainted, through Mr. Allen, in 1805. At the formation of Lord Grenville's Ministry, he had written, at my suggestion, a pamphlet, called "The State of the Nation." His early connection with the Abolitionists had familiarised him with the means of circulating political papers, and gave him some weight with those best qualified to co-operate in such an undertaking. His extensive knowledge and extraordinary readiness, his assiduity and habits of composition, enabled him to correct some articles, and to furnish a prodigious number himself. With partial and scanty assistance from Mr. Allen, myself, and two or three more, he, in the course of ten days, filled every bookseller's shop with pamphlets ; most London newspapers and all country ones, without exception, with paragraphs ; and supplied a large portion of the boroughs throughout the kingdom with handbills adapted to the local interests of the candidates ; and all tending to enforce the principles, vindicate the conduct, elucidate the measures, or expose the adversaries of the Whigs."

In November, 1808, Brougham was called to the bar.

He met at first with the ill-success which, by some law
of nature, seems to attend all famous lawyers at the
outset of their career, and went the Northern Circuit
without obtaining a single brief.  He made himself a
name, however, by the eloquence he displayed as counsel
before Parliament for the Liverpool merchants, who had
petitioned against the " Orders in Council; " the retaliatory
measure with which the British Government had replied
to Napoleon's attempt, in the Berlin and Milan decrees,
to ruin England by a commercial blockade.  The proceedings extended over six weeks, during which Brougham
delivered at the bar of either House a number of spirited
and forcible orations, which established his reputation as
a public speaker.  The want of stability in his character
had hitherto deterred the Whig leaders from bringing
him into Parliament; but they now acknowledged that
it was worth while to run a little risk to secure the
assistance of so redoubtable a champion, and accordingly,
early in 1810, he was returned to the House of
Commons for the borough of Camelford.  His maiden
speech was delivered on the 5th of March, in support of
Mr. Whitbread's motion, condemnatory of the conduct of
the Earl of Chatham, the " hero " of the disastrous
Walcheren expedition.  It did not fulfil the expectations
that his previous public efforts had excited ; but in the
course of the session his vast powers as a debater were
rapidly unfolded, and he soon became the acknowledged
rival and opponent of George Canning.  The subject of
negro slavery he made his own, taking it out of the
failing hands of the illustrious Wilberforce, and advocating the emancipation of the West Indian negroes with
all his most finished eloquence, and a sincerity which
even his enemies could not question.

On the dissolution of Parliament in 1812, Brougham boldly contested with Mr. Canning the representation of Liverpool, but was defeated, and for five years failed to obtain a seat in the House of Commons. In the interval he did not allow the public to lose sight of him. At the bar he practised with assiduity and success, increasing his fame by the strenuous eloquence with which he defended Leigh Hunt and his brother for an alleged libel in *The Examiner* on the Prince Regent. Having been introduced to the unfortunate and wayward Caroline of Brunswick, the Princess early distinguished him as her legal adviser, and he took up her cause with his usual fervor, partly, no doubt, from motives of ambition, but also, we verily believe, through a generous sympathy for a wronged and oppressed, if not wholly innocent, woman.

In 1816, through the influence of the Earl of Darlington, he was returned for Winchelsea, and he continued to represent that borough until 1830, when he resigned it, owing to a difference between himself and its patron. His long repressed activity now made itself felt on every question of the day; and as the champion of constitutional government and the liberties of the subject, he drew around him a constantly enlarging circle of admiring supporters. It is no exaggeration to say that he became a power in the land. His speeches exhibited all the gifts and graces of a great orator, save judgment and moderation; invective, ridicule, animated apostrophe, spirited declamation, ingenious argument, fertile illustration—all were combined and poured out together in a torrent of resistless eloquence. On the death of George III., and the consequent accession to the throne of George IV. and Queen Caroline, the latter

appointed him her Attorney and Solicitor-General, and
Brougham entered at once on a career of amazing popularity.  We need not remind the reader of the scandal
attending the "delicate investigation" into the Queen's
conduct; an investigation which showed her to have
been indiscreet, but had not proved her to be guilty.
Her royal husband, however, hated her with an un-
quenchable hatred, and seized every opportunity of
lavishing insult and outrage upon her.  On coming to
the throne, he insisted on the omission of her name
from the liturgy; and instructed his ministers to offer
her, through Mr. Brougham, an annuity of £50,000 a
year, provided she took an engagement not to come into
any part of the British dominions, and to assume some
other name or title than that of Queen.

It is known that Brougham never communicated this
proposal to the Queen.  Caroline was not deficient in
spirit, and he may have hesitated to be the medium of
conditions so insulting and dishonourable.  At all events,
it is certain she would have rejected them.  But, meanwhile, from her residence at Rome, she wrote to the
king's ministers, demanding the insertion of her name
in the liturgy, and announcing her intention of immediately
returning to England.  She landed at Dover, on Tuesday,
the 6th of June, and was received with an enthusiastic
welcome by an immense multitude.  "Her promptitude
and courage confounded her opponents, and gained her
the favour of the people.  Whatever one may think of
her conduct in other respects, it is impossible not to give
her credit for these qualities."  From Dover to London
her progress was one continued triumph; and as she
passed through the thronged streets of the metropolis,
the air was rent with shouts of tumultuous applause.

In a fury of wrath the King urged on his ministers to further steps; and a message was sent to the Lords, recommending another inquiry, in order to the adoption of "that course of proceeding, which the justice of the case, and the honour and dignity of his Majesty's crown, may require." Lord Liverpool, the Prime Minister, then laid on the table a "green bag" containing the papers collected during the "delicate investigation." The message was read, and the green bag produced in the Lower House, by Lord Castlereagh. Next day, Brougham read a message from the Queen, declaring that she had been induced to return to England for the maintenance of her character and the defence of her rights; that during the fourteen years that had elapsed since the charges were first brought against her, she had ever been ready to meet her accusers, and court the fullest inquiry into her conduct; and that now she demanded a public inquiry, instead of the formation of a secret tribunal to examine documents privately prepared by her adversaries. She relied, she said, with full confidence upon the integrity of the House of Commons, for defeating the only attempt she had any reason to fear.

Lord Castlereagh having moved that the papers in the green bag should be referred to a Select Committee, Brougham rose and delivered a very able and ingenious speech, in order to obtain delay and bring about an advantageous compromise. He felt that no private good, and much public harm, must be the result of a painful and demoralising investigation, and in the interest both of the King and Queen, was honestly anxious to avert it.

"The Queen," he said, "thinks it necessary for the clearing of her own honour, that the inquiry should be persisted in to the end; she shrinks not from it; she courts it; she is prepared to meet it; she comes from safety into—I will not say jeopardy, because the innocent in this land of law and liberty can know no jeopardy—but trouble, vexation, and anxiety. I have the honour of being a servant of her Majesty; I have also the honour of being a member of this House. As her Majesty's servant, I would not disobey her commands, and when her honour is at stake, I would do my best to defend it; but, in the upright performance of my duty in this House, I feel called upon even to thwart her Majesty's inclination, and I would tell her—'Madam, if negotiation yet be possible, rather go too far, and throw yourself upon your country and upon Parliament for your vindication, than not go far enough; if yet it be possible to avert the ruin which threatens the nation, your honour being safe, be ready to sacrifice all besides.' If I might advise those who stand in a similar situation with respect to the king, I would say to them—'Act like honest men, and disregard all consequences; tender that counsel to your sovereign which the case demands, and do not fear that Parliament will betray you, or the country desert you. Do not apprehend that even political calamity will attend you; for if successors must be appointed to your places, be sure that they will not be found within these walls.'"

The House was much influenced by this appeal, and in order to give time for negotiation, the debate was adjourned. On the part of the Queen, Mr. Brougham and Mr. Denman, and on the part of the King, the Duke of Wellington and Lord Castlereagh, met at the Foreign Office, and endeavoured, but in vain, to arrange a treaty of peace. The Queen was willing to live abroad, but insisted on the retention of her name in the liturgy,— the very point which the King was obstinately resolved not to concede. On the 19th of June, Parliament was informed that no terms of agreement could be settled. These proceedings, however, had greatly improved the

Queen's position, and as sensibly weakened the King's. She appeared before the nation as a queen, a claimant for justice, and an oppressed woman; and the popular sympathy manifested itself in a thousand ways. It was felt that, whatever might have been her errors, the last person who could rightly complain of them was the husband who had denied her his protection, and blackened her character, while himself living a life of the utmost license, and openly and notoriously violating—not once or twice or thrice, but continually—his marriage vows.

On the 4th of July, the Secret Committee of the Lords reported that the evidence affecting the honour of the Queen was such as to require, for "the dignity of the crown, and the moral feeling and honour of the country," a solemn inquiry, which might "be best effected in the course of a legislative proceeding, the necessity of which," said the Committee, "they cannot but most deeply deplore." The Queen, next day, in a petition to the Lords, declared that she was ready to defend herself, and prayed to be heard by counsel, in order to detail some weighty matters, which it was necessary to state in preparation for the inquiry. Her petition was refused; and on the 5th of July, Lord Liverpool, to "the everlasting disgrace of his administration," introduced "A Bill to deprive her Majesty, Queen Caroline Amelia Elizabeth, of the title, prerogatives, rights, privileges, and exemptions of Queen - Consort of this realm, and to dissolve the marriage between his Majesty and the said Caroline Amelia Elizabeth." It was immediately read a first time, and a copy of it ordered to be sent to the Queen. Next day she petitioned that her counsel might be heard against its principle and the mode of procedure adopted. The Lords assented, and Mr. Brougham appeared at the bar.　He complained that her Majesty was being treated with an injustice that would not have been inflicted on the meanest of her subjects :—

" Before such a bill could have been introduced against any other individual, there must have been a sentence of divorce in the Consistory Court, there must have been a verdict of a jury who might have sympathised with her feelings, who, being taken from the same rank of life as herself, and knowing that the evidence produced against her might, under similar circumstances, be produced against their wives and daughters, would have been influenced by a desire to guard against a common danger.　There would then have been among her judges none who were the servants of her husband, for her counsel would have had the right of challenging all such—none who were hired by him during his pleasure—none who were placed in a situation to feel gratitude for the past or expectation for the future favours which he had it in his power to bestow.　She would have been tried by twelve honest, impartial, and disinterested Englishmen, —at whose doors the influence which may act upon her present judges might agitate for years, without making the slightest impression either upon the hopes or the fears which it was calculated to excite. . . . With the confidence of injured innocence she flings herself upon the House, and trusts that no mixture of party—no pressure of interested persons—no adventitious influences exercised out of doors—no supposed want of sympathy with the feelings of the country—no alleged, though falsely alleged, tendency on the part of your Lordships to truckle to royal favour, will stand between the Queen and justice, or prevent her case from receiving a fair, impartial, and unprejudiced decision."

As might be expected, the House supported the proceedings of the Government, and fixed the second reading of the Bill for 17th August.　At this stage the Attorney-

2 A

General brought up the charges on the part of the crown,
and tendered the crown's witnesses.   Thenceforward, day
after day, until the 8th September, "indecent tales were
told by a party of Italian domestics—tales such as, at
other times, are only whispered by the dissolute in
private, and are never offered to the eye or ear of the
moral and modest, who compose the bulk of the English
nation.   These tales were now translated by interpreters
at the bar of the House of Lords, given in full in the
newspapers, and spread through every town, hamlet, and
lone house within the four seas."   Brougham next
examined the King's witnesses with infinite skill and great
severity, and succeeded in fatally discrediting their testimony; but a majority of the Lords remained firm in their
resolve to support the Bill.   Copley, the King's Solicitor-
General (afterwards Lord Lyndhurst), summed up in a
powerful speech on the 9th of September; after which
the Queen's counsel obtained an adjournment to Tuesday,
the 3rd of October.   Brougham then replied for the
defence in a most masterly oration, the conclusion of which
he is said to have written seventeen times over.   It ran
as follows :—

"Such, my lords, is the case now before you!   Such is the
evidence in support of this measure—evidence inadequate to
prove a debt—impotent to deprive of a civil right—ridiculous to
convict of the lowest offence—scandalous if brought forward to
support a charge of the highest nature which the law knows—
monstrous to ruin the honour, to blast the name of our English
Queen!   What shall I say, then, if this is the proof by which
an act of judicial legislation, a parliamentary sentence, an *ex
post facto* law, is sought to be passed against this defenceless
woman?   My lords, I pray you to pause.   I do earnestly beseech
you to take heed!   You are standing upon the brink of a

precipice—then beware! It will go forth as your judgment, if
sentence shall go against the Queen. But it will be the only
judgment you ever pronounced which, instead of reaching its
object, will return and bound back upon those who give it.
Save the country, my lords, from the horrors of this catastrophe
—save yourselves from this peril—rescue that country, of which
you are the ornaments, but in which you can flourish no longer,
when severed from the people, than the blossom when cut off
from the roots and the stem of the tree. Save that country, that
you may continue to adorn it—save the Crown, which is in
jeopardy—the aristocracy, which is shaken—save the Altar,
which must stagger with the blow that rends its kindred throne!
You have said, my lords, you have willed—the Church and the
King have willed—that the Queen should be deprived of its
solemn services. She has instead of that solemnity, the heart-
felt prayers of the people. She wants no prayers of mine. But
I do here press forth my humble supplications at the Throne of
Mercy, that that mercy may be poured down upon the people in
a larger measure than the merits of its rulers may deserve, and
that your hearts may be turned to justice."

Witnesses were afterwards heard on the Queen's behalf,
and on the 6th of November the Lords proceeded to vote
on the second reading of the Bill, which was carried by the
small majority of 28. A difference of opinion then arose
among its supporters,—some of whom, perhaps, were
influenced by the roar and storm of public indignation
which was fast gathering up from all parts of the country,
—so that the third reading showed a majority reduced to
9. Lord Liverpool at once recognised the fact that, with
so small a majority in its favour in the Lords, the stronghold of ministerial power and crown influence, it would
be madness to introduce the Bill into the Lower House,
where popular opinion would be more largely and
faithfully represented, and instead of moving " that this

bill do pass," he adjourned its further consideration for six months,—in other words, abandoned it.

Thus ended this *cause célèbre;* an episode in our parliamentary history of which no Englishman can feel proud. The only person who emerged from it with increased character and reputation was Henry Brougham, and at the time he was, I suppose, the most popular man in the country. The most honourable corporations voted him their "freedoms" in gold boxes; his bust might be seen in almost every shop window; public-houses hung out as a new sign the "Brougham's Head"; and a splendid candelabrum was presented to him, the cost of which had been defrayed by a penny subscription from artisans, mechanics, and labourers. His practice at the bar was largely augmented. "When he next appeared on the Northern Circuit, the attorneys crowded round him with briefs, that they might be privileged to converse with Queen Caroline's illustrious advocate. During one whole round of the assizes at York, Durham, Newcastle, Carlisle, Appleby, and Lancaster, crowds came from distant parts to see and to listen to him, and the Civil Court and the Crown Court were respectively overflowing or deserted as he appeared in the one or in the other." As was natural, his reputation as a successful and popular advocate greatly strengthened his ascendancy in the Commons; and he became in fact, if not in name, the leader of the Opposition.

It was contrary to his advice that the Queen, on the day of the coronation of George IV., attempted to force her way into Westminster Hall, to be present at a ceremony in which she had been denied a share. This step was a grave mistake, and exposed her to an ignominy which she felt acutely. The fever of mind and agitation of spirit it induced brought on an internal inflammation, against which her enfeebled frame could make no long resistance, and her chequered career terminated, after an illness of only a few days, on the 7th of August.

Throughout the kingdom the news of Queen Caroline's death was received with the marks of respect usually paid on the death of a member of the Royal family; and from tower and spire tolled the mourning bell, everywhere except in the cathedral-city of Durham. This ill-judged omission was not unnaturally made the subject of severe comment in the *Durham Chronicle.* Though the language employed certainly did not transgress the bounds of good taste, the Durham clergy waxed indignant at a layman's presumption in censuring them, and brought an action for libel against the proprietor, a Mr. Williams, at the Durham summer assizes, 1822. Brougham undertook the defence, and on this occasion made what Lord Campbell considers " by far the best speech he ever delivered either at the bar or in Parliament." Such is not my opinion; but unquestionably it was *one* of his best, and no other man of his time could have made a better, such pungency was there in its ridicule, such force in its sarcasm, such strength in its declamation. The following is a specimen of its effectiveness in attack; it refers to the " progress " which George IV. was then making through Presbyterian Scotland :—

" If any hierarchy in all the world is bound on any principle of consistency—if any Church should be forward not only to suffer but provoke discussion, to stand upon that title and challenge the most unreserved inquiry—it is the Protestant Church of England : first, because she has nothing to dread from it ; secondly, because she is the very creature of free inquiry—the offspring of repeated revolutions, and the most reformed of the reformed Churches of Europe. But surely if there is any one corner of Protestant Europe where men ought not to be rigorously judged in ecclesiastical controversy—where a large allowance should be made for the conflict of irreconcilable opinions—where the harshness of jarring tenets should be patiently borne, and strong, or even violent language be not too narrowly watched—it is this very realm, in which we live under three different ecclesiastical orders, and owe allegiance to a sovereign who, in one of his kingdoms, is the head of the Church, acknowledged as such by all men ; while, in another, neither he nor any earthly being is allowed to assume that name—a realm composed of three great divisions, in one of which prelacy is favoured by law and approved in practice by an Episcopalian people ; while, in another, it is protected indeed by law, but abjured in practice by a nation of sectaries, Catholic and Presbyterian ; and, in a third, it is abhorred alike by law and in practice, repudiated by the whole institutions of the country, scorned and detested by the whole of its inhabitants.

" His Majesty, almost at the time in which I am speaking, is about to make a progress through the northern provinces of this island, accompanied by certain of his chosen counsellors, a portion of men who enjoy unenvied, and in an equal degree, the admiration of other countries and the wonder of their own ; and there the prince will see much loyalty, great learning, some splendour, the remains of an ancient monarchy, and of the institutions which made it flourish. But one thing he will not see. Strange as it may seem, and to many who hear me as incredible, from one end of the country to the other he will see no such thing as a bishop ;* not such a thing is to be found, from the Tweed to John-o'-Groat's ; not a mitre—no, nor so much as a minor canon, or even a rural dean ; and in all the land not one

---

* This assertion was true only in a limited sense. There were no bishops recognised *by law ;* but the ancient Episcopal Church of Scotland, then as now, had its bishops, deans, canons, and curates, all of due ecclesiastical appointment.

single curate—so entirely rude and barbarous are they in Scotland ; in such outer darkness do they sit, that they support no cathedrals, maintain no pluralists, suffer no non-residence ; nay, the poor benighted creatures are ignorant even of tithes. Not a sheaf, or a lamb, or a pig, or the value of a plough-penny, do the hapless mortals render from year's end to year's end !* Piteous as their lot is, what makes it infinitely more touching, is to witness the return of good for evil in the demeanour of this wretched race. Under all this cruel neglect of their spiritual concerns, they are actually the most loyal, contented, moral, and religious people anywhere, perhaps, to be found in the world. Let us hope (many, indeed, there are, not far off, who will with unfeigned devotion pray) that his Majesty may return safe from the dangers of his excursion into such a country—an excursion most perilous to a certain portion of the Church, should his royal mind be infected with a taste for cheap establishments, a working clergy, and a pious congregation.

" But compassion for our brethren in the north has drawn me aside from my purpose, which was merely to remind you how preposterous it is, in a country of which the ecclesiastical polity is framed upon plans so discordant, and the religious tenets themselves are so various, to require any very measured expressions of men's opinions upon questions of Church government. And if there is any part of England in which an ample licence ought more especially to be admitted in handling such matters, I say without hesitation it is this very bishopric, where, in the nineteenth century, you live under a palatine prince, the Lord of Durham ; where the endowment of the hierarchy—I may not call it enormous, but I trust I shall be permitted without offence to term it splendid ; where the establishment I dare not whisper proves grinding to the people, but I will rather say is an incalculable, an inscrutable blessing—only it *is* prodigiously large—

---

* This, too, was not absolutely accurate. The Established Church of Scotland levies a yearly assessment for the building and repair of its churches, manses, &c.

showered down in a profusion somewhat overpowering, and laying the inhabitants under a load of obligation overwhelming by
its weight. It is in Durham where the Church is endowed with
a splendour and a power unknown in monkish times and popish
countries, and the clergy swarm in every corner, an' it were the
patrimony of St. Peter. It is here, where all manner of conflicts
are at each moment inevitable between the people and the
priests, that I feel myself warranted on *their* behalf and for
*their* protection—for the sake of the Establishment, and as the
discreet advocate of that Church and that clergy — for the
defence of their very existence—to demand the most unrestrained
discussion for their title and their actings under it. For them,
in this age, to screen their conduct from investigation, is to
stand self-convicted ; to shrink from the discussion of their title,
is to confess a flaw ; he must be the most shallow, the most
blind of mortals, who does not at once perceive that if that title
is protected only by the strong arm of the law, it becomes not
worth the parchment on which it is engrossed, or the wax that
dangles to it for a seal.

"I have hitherto all along assumed that there is nothing
impure in the practice under the system ; I am admitting that
every person engaged in its administration does every one act
which he ought, and which the law expects him to do ; I am
supposing that up to this hour not one unworthy member has
entered within its pale ; I am even presuming that up to this
moment not one of those individuals has stepped beyond the
strict line of his sacred functions, or given the slightest offence
or annoyance to any human being. I am taking it for granted
that they all act the part of good shepherds, making the welfare
of their flock their first care, and only occasionally bethinking
them of shearing, in order to prevent the too luxuriant growth
of the fleece proving an incumbrance, or to eradicate disease.

"If, however, these operations be so constant that the flock
actually live under the knife ; if the shepherds are so numerous,
and employ so large a troop of the watchful and eager animals

that attend them (some of them, too, with a cross of the fox, or even the wolf, in their breed), can it be wondered at if the poor creatures thus fleeced, and hunted, and barked at, and snapped at, and from time to time worried, should now and then bleat, dream of preferring the rot to the shears, and draw invidious, possibly disadvantageous, comparisons between the wolf without, and the shepherd within the fold? It cannot be helped; it is in the nature of things that suffering should beget complaint; but for those who have caused the pain to complain of the out-cry, and seek to punish it—for those who have goaded, to scourge and to gag—is the meanest of all injustice. It is, moreover, the most pitiful folly for the clergy to think of retaining their power, privileges, and enormous wealth, without allowing free vent for complaint against abuses in the Establishment and delinquency in its members; and in this prosecution they have displayed that folly in its supreme degree."

Doubts have often been cast upon Brougham's sincerity; and it is too true that he was led by his restless ambition and his impetuosity of temper into the advocacy of many measures and the support of many opinions in which he had no real faith. But certain subjects there were on which his convictions were sound, fixed, and lasting. Such were law reform, the abolition of slavery, the extension of education, and the better administration of public charities. These he made his own, and championed vigorously and strenuously in and out of season. His educational schemes were crude, ill-digested, and not not always practicable, but at least they had what was then the singular merit of contemplating the education of the whole people. To this great principle he was unalterably faithful throughout his public career; and no plan, or project, or measure which aimed, directly or indirectly, at the diffusion of knowledge ever failed to command his hearty support. The Education Act of

1874 was the necessary and natural consummation of
the educational movement which Brougham initiated
in 1806, and sustained in 1820. And his noble labours
in this direction may surely be allowed in some degree
to counterbalance his many failings and occasional
deviations from the path of political rectitude. As the
founder of the London University—for such he was in
effect, if not in name—and the source, and mainstay,
and vitality of the Society for the Diffusion of Useful
Knowledge, he has claims upon our gratitude which his
inconsistency, and egotism, and irritability of character
must not make us forget. We know that with his vast
powers he might have done much more—might have set
his mark upon our legislature and literature, as he has
done upon our political history; but this knowledge must
not prevent us from recognising the good he did do.

Continuing our biographical summary, we must briefly
advert to his quarrel with Canning, in the session of
1823. In the course of debate, Canning had observed
that, in the then state of Parliament and the country,
it seemed to him impossible to form a Ministry which
should agree upon the Catholic and "other burning
questions," so as to be able to carry on the business of
the country. This remark was construed as an admission
that he considered the cause of the Catholics hopeless;
though he had not said, nor did he mean, that it was
necessary that, in order to carry them, the whole Ministry
should be in their favour. On the 17th of April, on
the occasion of a petition in support of their claims
being presented, a hot discussion took place, in which
Mr. Tierney charged Canning with the ruin of the
Catholic hopes, because he had taken office without
making Emancipation an essential condition. Other

speakers followed with language even more violently personal, and at last Brougham poured out one of his copious and vehement invectives. Canning sat with flashing eye, quivering nostrils, and flushed cheeks, compelling himself to be silent, until Brougham dropped the words, " monstrous truckling," and " political tergiversation." Then, springing to his feet, he exclaimed, " I rise to say that is false." For some seconds the House was still; even the Speaker seemed paralysed. On recovering himself, he said, in a low tone, that the expression used by Mr. Canning was in violation of the laws and customs of the House, and he hoped it would be retracted. The Minister refused to withdraw the " sentiment," and Mr. Brougham would not explain away his imputation. After much angry discussion, the difficulty was solved by Brougham's consenting to declare that his charge referred to Mr. Canning's political, and not his private character.

This incident was forgotten by Brougham when Canning became Prime Minister, and the latter received his hearty and persistent support. It was a disinterested support, for he declined the office of Chief Baron of the Exchequer. After Canning's death he maintained a steady opposition to the Wellington Government, while not desisting from his labours as a reformer. In 1828, his perseverance obtained the appointment of two royal commissions— one to inquire into the mode of procedure in the common law courts, and the other into the condition of the law of real property. Both led to large and real improvements in our juridical institutions. About this time, differing in political views from its patron, the Earl of Darlington, he resigned his seat for Winchelsea, but was immediately returned for Knaresborough, through the influence of the Duke of Devonshire. In 1829 he gave his strenuous assistance to the Government in carrying the great measure of Catholic Emancipation, of which he had been an advocate ever since his first appearance in Parliament. When, after the accession of William IV., the struggle began for a reform of the House of Commons, so that it might more fully represent the interests, feelings, and opinions of the people, he took up the question with his customary vehemence. At the dissolution of Parliament he boldly contested the county of York against Mr Stuart Wortley, who stood in the interest of the great landholders; and, in spite of a thousand difficulties, carried his election triumphantly.* He had no sooner taken his seat in the House than he gave notice in the Commons of his intention to bring forward, in a fortnight, the question of parliamentary reform; but before the fortnight had elapsed, the Wellington Government was a thing of the past; and Earl Grey, the Whig leader, was engaged in forming an administration.

Of that administration it was inevitable that Brougham should be a member, but it was a surprise to everybody when it was found that the office selected for him, or rather, the office he had selected, and upon which he insisted, was that of Lord Chancellor.

"It was amusing," says a contemporary historian, "to see how that announcement was everywhere received with a laugh; in most cases with a laugh which he would not have objected to,

---

* This was the high-water mark of Brougham's career; thenceforward he gradually declined. I think the success was too much for his excitable nature, and *intensified* his temper of jealousy and irritability, his restless and insatiable vanity. From this time he lost more and more of his never very large measure of self-control.

—a laugh of mingled surprise, exultation, and amusement. The anti-reformers laughed scornfully, dwelling upon certain declarations of his against taking office, and upon his incompetency as an equity lawyer—facts which he would not himself have disputed, but which his party thought should be put aside by the pressure of the time. To his worshippers, there was something comic in the thought of his vitality fixed down upon the woolsack, under the compression of the Chancellor's wig. Some expected a world of amusement in seeing how he got on in a position so new—how the wild and mercurial Harry Brougham would comport himself among the peers, and as the head of the law. Some expected from him the realisation of all that he had declared ought to be done by men in power, and as the first and most certain boon, a scheme of national education, which he would carry with all the power of his office and his pledged political character. Others sighed while they smiled—sighed to give up the popular member for Yorkshire, and found that his country had had the best of him." *

This was indeed true.† Never was any man more discredited by the difference between promise and performance than Henry Brougham, and never was a popular hero more quickly dethroned from his place in the affections of the people.

Brougham became Lord Chancellor, and, as a matter

---

* It was the feeling of his mother. When Parliament adjourned, Brougham took a journey to Brougham Hall, in Westmoreland, to visit her, and ask her blessing on a Lord Chancellor. The good old lady was still in the full enjoyment of all her rare faculties. While she reciprocated her son's warm affection, and was proud of his genius and services, and the glorious position he had attained, she could not help saying to him, "My dear Harry, I would rather have embraced the member for Yorkshire; but God Almighty bless you!"

† H. Martineau, "History of the Peace," ii. 410.

of course, received a peerage with the title of Baron Brougham and Vaux.

Parliamentary reform and Chancery reform engaged the attention of the active Chancellor when he escaped from the laborious duties of his court, and in the debates of the Upper House and the councils of the Cabinet his irrepressible energy soon secured him a prominent position.

The famous Reform Bill was introduced into the House of Commons, on the 2nd of March, by Lord John Russell. I need not dwell on the sweeping nature of its provisions; on the dismay and wrath it excited in the breasts of Tory borough-mongers and the privileged classes generally; or the enthusiasm it awakened among the great body of the people. In the Lower House it was fiercely opposed, and, on the occasion of the second reading, ministers were defeated by a majority of eight. On the following day the Opposition declined to go into committee on the Ordnance Estimates, which virtually amounted to a refusal of the supplies. Ministers offered their resignations; the king refused to accept them. They then demanded a dissolution of the new Parliament. To this the king not unnaturally objected; but on fresh representations from Lord Grey he yielded. He would go instantly, he would go that moment, and dissolve Parliament by his own voice (22nd April.) "As soon as the royal carriages could be got ready," said his ministers. "Never mind the carriages; send for a hackney coach," replied his Majesty; and the saying spread over the kingdom, and greatly enhanced the popularity of the "Sailor King."

At the gate Lord Durham, the Lord Privy Seal, found but one carriage waiting—the Lord Chancellor's. He gave orders to drive first to Lord Albemarle's, the Master of the Horse. Lord Albemarle, who was breakfasting, started up on the entrance of Lord Durham, asking what was the matter. " You must have the King's carriages ready immediately." " The King's carriages ! Very well; I will just finish my breakfast." " Finish your breakfast ! Not you; you must not lose a moment. The King ought to be at the House." " Lord bless me ! Is there a revolution ? " " Not at this moment; but there will be if you stay to finish your breakfast." This was enough ; and in a wonderfully brief space of time the royal carriages drove up to the Palace. The King was ready and impatient ; he walked with an unusually brisk step; " and so did the royal horses, in their passage through the streets, as was observed by the curious and anxious observers."

Now turn we to the Lower House. The picture it presented is thus described by a contemporary historian :—

" It was crowded, expectant, eager, and passionate. Sir Richard Vyvyan was the speaker of the Opposition, and a very strong one. A question of order arose as to whether he was or was not keeping within the fair bounds of his subject, which was a reform petition, whereas he was speaking on ' dissolution or no dissolution.' The Speaker appears to have been agitated from the beginning, and there were several members who were not collected enough to receive his decision with the usual deference. Honourable members turned upon each other, giving contradictions, sharp, angry, even abusive. Lord John Russell attempted to make himself heard, but in vain : his was no voice to pierce through such a tumult. The Speaker was in a state of visible emotion. Sir Richard Vyvyan, however, regained a hearing ; but as soon as he was once more in full flow, boom ! came the cannon which told that the king was on his way, and the roar drowned the conclusion of the sentence. Not a word

more was heard for the cheers, the cries, and even shouts of
laughter—all put down together, at regular intervals, by the
discharges of artillery.　At one moment Sir Robert Peel, Lord
Althorp, and Sir Francis Burdett, were all using the most vehement action of command and supplication in dumb show, and
their friends were labouring in vain to procure a hearing for
them.　The Speaker himself stood silenced by the tumult, till
the cries took more and more the sound of ' Shame ! Shame !'
and more eyes were fixed upon him till he could have made
himself heard, if he had not been too much moved to speak.
When he recovered voice, he directed that Sir Robert Peel was
entitled to address the House.　With occasional uproar, this
was permitted ; and Sir Robert Peel was still speaking when
the Usher of the Black Rod appeared at the bar to summon the
Commons to his Majesty's presence."

Meanwhile, in the House of Lords, the Peers had
assembled in unusual numbers.　Brougham had left the
woolsack, and the Earl of Shaftesbury had temporarily
occupied the chair as Speaker.　Lord Wharncliffe rose
to move an address to the King, praying that he would
not dissolve the present Parliament.　The Ministerialists
interrupted him ; and no fewer than five peers were on
their feet at once, each endeavouring to gain a hearing.
At last, Lord Wharncliffe was permitted to make his
motion, and it seemed possible that it might be carried
by acclamation, when Lord Shaftesbury was compelled
to vacate the woolsack by the appearance of the Lord
Chancellor in a state of much excitement, and crying
out, with strident voice : " I never yet heard that the
Crown ought not to dissolve Parliament whenever it
thought fit, particularly at a moment when the House
of Commons had resorted to the extreme step of refusing
the supplies."

Thinking he had effectually checked the course of the debate, Lord Brougham again disappeared. But no sooner was he gone, than Lord Shaftesbury was replaced on the woolsack, and Lord Mansfield was bitterly inveighing against the dissolution and the Reform Bill, when shouts were heard of—"The King! the King! God save the King!" The large doors on the right of the throne were flung wide, and his Majesty, accompanied by the Chancellor and other great officers, entered the House, and took his seat. The Commons were summoned, and when they had arrived, his Majesty began :—

"My Lords and Gentlemen, I have come to meet you for the purpose of proroguing this Parliament, with a view to its immediate dissolution. I have been induced to resort to this measure, for the purpose of ascertaining the sense of my people, in the way in which it can be most constitutionally and most authentically expressed, on the expediency of making such changes in the representation as circumstances may appear to require; and which, founded upon the acknowledged principles of the Constitution, may tend at once to uphold the just rights and prerogatives of the crown, and to give security to the liberties of the people."

Thus was a great political peril—perhaps a revolution of portentous dimensions—happily averted.

## II.

The new Reform Bill passed its second reading in the House of Commons by a majority of 136, on the 7th of July, and its third on the 21st of September, by a majority of 109. The great question then arose, as it has often since arisen, "What will the Lords do?" In the Upper House, the crucial debate—that on the second reading—took place on the 3rd and extended to the 7th of October. On the last night of the debate, the Lord Chancellor delivered, in support of the bill, one of his finest speeches, in which he analysed, with a power of criticism he did not always exhibit, the arguments of its opponents, emphasized those of its supporters by a variety of illustrations, and concluded with an eloquent and dignified peroration :—

"Among the awful considerations," he says, "that now bow down my mind, there is one which stands pre-eminent above the rest. You are the highest judicature in the realm ; you sit here as judges, and decide all causes, civil and criminal, without appeal. It is a judge's first duty never to pronounce sentence, in the most trifling case, without hearing. Will you make this the exception ? Are you really prepared to determine, but not to hear, the mighty cause upon which a nation's hopes and fears hang ? You are. Then beware of your decision ! Rouse not, I beseech you, a peace-loving but a resolute people ; do not alienate from your body the affections of a whole empire. As your friend, as the friend of my order, as the friend of my country, as the faithful servant of my sovereign, I counsel you to assist with your uttermost efforts in preserving the peace, and upholding and perpetuating the Constitution. Therefore, I pray and I exhort you not to reject this measure. By all you hold most dear, by all the ties that bind every one of us to our common order and our common country, I solemnly adjure you—I warn you—I implore you—yea, on my bended knees, I supplicate you—reject not this bill !"

But, in spite of warning, remonstrance, and argument, the Lords threw it out by a majority of 41. A flame of wrath at once lit up the country, from John-o'-Groat's House to Land's End ; and for a time the fate of the

Constitution hung in the balance. Various solutions of
the difficulty were proposed; the most popular was the
creation of a number of peers sufficient to outvote the
hostile majority. This bold and revolutionary proposal,
which involved a direct degradation of the dignity and
authority of the Upper House, was made by Brougham,
accepted by ministers, and urged upon the King, who
very reluctantly gave a verbal assent. The Government
then introduced their bill into the House of Commons,
on the 12th of December, and it passed through its
various stages with immense majorities. In the Lords,
the indignation of the country and the threatened creation of new peers had not been without good effect; and
on the second reading, ministers secured a majority of
nine. The bill then went into committee, where the
facilities for "maiming and delaying a measure of great
magnitude and intricacy" proved too much for the moderation and self-control of the Lords. The King, moreover,
had receded from his original ardour in the work of
reform, and refused to adopt the expedient by which a
minority in the Upper House might have been converted
into a majority. There was no alternative for Earl
Grey and his colleagues but resignation; and the Duke
of Wellington, with what his admirers called courage,
but cooler critics audacity, stood forward to meet the
storm. But he could get no colleagues in his Cabinet,
no majority in the Commons, and no soldiers to fight for
him in the streets; and it was soon clear that without
fighting, and hard fighting, he could not prevent the
people from carrying reform. The crisis lasted a week.
Then the Duke resigned; Earl Grey was recalled; the
King addressed a curious but significant circular letter
to the Opposition peers; and on the 7th of June the

Reform Bill received the royal assent, and became an Act of Parliament.

It is unnecessary to dwell on Brougham's personal share in this protracted struggle. What is certain is, that his boldness and decision contributed largely to the steadfast action of the ministry, and that the final triumph was in no small degree due to his consummate energy. In reference to the proposed creation of peers, he discusses, in his " Political Philosophy," the question : Whether, if the peers had persisted in their opposition, this swamping process would have been adopted, and he replies :—

"I cannot, with any confidence, answer it in the affirmative. I had a strong feeling of the necessity of the case in the very peculiar circumstances we were placed in. But such was my deep sense of the dreadful consequences of the act, that I much question whether I should not have preferred running the risk of confusion that attended the loss of the bill as it then stood ; and I have a strong impression on my mind that my illustrious friend [Earl Grey] would have more than met me half-way in the determination to face that risk (and, of course, to face the clamours of the people, which would have cost us little) rather than expose the Constitution to so imminent a hazard of subversion."

But this was written long after the victory had been gained, and when the excitement of battle was over. There can be little doubt that if Wellington had "stood to his guns," this bloodless revolution must have eventually been wrought, if only to prevent the outbreak of a sanguinary one.

At no time of his life was Lord Brougham more popular than now, and never had he more deserved popularity. He had exhibited all his best qualities—his

intellectual activity, his courage, his promptitude of resolution—in their fullest measure, and none of his worst.
But his was not a character that throve in prosperity ; it
lacked moderation, self-control, composure.  His intense
egotism began to prevail over his judgment ; his irritability of temperament over his discretion.  On these
meaner things, however, I do not care to dwell ; I
remember too keenly the magnitude of his services.
Even during the two years of his Chancellorship, from
1832 to 1834, he introduced and successfully carried
out several legislative measures of importance.  The
Judicial Committee of the Privy Council—a tribunal of
appeal in ecclesiastical cases, was his creation.  He
suggested the establishment of those local centres of civil
jurisdiction which, under the designation of " County
Courts," have proved so useful to the community.  The
reform of the Scottish municipal corporations, the settlement of the Bank Charter, the partial reform of the
Church of Ireland—these measures bore the impress of
his versatile energy.

In 1834, Lord Grey and Lord Althorpe resigned office;
but through Brougham's vigour and singular readiness
the Whig Ministry was almost immediately reconstructed,
with Lord Melbourne as Premier.  At this time, before
a committee of the House of Commons, he proved that
office had not deadened his sympathy with the great
cause of popular education, by strenuously advocating
the repeal of the stamp duty on newspapers, the tax
upon advertisements, and all duties upon paper—a wise
and truly liberal proposal, which it was reserved for
Mr. Gladstone to carry out some thirty years later.  But
he was now offending his colleagues by his injudicious
pretensions and the King by his brusque familiarity ; and

his popularity out-of-doors was steadily declining through
a variety of causes, except, indeed, in Scotland. Thither
during the recess of 1834, he accordingly betook himself, making what was little short of a royal progress, and
being received with true Scotch fervor by a people
who, it must be owned, had good reason to be proud of
their illustrious fellow-countryman. Unfortunately, it
threw the Chancellor off his balance ; and at Inverness
he had the bad taste to say he would write "by that
night's post" to the King an account of his reception.
At Edinburgh, speaking at a dinner given to Earl
Grey, his egotism was also manifested indiscreetly. He
returned to London, inflated by the homage he had
received ; but, alas, in a few weeks the Melbourne
Ministry was a thing of the past. By an arbitrary and
unusual exercise of his prerogative, the King called the
Conservative leaders to his councils (November 1834).

The new Lord Chancellor was Lord Lyndhurst, and
with a singular want of dignity, Brougham wrote to him,
soliciting (without salary) the office of Chief Baron of the
Exchequer. This action provoked, however, such very
general disapprobation that Brougham was compelled to
recall it. The Peel Cabinet did not long retain the reins
of power. On a dissolution of Parliament it was found
that the country had not wholly withdrawn its confidence
from the Whig leaders, and Peel, being defeated in the
Commons on Lord John Russell's motion respecting the
Irish Church, sent in his resignation (April 8, 1835),
Melbourne was again sent for, and Brougham began to
exult in the prospect of regaining the Great Seal ; but
the Whig Prime Minister had suffered so much from his
indiscretion, his vanity, his insubordination, and his
petulance, that he resolved, at whatever risk, to exclude

him from his Government. " Although he will be dangerous as an enemy," said Melbourne, " he would be certain
destruction as a friend. We may have small chance
of going on without him, but to go on with him is
impossible." To pacify him for a time, the Great Seal
was put in commission, so that Brougham did not absolutely abandon the hope of again taking his place on the
woolsack, and throughout the session of 1835 he vigorously supported Lord Melbourne. In truth, it was entirely
through his perseverance and courage that the Municipal
Reform Bill passed through the Lords. Some idea of
his untiring activity may be found from the subjects of
debate which, in this one session, he discussed with all his
characteristic force and eloquence. The list compels our
admiration of his versatility :—

" Address to the King—Administration of Justice in Ireland—
Admission of Ladies—Agricultural Distress—Breach of
Naval Discipline — Bribery at Elections — Borough
Reform in Scotland—Business, Delay of—Canada Cen-
tral Criminal Court—Charities—Church of Ireland—
Church of England—Church of Scotland—Church Pro-
perty—Church Rates—Commissioners of Law Inquiry—
Commissioners of Public Instruction—Committees of
Privilege—Constabulary of Ireland—Corporation Com-
mission — Corporation Reform—Corn Laws — Counsel
for Prisoners—Dissenters' Marriages—Dissolution of the
Ministry—Dublin Police—Duty on Paper—Ecclesiastical Courts—Education—Entails in Scotland—Houses
of Parliament, New—Imprisonment for Debt—Indemnity
to Witnesses—Islington Market—London University—
Marriage Law—Music and Dancing—Newspaper Stamps
—Oaths Abolition Bill—Patents—Poor Law, the New
—Post Office—Prison Discipline—Processions in Ireland—Russia and Austria—Sheriff's Accounts—Slavery

—Spain—Stoke Pogis—Taxes on Knowledge—Tithes, Recovery of — Tithes of Turnips Exemption Bill — University Oaths—Western, Great, Railway—Wills, Execution of—Writ of Certiorari, Abolition of."

Towards the end of the year, Sir Charles Pepys was made Lord Chancellor, and raised to the peerage as Lord Cottenham. This was a very severe blow to Brougham. I am disposed to think that he was not very well used ; that his great services to the Liberal party might and should have been allowed to counterbalance his unfortunate peculiarities of temper and character ; but when this admission has been made, I can see no justification for the spirit of hostility in which he thenceforth acted towards the Whig Government. A private wrong cannot excuse an abandonment of public duty ; and it was an unedifying spectacle to see a man who had been one of the foremost leaders of the Whigs, now pouring out upon them all the vials of his bitterest acrimony. In the first session of Queen Victoria's first Parliament his opposition was so violent as to destroy its own influence. His unscrupulous and sarcastic eloquence wounded the feelings of many, but gained the votes of none. Who could believe in his sincerity ? Who could credit his protestations of disinterested zeal for the public good ? The *spretæ injuria formæ* rankled in every speech, and oblivious of principle, oblivious of self-respect, oblivious of his obligations to the Liberal cause, he "squandered the remains of his public character" in efforts to ruin the party of which he had once been the pride and ornament. On one occasion he attacked his former colleagues with exceptional virulence:—

"They rush," he said, "unheeding, unhesitating, unreflecting, into resolutions upon which the wisest and readiest of mankind would hardly pause and ponder too long. But when all is determined, when every moment's delay is fraught with peril, then comes uncertainty and irresolution. They never pause until the season has arrived for action, when all faltering, even for the twinkling of an eye, is fatal, then it is that they relapse into supineness and inactivity—look around them and behind them, and everywhere but before them, and sink into repose as if all had been accomplished at the moment when everything remains to be done. If I were to ransack all the records to which I have ever had access of human conduct in administering great affairs, whether in the annals of our own time or in the ages that are past, I should in vain look for a more striking illustration of the Swedish Chancellor's famous saying to his son, departing to assist at a congress of statesmen, ' *I, fili mi, ut videas quantulâ sapientiâ regatur mundus.*' "

Well might Lord Melbourne condemn, in terms of dignified reproval, " the torrent of invective and sarcasm with which the noble and learned lord had overwhelmed the officers of her Majesty's Government, and that most laboured and most extreme concentration of bitterness which had been poured forth on this occasion."

It is pleasant to turn from this disagreeable spectacle to a brighter aspect of his indefatigable activity. As President of the Society for the Diffusion of Useful Knowledge (founded in 1826), he did good work; the publication of the *Penny Magazine* and the *Penny Encyclopœdia*, gave the first impulse to a beneficent movement which, in our own time, has attained to almost colossal proportions. He wrote leading articles and pamphlets, and contributed with Briarean activity to the *Edinburgh Review.* The mistrust, however, with which the editor and the chief writers in that time-honoured organ of Whig politics regarded him, is

developed in a letter from Lord Macaulay to Macvey
Napier (20th July, 1828):—

"As to Brougham," he writes, "I understand and feel for
your embarrassments. I may, perhaps, repine too much ; but I
should say that this strange man, finding himself almost alone
in the world, absolutely unconnected with either Whigs or
Conservatives, and not having a single vote in either House of
Parliament at his command except his own, is desirous to
make the *Review* his organ. With this intention, unless I
am greatly deceived, after having during several years contributed little or nothing of value, he has determined to exalt
himself as if he were a young writer struggling into note, and
to make himself important to the world by his literary services.
And he certainly has succeeded. His late articles have very
high merit. They are, indeed, models of magazine writing as
distinguished from other sorts of writing. . . . His wish,
I imagine, is to establish in this way such an ascendancy as may
enable him to drag the *Review* along with him to any party to
which his furious passions may lead him ; to the Radicals ; to
the Tories ; to any set of men by whose help he may be able to
revenge himself on old friends, whose only crime is that they
could not help finding him to be an habitual and incurable
traitor."

It will be seen that if Brougham did not love the
Whigs, the Whigs had no love for Brougham ! But to
stigmatise him as " an habitual and incurable traitor "
is, I think, an exaggeration. His temperament was not
that of a traitor ; he was mentally and morally incapable
of carrying on a subtle, continuous, and protracted conspiracy. His desertion of the Whigs was due to the angry
impulse of an excitable man of great parts and greater
vanity. Conceiving himself to have been ill-used and
humiliated by them, he was anxious to be revenged, and to

show them that he would be as potent as an enemy as he had been as an ally. And after all, we must remember that to the cause of education, of law reform, of popular enlightenment, he was never unfaithful, not even in his wildest anti-Whiggish moods. Nor did he swerve in his advocacy of Free Trade, and that, too, at a time, when by the Whig leaders themselves it was only partially accepted and imperfectly understood (1839).

I have not thought it necessary to dwell upon his rivalries and contentions with Lord Lyndhurst and Lord Campbell. They made no mark on the history of the time, and had no important or permanent results. That Brougham was frequently in the wrong may be admitted; but Lord Campbell, in his malicious biography of his "noble and learned friend," has abundantly proved that the ex-Chancellor had very good reason for doubting *his* sincerity. We do not believe that Brougham, with all his faults—and they were many—would ever have stooped to Campbell's malignant meanness; or that if he had survived Campbell, he would have disgraced himself by flinging mud upon his grave.

In 1840, Brougham purchased a small estate near Cannes, in the south of France, and built upon it a convenient residence which he called by the name of his well-loved daughter—Château Eleanor Louise. There he spent several months every year to the close of his busy life—not forgetting to pay a regular visit to Paris, that he might attend the meetings and take part in the scientific deliberations of the Institute; for with all his political, judicial, and parliamentary labours, he found time, or made time, to continue his literary and scientific pursuits. In the Lords, while having few opportunities of attacking a ministry which, in its incapacity and negligence, was always laying itself open to attack, he continued to advocate the repeal of the Corn-Laws, a more expeditious administration of criminal justice, the reform of charitable trusts, and kindred subjects. When Sir Robert Peel came into power in August, 1841, Brougham warmly supported him, and when the Corn Law Abolition Bill came before the Lords in 1846, passed upon the great minister a fine eulogium :—

"I should fail of discharging a duty which I owe as a citizen of this country, and as a member of this House—a debt of gratitude on public grounds, but a debt of strict justice as well—did I not express my deep sense of the public virtue, no less than the great capacity and the high moral courage which my right honourable friend at the head of the Government has exhibited in dealing with this question. He cast away all personal and private considerations of what description soever, and, studiously disregarding his own interest in every stage and step of his progress, he has given up what to a political leader is the most enviable of all positions—the calm, unquestioned, undivided support of Parliament; he has exposed himself to the frenzy of the most tempest-troubled sea that the political world in our days perhaps ever exhibited. He has given up what to an ambitious man is much—the security of his power; he has given up what to a calculating man is much—influence and authority with his party; he has given up what to an amiable man is much indeed—private friendships and party connections; and all these sacrifices he has voluntarily encountered, in order to discharge what (be he right or be he wrong) he deemed a great public duty. He, in these circumstances—he, in this proud position—may well scorn the sordid attacks, the wretched ribaldry with which he is out of doors assailed, because he knows that he has entitled himself to the gratitude of his country, and will leave—as I in my conscience believe—his name to after ages as one of the greatest and most disinterested ministers that ever wielded the destinies of this country."

There is an evident ring of sincerity in these words which are not less honourable to Brougham than to Peel.

Some ridicule was excited in 1848 by one of those escapades into which his restlessness and mental excitability sometimes impelled him. After the deposition of Louis Philippe, and the establishment in France of a Republican Government, he announced himself as a candidate to represent the department of Var (in which his château was situated) in the National Assembly. But he soon discovered that he must first become naturalised, and addressed the necessary form of application to the Minister of Justice. Great was his chagrin when he learned that he would have to abandon "all titles of nobility, all privileges and advantages," which he possessed as an Englishman; that he would have to cease to be an Englishman before he could become a Frenchman. He wisely decided that *le jeu ne vaut pas la chandelle,* and returned to his duties in the House of Lords.

In the following year he demonstrated the flexibility of his genius by lecturing before the Institute, in French, on the result of a long series of experiments which he had made upon light. The worst of it was that, in science as in so much else, his knowledge was not profound, and he fell into errors which the exaggerated character of his pretensions made all the more deplorable.

But our space is wholly inadequate to a yearly chronicle of all the sayings and doings of this extraordinary man, and we must pass rapidly onward to the close of his tumultuous career. This is all the more easy, because he promised so much and performed so little. He was always introducing bills which perished stillborn, and motions which he never carried to a division,

and schemes of legislation which never ripened into
fruition. The *cacoethes loquendi* ruined him; he
drowned his reputation and himself in floods of talk.
His influence in Parliament left him as his popularity
had left him; and, except in the cartoons of Mr. *Punch*,
he attracted little public attention. As President of the
Law Reform Society he did good service—better, perhaps, as President of the Social Science Association, the
annual meetings of which he attended from 1857 to
1866. In the autumn of 1858 he delivered an eloquent address at the inauguration of a statue of Sir
Isaac Newton at Grantham, his birthplace. Gradually
he withdrew more and more from the political arena,
and occupied his still immense energies in cultivating
more peaceful fields. Old age did not seem to dim his
faculties; his mind was alert and clear to the very last,
though he was in his ninetieth year, when, after a life of
unparalleled intellectual effort, he expired, at his château
near Cannes, on the 7th of May, 1868.

In conclusion, I must briefly advert to his literary productions. These, like his legislative efforts, are marked
by crudeness and imperfectness. They do not seem to
have been "thought out." The impression which the
reader derives from their perusal is that their author has
dashed them off, *currente calamo*, without any adequate
preparation. Hence his style is generally careless,
inelegant, involved; his arguments are defective; his
facts huddled and heaped together without any regard to
method or system. His scientific knowledge is often
deficient, as, perhaps, was necessarily the case with a man
whose life was chiefly given up to public affairs. In
literature, as in science and in politics, Brougham failed,
from attempting too much. He was always trying to

drive six horses abreast ! In his ambition to demonstrate his versatility he forgot the essential condition of thoroughness. The best of his works I take to be his "Sketches of Statesmen who Flourished in the Time of George III." There was no continuous labour required upon these desultory chapters, no political research or studious investigation; and, therefore, Brougham is seen at his worthiest. His insight into character was not very deep, but, on the whole, it was accurate. The novel which is ascribed to his pen, "Albert Lunel ; or, The Château of Languedoc," suppressed on the eve of its publication (1844), but reprinted in 1872, is dreary reading. His "Dialogue on Instinct" (1849) had at one time a considerable reputation ; but is now interesting only as the work of a man of extraordinary capacity. A higher rank may be claimed for his "Discourse on Paley's Natural Theology ; " it contains some just reflections and apposite illustrations. The following passage may be taken as a specimen :—

"A comparative anatomist, of profound learning and marvellous sagacity, has presented to him what to common eyes would seem a piece of half-decayed bone, found in a wild, in a forest, or in a cave. By accurately examining its shape, particularly the form of its extremity or extremities (if both ends happen to be entire), by close inspection of the texture of its surface, and by admeasurement of its proportions, he can with certainty discover the general form of the animal to which it belonged, its size as well as its shape, the economy of its viscera, and its general habits. Sometimes the investigation in such cases proceeds upon chains of reasoning where all the links are seen and understood ; where the connection of the parts found with other parts and with latitudes is perceived, and the reason understood—as that the animal had a trunk, because the neck was short compared

with its height; or that it ruminated, because its teeth were
imperfect for complete mastication.   But frequently the inquiry
is as certain in its results, although some links of the chain are
concealed from our view, and the conclusion wears a more
empirical aspect—as gathering that the animal ruminated, from
observing the print of a cloven hoof; or that he had horns, from
his wanting certain teeth; or that he wanted the collar-bone,
from his having cloven hoofs.

"The discoveries already made in this branch of science are
truly wonderful, and they proceed upon the strictest rules of
induction.   It is shown that animals formerly existed on the
globe, being unknown varieties of *species* still known; but it
also appears that *species* existed, and were *genera*, wholly
unknown for the last five thousand years.   These peopled the
earth, as it was, not before the general deluge, but before some
convulsion long prior to that event had overwhelmed the
countries then dry, and raised others from the bottom of the sea.
In these curious inquiries, we are conversant, not merely with the
world before the flood, but with a world which, before the flood,
was covered with water, and which, in far earlier ages, had been
the habitation of birds, and beasts, and reptiles.   We are carried,
as it were, several worlds back, and we reach a period when all
was water, and slime, and mud, and the waste, without either
man or plants, gave resting-place to enormous beasts like lions
and elephants and river-horses, while the water was tenanted by
lizards the size of a whale, sixty or seventy feet long, and by
others with huge eyes having shields of solid bone to protect
them, and glaring from a neck ten feet in length, and the air
was darkened by flying reptiles covered with scales, opening the
jaws of the crocodile and expanding wings, armed at the tip with
the claws of the leopard.   No less strange, and yet no less proceeding from induction, are the discoveries made respecting the
former state of the earth, the manner in which these animals,
whether of known or unknown tribes, occupied it, and the
period when, or at least the way in which, they ceased to exist."

It is needful to note that Lord Brougham wrote before Mr. Darwin had propounded his theory of evolution. Among his other works we find:—"Lives of Men of Letters and Science in the reign of George III.," a less successful effort than the "Memoirs of the Statesmen;" a manual of "Political Philosophy," written for the Society for the Diffusion of Useful Knowledge; his "Analytical View of Sir Isaac Newton's *Principia*;" a collection of his "Speeches, with Historical Introduction and Dissertation upon the Eloquence of the Ancients;" several pamphlets on "Law Reform;" "Contributions to the *Edinburgh Review*" (1857); and "Recherches Analytiques et Expérimentales sur les Alveoles des Abeilles," published in 1859. His "Autobiography," a Memoir of his Life and Times, begun when he was in his eighty-fourth year, was published after his death (in 1871), under the editorship of his brother. It contains some interesting and even valuable documents and letters, and much information on subjects previously unknown to, or imperfectly understood by, the public; but the mis-statements are so numerous and so serious, and the prejudices and antipathies so bitter and even unscrupulous, that its authoritative value is considerably diminished.

Lord Brougham's works have been published in ten volumes. A biographical list of them was issued in 1873.

For particulars of his extraordinary career, the reader will consult the various "diaries" and "journals" issued by his contemporaries down to that of Mr. Charles Greville; the volumes of *Punch* from 1842 downwards (he figures in many of its cartoons, with his strongly-marked countenance and prominent nose, his ill-fitting coat and Ettrick tweed trousers); the columns of *The*

2 C

*Times* (at first his great friend and supporter, but from about 1834 his open and relentless enemy and critic) ; J. A. Roebuck's " History of the Whig Ministry of 1830 ;" Rev. W. N. Molesworth's " History of England since the Reform Bill ;" Miss Martineau's " History of the Thirty Years' Peace ;" Trevelyan's " Life and Letters of Lord Macaulay ;" Lord Campbell's " Lives of Lord Lyndhurst and Lord Brougham ;" Fonblanque, " England under Seven Administrations," &c.

# INDEX.

387

S. W. PARTRIDGE AND CO., 9 PATERNOSTER ROW, LONDON.